Reconstructing Woody

Reconstructing Woody

Art, Love, and Life in the
Films of Woody Allen

Mary P. Nichols

ROWMAN & LITTLEFIELD PUBLISHERS, INC.
Lanham • Boulder • New York • Oxford

ROWMAN & LITTLEFIELD PUBLISHERS, INC.

Published in the United States of America
by Rowman & Littlefield Publishers, Inc.
4720 Boston Way, Lanham, Maryland 20706

12 Hid's Copse Road
Cumnor Hill, Oxford OX2 9JJ, England

British Library Cataloguing in Publication Information Available

Library of Congress Cataloging-in-Publication Data

Nichols, Mary P.
    Reconstructing Woody : art, love, and life in the films of Woody
Allen / Mary P. Nichols.
        p.   cm.
    Includes bibliographical references and index.
    ISBN 0-8476-8989-1 (alk. paper)
    1. Allen, Woody—Criticism and interpretation.   I. Title.
PN1998.3.A45N53   1998
791.43'092—dc21   98-7452
                                                        CIP

Printed in the United States of America

♾ ™ The paper used in this publication meets the minimum requirements of
American National Standard for Information Sciences—Permanence of Paper
for Printed Library Materials, ANSI Z39.48—1984.

Contents

Acknowledgments   vii

Preface   ix

1. The Interpreter and the Artist   1

2. The Hero and the Klutz (*Play It Again, Sam*)   19

3. The Anhedonist and the Singer (*Annie Hall*)   33

4. The Interior Decorator and the Vulgarian (*Interiors*)   49

5. The Director and the Fan (*Stardust Memories*)   65

6. The Empiricist and the Image Maker (*A Midsummer Night's Sex Comedy*)   83

7. The Changing Man and the Psychiatrist (*Zelig*)   99

8. The Actor and the Character (*The Purple Rose of Cairo*)   115

9. The Eavesdropper and the Patient (*Another Woman*)   131

10. The Ophthalmologist and the Filmmaker (*Crimes and Misdemeanors*)   149

11. The Detectives (*Manhattan Murder Mystery*)   165

12. The Murderer and the Playwright (*Bullets over Broadway*)   179

13. The Sportswriter and the Whore (*Mighty Aphrodite*)   195

14. The Comic   211

Notes	223
Bibliography	245
Index	249
About the Author	255

Acknowledgments

Had it not been for my graduate students, this book would not have been written. It started in 1992 when my husband and I happened to rent Woody Allen's *Midsummer Night's Sex Comedy* for our evening entertainment. I was teaching Greek political thought at the time, including Aristophanes' *Clouds*. Similarities between the ancient comedian and the modern filmmaker jumped out. Each, for example, mocked a pompous professor of philosophy. While Socrates taught his students in the *Clouds* to reduce the Greek gods to natural phenomena, in *Sex Comedy* Leopold Sturgis pronounces in his university classes that nothing exists that cannot be "touched, tasted, felt, or in some scientific fashion proven." In both cases the philosophers are at the top of the world, boasters who do not foresee their comeuppance, and the comic poet lets their pretensions collapse in smoke. Was *Sex Comedy* saying today what the *Clouds* said over two thousand years ago? Was Woody Allen a modern-day Aristophanes? And why was philosophy a particularly good butt for the comic's laughter? My students would have to see this movie.

The next week I watched *Sex Comedy* again, with my students. Showtime at five, followed by pizza, and then discussion late into the night. It was the first of many "Woody Allen parties." The next semester I taught eighteenth-century political thought. We read Rousseau, Burke, and Kant and talked of the effect of romanticism, especially the new cult of the artist, on human life. Again, I invited students to my home for a movie. This time we watched *Interiors*.

vii

Over the years students have come and gone, but the parties have continued. At times, they were connected to my graduate courses; often it just felt like the right time in the semester to have a Woody Allen party. And newcomers to the program were as enthusiastic as the earlier students, or at least as tolerant of their teacher's enthusiasms. For their support, their willingness to discuss, and their tolerance, I am deeply grateful.

I am also grateful to friends who have read part of and in some cases the entire manuscript and who have offered me their extensive criticisms—Susan Benfield, Carly Kinsella, Dan Mahoney, Jeffrey Poelvoorde, Denise Schaeffer, and Catherine Zuckert. I am also grateful to my teacher Joseph Cropsey, who in addition to raising for me the enduring questions of poetry and philosophy, virtue and friendship, also cultivated my appreciation for stand-up comedy, and whose skepticism about this whole project no doubt spurred me to its completion. My husband David Nichols first introduced me to Woody Allen movies by taking me to see *Play It Again, Sam* before we were married and has enjoyed Allen's movies with me over the years, even for the umpteenth time we watched them together. He has helped me host the Woody Allen parties, has often discussed Allen's movies with me, and read my manuscript at its various stages. I am grateful for his encouragement and support in this as in everything. I would like to thank the Kobal Collection for permitting us to reproduce the stills from the movies, and Faber and Faber for their permission to reprint quotations from *Woody Allen on Woody Allen: In Conversation with Stig Bjorkman* (also published as *Woody Allen on Woody Allen: Woody Allen in His Own Words*). Finally, I am grateful to Woody Allen for allowing me to quote from his movies—within legal guidelines, of course—and, more important, for the hours of entertainment, thought, and discussion his movies have occasioned.

Preface

Film critics have often noted similarities between Woody Allen and the characters he plays. Allen himself has said that his characters' obsessions are his obsessions, that their problems are his problems. So, it is no surprise when commentators view Woody Allen's "art" as whining self-reflection and mock his "love affair with death" as "a metaphysical head cold."[1] Writing for *The New Yorker*, Pauline Kael has railed for years against Allen's adolescent complaints about life, and recently Maureen Dowd advised Allen to "grow up."[2]

No movie of Allen's since *Stardust Memories* has raised the hackles of reviewers so much as his 1997 offering, *Deconstructing Harry*. The movie is about a novelist, Harry Block (Woody Allen), a successful writer whose personal life appears despicable. Harry has cheated on several wives, including with a wife's sister and with another wife's patient. And he continues to engage in nasty fights with one of his former wives over their son. Not only are his relationships nothing to write home about, Harry writes them up for public consumption—in "fiction" that comes so close to life that Harry barely changes the names of those involved.

Deconstructing Harry comes in the wake of several years of adverse publicity about Allen's private life—from his affair with Mia Farrow's adopted daughter to unproven accusations of child molestation. When Harry wonders whether he is "the worst person in the world," critics therefore interpret this to be Allen "acknowledging, and even reveling in, his ill repute."[3] And when Harry admits that his protagonist is "me thinly disguised" and he is not going to "disguise it any more," the critics suppose that they are hearing Allen come clean. In the character of Harry, they say, Allen finally reveals himself as a "dirty old man."[4] Even those who like *Deconstructing Harry* see it as "brazenly autobiographical."[5]

Perhaps Allen is upbraiding the public for judging him by conventional moral standards. Dowd believes that the movie's message is that art overrides morality, and that "ordinary ethical standards do not apply to people who produce extraordinary art."[6] So, Allen is whining again, this time not about the inevitability of death, but about the public judgment of his private life. When one of Harry's former wives describes his life as nihilism, cynicism, sarcasm, and orgasm, he replies that "in France [he] could run on that slogan and win." Would that Americans were as liberated as the French, perhaps Allen sighs.

In *Deconstructing Harry*, the upstate college that once expelled Harry offers to hold a ceremony in his honor. But Harry is arrested before the honoring occurs. In the end he is honored only in a dream, and primarily by the characters he has created. It is easy to suppose that Allen is seeking vindication from the world of his imagination that the real world does not bestow. The last writing project that Harry imagines is about "a character too neurotic to function in life" who "can only function in art."

These interpretations, however, miss the joke underlying *Deconstructing Harry*, for Allen has given his most vociferous critics, who confuse his art with his life and judge both harshly, a version of the despicable person they imagine that he is. He holds out bait, and critics bite, identifying Allen with Harry and seeing their opinions confirmed. But to identify Allen with one of his characters is to confuse biography and fiction, life and art—one of the errors that the movie shows Harry himself making. Indeed, this is one of the worst things Harry does, at least according to the movie. His lover Lucy may faint when she hears Harry has left her for a younger woman, but it is when she sees herself in one of Harry's stories that she threatens to shoot him.[7] Critics thus accuse Allen of what Lucy accuses Harry—writing fiction that is only thinly disguised life. But that is a mistake, the movie shows, that might move a lover to kill.

Allen has the last laugh, just as surely he is grinning when Harry finds the floor in hell reserved for the media "all filled up."

Ed Siegel of the *Boston Globe* better appreciates Allen's irony. While he thinks that the movie could be seen as self-justification, or even a confession of wrongdoing, he finds it "more likely" that "Allen is having some fun at our expense for asking those questions [about the relation between this movie and his private life] in the first place."[8]

Making private matters public, one of Harry's sins, crosses a moral line, and Woody Allen is a very private man. He has not asked us to judge his private life. He has offered us over thirty movies that present a complex moral vision. At the same time they reflect on the relationship between art and life, and that relationship is too complex to be simple autobiography. Today, Allen's private life is in the public eye, and his movies tend to be viewed primarily in relation to his life. But like Woody Allen's life, this will pass. His movies will remain. At the end of *Harry*, the protagonist dreams of being honored, in front of his son, by the characters he creates. It is his art that will honor him—before posterity.

Audiences—including some of the morally outraged critics—also laugh at *Deconstructing Harry*.[9] Woody Allen has given us another very funny movie. Harry may not be the worst person in the world, but Allen clearly presents him as terribly flawed, reproached for his deeds not only by those once close to him but also by his own fictional characters who come to life. At one point, Harry objects to being "lectured by [his] own creation." When the media similarly reproaches Allen for his life, it forgets that Allen has created not only the flawed Harry Block, but also the characters from Harry's stories who lecture him. Allen is more aware than his critics that art does not merely imitate life but might lecture life. Art might serve as life's best self.

There is no question that Allen's movies are self-reflective. But self-reflection can mean examination of one's own art as well as indulgent projection of private vice. In the pages ahead, I will show that Allen's movies attempt to improve contemporary life. In his own way, Woody Allen is fighting amorality, just as Harry in one of his short stories claims that he can beat the devil, if only because he is a greater sinner than the devil himself.

In what way, then, might Harry beat the devil? At the outset of *Deconstructing Harry*, Harry Block suffers from writer's block. His life is blocked by Allen's editing as well, as jump cuts make his conversations and deeds discontinuous. Harry's life does not flow from one moment to another; his time is disjointed, just as his character is flawed and his writing at a standstill. As the movie proceeds, he seems to be falling apart. Insofar as he lacks integrity, he is ripe for deconstruction. But by the end of the movie, Harry is writing again. He imagines that he descends into hell in search of his "one true love" who has been carried away by the devil, but he finds, forgives, and tries to rescue his father instead. When he "ascends" back to life after his attempt to rescue Faye from Larry's underworld domain, Larry and Faye rescue him from prison. They come directly from their wedding with his bail money. Harry sees that Larry is not the devil, for Harry comes to bless their marriage. Harry's life may have been ripe for deconstruction, but by the end he has begun a process of reconstruction. *Deconstructing Harry* shows that Allen is not simply or even primarily a deconstructionist.

My view therefore differs from those of Nancy Pogel and Sam B. Girgus who think that Allen's films undermine the world in which we live, from the moral platitudes we accept even to our belief in an objective reality. Pogel finds in Allen's "inconclusive" films a "dialogic imagination" that leaves "intersecting optimistic and pessimistic images . . . as unresolved possibilities." Allen thus "deconstructs [himself, his audiences, his critics, and his medium] even to the last frames of his film."[10] Similarly, Girgus argues that Allen's films "reveal a decentered world of displaced and dislocated characters," and "a fragmented consciousness."[11] Although these critics approve of the subversion of reality they find in Allen's films, others object, while characterizing Allen's films in the same vein. Thus Allan Bloom in *The Closing of the American Mind* claims that in Allen's work "the outer is dissolved and becomes formless in light of the inner, and the inner is a will-o'-the-wisp, a pure emptiness."[12]

I agree that Allen's films address these modern—or postmodern—positions. Indeed, in *Deconstructing Harry*, Allen's jump-cut technique reflects a postmodern consciousness, and Harry's final story involves a character who leads "a fragmented, disjointed existence." But Allen's films do not celebrate this lack of moral and intellectual coherence or give birth to myriad and contradictory interpretations that cannot be resolved because his films themselves lack any integrity. When Harry sees that Larry is not the devil that he imagined in his story, he recognizes that life is a standard for art. But if this is so, life and art do not dissolve into each other. The one time *Harry* refers to its own title it is in the words of a less sophisticated interpreter—only a graduate student—who likes "deconstructing [Harry's] books," because while "on the surface they all seem a little sad, underneath they're really happy." The graduate student's "deconstruction" of Harry, however, is not truly a deconstruction: far from finding in Harry's work only the play of shimmering surfaces and the irresolvable optimistic and pessimistic oppositions of a "dialogic imagination," it discovers the happiness underlying life's sadness.

In contrast to the majority of Allen's critics, Sander H. Lee argues that Allen is not the partisan of nihilism he is often taken to be. Although Allen finds no "ontological foundations" for "traditional ethical values," according to Lee, he remains torn between an "intellectual tendency toward atheism" and "a spiritual yearning for some sort of salvation." Most important, Allen remains committed to the necessity of individual moral responsibility in any meaningful human life. His heroes are free to choose the meanings of their lives and are responsible for the consequences of their choices, even though they must make a moral commitment in an amoral world.[13] As Lee writes, "Values must be chosen without reference to any ultimate guidance, since we are unable to prove that such guidelines exist."[14] To Lee, Allen is, in short, an existentialist, who "helps us identify the theories he is using" when he shows us Judy Roth in *Husbands and Wives* "holding a book with Sartre's name emblazoned on the cover," and when we see Gabe Roth express a desire to move to Paris to write in a cafe—to adopt a lifestyle associated with Sartre.[15]

Judy Roth, however, may read about existential commitments, but she also has great difficulty making any. And Gabe Roth's dream of a Sartrean lifestyle seems more of an escapist desire than an affirmation of responsibility for his life. Writing in a Paris cafe is, at any rate, a trite and pretentious imitation rather than authentic moral commitment. Allen pokes as much fun at Sartrean existentialism as he does at the postmodern theories of art that turn texts into infinite plays of meaning, reality into illusion, and illusion into reality.

Thus, I agree with Lee that Allen's work is essentially moral, contrary to the typical deconstructionist view, but I do not find its morality to be as ungrounded and arbitrary as Lee suggests. Although Allen's films begin with contemporary assumptions, nihilistic and existential, they move from them to reveal the potential of the human soul for fulfillment in deeds of virtue and love. The world in which this potential can be actualized is a moral one. Allen's work is evidence that the American mind is open to questions of truth and virtue and shows how a popular art form such as the film might provide society moral and intellectual education. His movies call not for deconstruction, but rather an interpretation that reveals their noblest import. To that end we must reconstruct our understandings of Woody Allen.

I will discuss twelve of Allen's movies that demonstrate Woody Allen's art and its implications for modern life. The movies I have chosen reveal the variety and the breadth of his production, beginning with a comedy relatively early in his career, the 1972 *Play It Again, Sam*, and concluding with his 1995 *Mighty Aphrodite*. We shall explore examples of both his comedies and his "serious dramas," such as *Interiors* and *Another Woman*. We shall examine the ones he regards as his favorites, such as *Stardust Memories* and *The Purple Rose of Cairo*, as well as ones he claims are merely "trivial," such as *Manhattan Murder Mystery*. And we shall look at some the critics loved (like *Bullets over Broadway*) and some the critics hated (like *Interiors*). I have nevertheless not aimed at variety for its own sake. While other movies might have been selected, the ones I shall discuss are all relevant to understanding Woody Allen's art and its implications for our lives.

1

The Interpreter and the Artist

Any interpretation of Woody Allen's movies, especially one that takes as its concern such serious topics as truth and virtue, runs the risk of overinterpretation. Allen himself often mocks those who look for more meaning in films than is there. In *Stardust Memories*, for example, overenthusiastic critics are rebuked by film director Sandy Bates (Woody Allen) when they ask him what he is "trying to say" in his films. He was "just trying to be funny," he tells them.[1] Near the end of that movie, an audience watches and then discusses the meaning of Sandy's latest movie. When one of the viewers wonders about "the significance of the Rolls-Royce" driven by the director in the movie, her companion responds that he thinks that "it represents his car."

Allen himself warns "against interpretation" by including an interview with novelist and literary critic Susan Sontag in his mock documentary *Zelig*. Susan Sontag, Allen tells us in the caption on the screen, is the author of *Against Interpretation*. In that book, Sontag inveighs against "the hypertrophy of the intellect at the expense of energy and sensual capability." Interpretation is one illustration of this hypertrophy; it is "the revenge of the intellect upon art." Interpretation, she writes, "excavates, and as it excavates, destroys; it digs 'behind' the text, to find a sub-text which is the true one." She puts "behind" in quotation marks to imply that there is no "behind" the text, there is only the text. The "most celebrated and influential . . . systems of hermeneutics," according to Sontag, are Marx's and Freud's "aggressive and impious theories of interpreta-

1

tion," thrusting aside the "manifest content" in order to discover "the true meaning."[2] Since Allen refers in *Zelig* to both Marxist and Freudian interpretations of the Zelig phenomenon, Sontag's presence can be understood as a warning. The viewer who responds in *Stardust Memories* that the Rolls-Royce represents a car makes an observation worthy of Susan Sontag. Allen lets his response illustrate in his unreflective way Sontag's impassioned cry, "Away with interpretation."

On the other hand, does Allen want us to apply the attitude of the viewer who sees no more than a car in Sandy's Rolls-Royce to everything in Allen's movies? The viewer in question, Allen tells us, is a lawyer. Could Allen be poking fun at the legalistic and prosaic mentality of the lawyer? The woman who wonders about the significance of the Rolls-Royce is an actress. Is the actress or the lawyer better able to appreciate Sandy's movie? To proclaim "do away with interpretation" is to assert that there is "nothing more than meets the eye," as does the pompous professor in *A Midsummer Night's Sex Comedy*, who learns enough by the end of the movie to retract his claim. Moreover, Sontag herself, in spite of her book's title to which Allen calls our attention, gives an interpretation of Zelig in Allen's movie. Allen says, in effect, that we cannot avoid interpretation.

When Sandy Bates answers the question about what he meant to say in his movie with the quip that he just meant to be funny, how seriously should we take him? It is after all a funny comment, and his audience laughs. Even trying to be funny, however, "says" something, for it indicates that there are certain things at which others can or should laugh. When the studio executives hear that Sandy wants to make serious movies rather than comedies, one of them objects, "Doesn't the man know that he's got the greatest gift that anyone could have? The gift of laughter?" One may have the gift of laughter, like Sandy Bates, and choose not to use it because the world as he sees it is too full of human suffering. Sandy Bates's earlier choice to use his gift of laughter, his intention to make funny movies, "says" something about how he viewed the world and what he thought was the appropriate reaction to it. So does his decision not to make more comedies. Sandy's "funny" comment is not a put-down of interpretation; rather it is an answer, however brief, to the question of what he meant to say in his movies.

Woody Allen, however, claims that unlike Sandy he never wanted to stop making comedies altogether. He claims that Sandy's rejection of comedy fit the character in the movie, but that he himself did not feel that way, and that while he wanted to make comedies, he occasionally wanted to make a more serious film.[3] Indeed, one of Allen's complaints against interpreters of *Stardust Memories* is that they took the film literally. He was simply not the lead character, and Sandy's sentiments were not his own.[4]

The erring critics understood the movie as if it were a simple reflection of reality, as if Allen had held a mirror up to himself, his fans, and his critics, and presented the reflection in *Stardust Memories*.[5] Indeed, they assumed that the artist does no more than what Socrates attributes to him in the *Republic* when he compares the artist to someone carrying around a mirror and reflecting everything in the world (*Republic*, 596d). This analogy suggests that artists or poets in the broad sense present "nothing more than meets the eye," for a mirror reflects no more than the eye reflects. But if poets simply re-presented the world, as this mirror image suggests, their representations would be superfluous. Art would add nothing to what we see, and we would have no desire to look through the eyes of the artist; art would have no appeal.

On the other hand, if the artist shows us what we cannot see by ourselves—if, for example, we need Mozart's music to hear what Mozart heard, and even someone to teach us how to listen to Mozart, as the professor does for his fiancee in *A Midsummer Night's Sex Comedy*—Socrates' analogy between the poet and the man carrying around a mirror would not hold.[6] Throughout *Sex Comedy*, its protagonist Andrew insists that "there is more than meets the eye," and tries to capture this by means of his spirit ball. He tries to do what a good poet or artist does more successfully. Because "there is more than meets the eye," what does meet the eye must be interpreted. The eye of the poet is no ordinary mirror, for it helps us to understand what does meet the eye. And because poetry is no ordinary mirror, it requires interpretation, whether it be the interpretation of the moviegoer, for example, or of the most experienced film critic. This means that poetry can mislead us about the world and interpretation can mislead us about poetry, just as much as they can serve as our access to the world and its meaning.

When Allen insists that he is not Sandy Bates, and indeed that he has never been the character he has played, he implies that interpretation is necessary. The critics, paradoxically, fail to interpret when they assume that they are seeing Allen on the screen, and that Sandy's sentiments are Allen's. They do not understand that art is not simply a mirror of reality. As Allen says, "most people . . . can't understand an act of imagination. So every film I make, they feel is an autobiography. . . . Therefore I have to explain to them, that *Annie Hall* wasn't, that *Manhattan* wasn't, that *Husbands and Wives* wasn't."[7] Allen is referring to those, for example, who see *Annie Hall* as a reflection of his relationship with Diane Keaton, or *Husbands and Wives* as a reflection of his breakup with Mia Farrow and his attraction to a woman young enough to be his daughter.

But even if personal events triggered Allen's reflections that underlie these movies, they could fully explain the movies only if art were not art, only if art were a simple mirror of reality.[8] Art is, as Allen says, "an act of imagination." And because art is itself interpretation of the world, it too must be interpreted. Allen is thus "for interpretation," not "against" it when he objects to the critics of *Stardust Memories*. Just as the world requires poetic reflection in order to be understood, poetry and art require interpretation.

This does not mean that the artist is always the best interpreter of his or her own work. Allen recounts the critics' reaction to the fact that *Stardust Memories* is one of his favorite movies: "Everybody said to me, 'Of course it's your favorite film, because nobody liked it. You're protecting your child, even if it's crippled, or blind.' " Allen denies that this is the case, but says that his disagreement with his critics is indecisive: "Only time will tell. What is of lasting value will remain, and what is not will not."[9] Allen's perhaps uncharacteristic optimism here suggests that others, over time, are authoritative judges of an artist's work. If "time will tell," however, it is worth contributing to what "time will tell." Allen asks for no less.

There are nevertheless limits to interpretation of art, imposed by the work of art itself. Art should serve as an authority for its own interpretation. An interpreter can be guided by the work she interprets by attempting to understand its integrity. Commenting on various aspects of his movies, Allen speaks of what "fits" or is "correct for the film." For example, the painting of the pregnant woman that he uses in *Another Woman*, he says, "just looked right, it just had the right feel for the movie." Of course, there are any number of reasons why the painting might feel right for the film. Allen himself mentions that the protagonist is a professor of German philosophy, and so "I was trying to find someone fitting as an artist." And a painting of a pregnant woman calls up memories for the professor of her own aborted pregnancy. Moreover, the woman in the painting is naked, or exposed, like that other woman on whom the professor has been eavesdropping, and unlike the self-protected professor. The picture "fits" the film in that it contributes in complex ways to the problems the filmmaker presents.

Similarly, in *Zelig*, Allen interviews a number of intellectuals, not only Susan Sontag, but also Saul Bellow, Irving Howe, and others, who comment on Zelig and his significance. They were, Allen says, "correct for the film." They give it "the patina of intellectual weight and seriousness."[10] One could add countless examples. The whole serves as an authority for the parts that constitute it. And good art is a whole. In *Bullets over Broadway*, Allen presents a young playwright and director who loses control of his play by letting the parts, the individual actors and actresses, serve as authorities for the whole. The play loses its integrity, and nothing "fits."

Works of art are wholes, however, not merely because of internal consistency but because of the comprehensiveness of their vision. The parts that "fit" a film are ultimately "correct for the film" if they contribute to their film's "fitting" the world. We shall see why Pearl, for example, "fits" *Interiors*—although Arthur's daughters do not at first think that their father's fiancee fits at all in the family—and makes it more complete. And in *Bullets*, the artist's play is imperfect or partial due not simply to the incoherence of its parts but to its author's poor understanding of human character. A work of art is a "whole," paradoxically, because it serves as a medium between the world, especially the human and moral world, which it interprets, and those whom it addresses, who must interpret it in turn. Its being a whole thus finally depends on its being a part of an ongoing process that links its audience to a world and itself to both.

While the whole he is creating serves as the artist's authority for the parts with which he constitutes it, the artist does not necessarily see the whole from the beginning or plan all the parts from the outset. The whole takes shape as more and more of the parts fall into place. Allen discusses his use of eyes, seeing, and blindness in *Crimes and Misdemeanors*, for example, which is a movie about "people who don't see": "They don't see themselves as others see them. They don't see the right and the wrong of situations." While one of the characters literally goes blind in the course of the film, others lack "emotional vision" and "moral vision." Allen's use of this theme of seeing, he says, was "instinctive." He explains that he took no special notes on it. "You feel," he says, "when writing the script, when it should surface again. When one feels it's correct for it to surface, you let it happen." Thus, he first thought of making Judah in *Crimes* an eye doctor "before [he] thought of the eye metaphor. That was the first instinct for it."[11]

It is because the whole evolves during the process of its creation that Allen makes changes during the filming of a movie, even changing the sequence of scenes during editing.[12] In *Interiors*, for example, Allen moved the scene in which the husband's voice-over explains his past life with Eve and their daughters from a later point in the movie to the beginning. "That's happened to me before on other films," Allen explains, "where a scene meant for another part of a picture is moved elsewhere. I just get a sudden idea. I could be walking down the street, and suddenly rearrangements like this enter my mind. And it's great. It gives the film a certain vitality, because it's spontaneous."[13]

It is no wonder that many thinkers have claimed that poets are inspired. The inspiration, however, comes only after much hard work and discipline. And it comes only after much "thought." Describing the act of imagination, Allen says, "I start to think. . . . I take a walk. . . . And I think and think. Then just by the sweat of the brow, eventually something comes."[14] Moreover, as he acquires more and more experience in his art, as he matures, a good artist can rely on his instincts more and more. Allen is also aware of this, and he has explained that "as time goes on, you get more and more knowledgeable and experienced and . . . you let your instincts operate more freely."[15]

When Allen first started writing plays, he admits he "was not very good at it," for he "had not yet developed enough craft," he "was not educated enough. . . . not . . . literate, not that familiar with literature, not an habitual reader." Consequently it "took a while to absorb things, to read a lot, to see a lot of theater." An artist must have natural talent, but he also has much to learn, which he does, according to Allen, as "an act of love": "You love it . . . and gradually you learn. . . . It's the same way with play-writing, or movie-directing, or acting [as with being a musician]. You love either reading or watching films or plays or listening to music. And in some way, over the years, without making any attempt, it gets into your blood, into the fibre of your body."[16] That is why the mature artist can rely on instinct, for it is not an untutored, raw instinct.

From the vantage of his more experienced "pure writer's instinct," Allen would do some things in his earlier movies differently, such as introduce "the other woman," Pearl, earlier in *Interiors*.[17] Instinct, or inspiration, is not unerring and requires, as Allen admits, experience and knowledge. The greater the artist, and the more mature, the more he can rely on instinct to guide him to the whole that he glimpses. Some things fit, others do not. Some are correct for the film, others are not. The artist's choices are not simply arbitrary, even if the reasons for them are at times "unconscious."[18] That is why authors have said, "trust the tale, not the teller,"[19] and that is why the work of art itself can serve as an authority for its own interpretation.

Interviewing Allen about his movies, Stig Bjorkman asked him whether the "jump-cut technique" he used in *Husbands and Wives*, focusing on a character and then quickly cutting to another shot where the character is in a slightly different position, is indebted to Godard's early films. While Allen quite clearly intended the technique to produce "a jagged, nervous feeling" that reflected the "internal, emotional and mental states of the characters," he did not consciously have Godard in mind. He does not know whether using this technique simply came to him one day, or whether he learned about it from Godard. Godard is certainly "part of the rich treasure of wonderful film-makers that have contributed to the vocabulary of the film." Allen is aware that sometimes he does something in a film that is "stimulating and exciting" and that "just couldn't be related to anybody else having done [it]," and other times "it's in the tradition of the vocabulary that other film-makers have given us." And he is not always sure when it is one way rather than the other.[20] This is why we should trust the tale, which is of course more or less trustworthy depending on the greatness of its source, the artist's "pure, artist's instinct," his familiarity with the traditions in which he works, and his reflections upon life. To whatever extent art requires interpretation for its completion, interpretation feeds upon art, just as art does upon life.

When Allen speaks of the heritage of film literature that comes into play in his own work,[21] he means many classical American filmmakers and comic actors, such as Orson Welles, Alfred Hitchcock, Charlie Chaplin, Buster Keaton, Bob Hope, and the Marx Brothers. He is also referring to European directors—Bergman, Renoir, Fellini, and Godard, for example. Allen does not depreciate entertainment, and he even admits that some of his films are merely entertainment, but he also aspires to the greatest art.[22] And the greatest art, as he understands it, places itself within a tradition, both deliberately and instinctively, in some ways deviating from it, in others affirming it, but always building on it.

Allen's heritage, however, is not limited to film. Underlying Allen's movies is not simply the rich treasure of filmmakers to whom he is consciously and unconsciously indebted, but also a trove of poets and philosophers. In an early sketch, for example, his "Apology," he occupies the place of Socrates.[23] And he singles out Russian novelists such as Dostoyevsky and Tolstoy as "greater than other novelists" because they treat "the so-called existential themes, the spiritual themes," which "to me are still the only subjects worth dealing with." The question of "our position in life and in the world" is "the only interesting theme to me," he maintains, and mentions Kierkegaard especially, whose themes are "the natural material of a dramatist."[24] Allen's heritage, which he addresses through his movies, is also the heritage of Western civilization, of its philosophy and literature.

Allen addresses this tradition in a variety of ways. Consider, for example, his titles and plots. *Love and Death* portrays a failed attempt of a Russian peasant to assassinate Napoleon. Like Tolstoy's *War and Peace*, which the movie deliberately recalls, *Love and Death* considers the existential issues that haunt Tolstoy's characters. With *A Midsummer Night's Sex Comedy*, Allen remakes Shakespeare's *Midsummer Night's Dream*: the movie's mix-up of lovers in the country outside the city mirrors Shakespeare's confusion of lovers in the forest outside of Athens. *Crimes and Misdemeanors* treats the issue of justice and punishment raised by Dostoyevsky's *Crime and Punishment*. *Oedipus Wrecks*, Woody Allen's contribution to *New York Stories*, is about a man who attempts to deny his origins, but fails to do so. It thereby echoes Sophocles' ancient drama. The character that Allen plays is responsible for making his mother disappear just as Oedipus commits patricide, but in each case the parent nevertheless looms large in the child's life.

Allen in effect "replays" the old books, novels, and plays in order to make an implicit comment on them. He thus enters into the conversation between the greatest philosophers and poets. The conversation is more than intellectual. In one of his earlier sketches, "The Kugelmass Episode," an English professor employs magic to actually enter the novel *Madame Bovary*.[25] Imagine the surprise of the readers of this French classic when this strange little Jewish professor keeps turning up on its pages. The main character in this sketch serves as a paradigm for Allen himself, for he too enters into the books of the Western tradition when he replays them in his movies. There is a parallel between *Madame Bovary* with Kugelmass in it and *Oedipus Wrecks*, for example, which is like *Oedipus Rex* with Woody Allen in it.

"Replaying" the old in order to comment upon its relevance to life is also Allen's explicit device in one of his earlier movies, *Play It Again, Sam*. The line that forms the movie's title resembles that spoken by Ilsa Lund in *Casablanca*, when she asks the pianist Sam to "play it," referring to the song that she once shared with Rick and that now only calls attention to the changes that have occurred when "Time Goes By." The irony is bitter, for it is no longer "the same old story" between her and Rick, and the words of the song stand in sad contrast to the deeds of the former lovers.

Woody Allen picks up on this issue, raising by his own title the question of whether his movie, a replay of *Casablanca*, is the same old story, or whether fundamental things change as time goes by. Can Allen say to the maker of *Casablanca* what Ilsa Lund says to Sam? Can the old be repeated? Of course, *Play It Again, Sam* is not *Casablanca*. What effect does the "replaying" have on the original? Can art capture, in the words of "As Time Goes By," something "fundamental" that changes no more than the meaning of a kiss or a sigh? And can it capture the fundamental without denying the uniqueness of the new? The title of Allen's movie is itself only a partial repetition of Ilsa's words, for he adds "again" to her phrase. There is no simple repetition.[26] Allen thus enters a dialogue that has animated the most serious literary and philosophic works of the Western tradition, for even if everything has already been said, it nevertheless requires saying again. And that is the significance of the "Kugelmass Episode": the lovely Madame Bovary arouses the professor's love, and he enters the novel to have an affair with her. The old classic changes in time, as it affects its readers and they are drawn into it.

In this way Woody Allen responds to what Socrates many years ago called the "old quarrel between philosophy and poetry" (*Republic*, 607b). In Plato's *Republic*, Socrates criticizes the artist or the poet for binding human beings to the here and now, to their own personal lives, and thus for impeding their philosophic pursuit of eternal truths. The poet gives pleasure, and thus flatters his audience, and has little concern with telling the truth in his poetry. The philosopher, in contrast, pursues the truth no matter how unpleasant, for both others and himself. The distinction that Socrates makes between poetry, which aims at pleasure, and philosophy, which aims at truth, is similar to the distinction Allen first saw in the cinema of his childhood and teenage years, between the "entertainment and escapism" of American cinema and the "much more confrontational and grown up" European films.[27] The former resembles the kind of poetry that Socrates criticizes, while mature cinema is more reminiscent of the philosophy with which Socrates contrasts poetry.

Allen thus sees the possibility of a kind of "philosophic poetry."[28] It is one that addresses "our position in life and in the world," "the existential themes, the spiritual themes." Such a poetry does not avoid truth for the sake of entertainment. It does not flatter. Allen not only casts himself in the role of Socrates in his sketch, "My Apology," where he awaits execution because "the senate is furious over [his] ideas."[29] He also portrays in *Stardust Memories* a director who refuses to give people the mere escapist entertainment they crave and imagines himself being shot by a fan. In order to avoid escapist entertainment in that film, director Sandy Bates must confront not only his fans but also his producers. Sandy wants to give his film a realistic ending, but the producers insist that "too much reality is not what the people want." They want a "commercial," "upbeat" movie, for "human suffering does not sell movies in Kansas City."

In the course of *Stardust Memories*, however, Sandy discovers an ending for his movie that is acceptable both to the producers and to Sandy himself. Sandy's original ending, to his producer's consternation, showed the journey of life ending for everyone in a garbage heap. The producers, in contrast, wanted to show everyone going to a "Jazz Heaven." Sandy offers a new ending: while there are still "many sad people," it is not clear where they are going, but even if it is to that same junkyard, "we like each other . . . we have some laughs, and there's a lot of closeness." Sandy imagines that he is on that train, with a woman who is in love with him in spite of his doing "a lot of foolish things"; she realizes that he's not evil, "only floundering around . . . ridiculous, maybe . . . just searching." In other words, Sandy has discovered that life is good even if there is no Jazz Heaven of which we can be assured.

More important, even if a Jazz Heaven were possible, Allen suggests, it would not be desirable. *The Purple Rose of Cairo* shows that human life is good only because it is not perfect. In that movie the protagonist learns the problematic character of a "perfect" and flawless artistic creation with whom she falls in love. An artist who has a complex understanding of the goodness of imperfect and changing human life might be both entertaining and confrontational at the same time. He could both reconcile us to our human condition and also challenge the simple platitudes that view Jazz Heavens and whatever is analogous to them as either possible or desirable.

Sandy's resolution of his movie is a reflection of Allen's mature understanding, and an understanding that has been refined and deepened over his years of making movies. It is a combination of the American "entertainment" that he experienced in movie theaters as a boy and the "eye-opening" maturity of European cinema.[30] It is neither the escapism that might accompany entertainment nor the pessimism with which mature cinema might confront us. Like Zelig in the movie that bears his name, Allen both reflects others (the cinematic traditions that he loves, both American and European) and becomes "his own man."

Inasmuch as Allen's art is entertaining as well as confrontational, moreover, it does not merely follow Socrates in upbraiding the pursuit of pleasure. Rather, it indicates that the alternatives are not as stark as Socrates delineates in the *Republic*. Indeed, Socrates leaves open the possibility of reconciling philosophy and poetry when he hopes that some poet or lover of poetry might write a defense of poetry, showing that it's not only pleasant, but beneficial for societies and human life (607c–d). Aristotle provides just such a defense in his *Poetics* when he argues that poetry is "more philosophic than history." While history narrates particulars, events that have happened, poetry narrates events that might happen, Aristotle explains, showing their underlying causes or truths. Poetry reveals universal themes in the particular situations and characters it portrays and stories it tells (*Poetics*, viii.4–ix.4). Allen is a poet, I believe, whose poetry is true to Aristotle's observation that poetry is philosophic.

The characters of Allen's movies alone indicate the universality and importance of his themes. There is the philosophy professor in *A Midsummer Night's Sex Comedy* who opens the movie by denying that there are "ghosts, little spirits, or pixies." Woody Allen mocks his avowed empiricism by celebrating his intended marriage to the beautiful and pixielike Ariel. There are other characters who represent the spiritual life, from the inventor of the spirit ball in *A Midsummer Night's Sex Comedy* to the rabbi who believes in the ultimate justice of the universe in *Crimes and Misdemeanors*. Some of Allen's characters are philosophy professors who are successful in their careers but fail to understand themselves—not only in *Sex Comedy* but also in *Another Woman*. In other movies like *Bullets over Broadway* artists suffer the pitfalls of the life of imagination.

Not only are Allen's movies about philosophers and poets of various sorts. They constantly raise the question of the relation between life and art. Is art a means to escape life, as Cecilia uses movies during the Depression in *The Purple Rose of Cairo*, or does life imitate art for its own self-improvement, as Allan Felix attempts to imitate Bogart's Rick in *Play It Again, Sam*?

By raising the question of art or poetry, and in particular the question of movies, as Allen does in these two movies, he raises the question of his own activity in making movies. *Play It Again, Sam* opens with the camera focusing on Allan Felix in a movie theater watching *Casablanca*. What effect is the movie having on him? But we too are watching a movie, and is its effect on us like or unlike that of *Casablanca* on Allan Felix? The film need not have begun in a movie theater. The original play, from which Allen wrote the screenplay, began with Allan Felix watching a Bogart movie on television. The change highlights the fact that Woody Allen's films are self-reflective.[31] Whether or not Allen makes movies reflecting his personal life, his movies do reflect his life as an artist. Some of them are literally movies about movies, but most in one way or another concern the relation between art and life. It is thus the poet, to speak in ancient terms, who finds a way to self-knowledge, because he finds a way to reflect and thereby see himself. In *Another Woman*, we shall see a philosophy professor come to understand herself only with the help of poetry.

In the last of the "Selections from the Allen Notebooks," Allen writes, "Last night, I burned all my plays and poetry."[32] In doing so he casts himself as that disciple of Socrates, Plato, who was rumored to have burned all of his plays and poetry after he met Socrates.[33] Presumably Plato heard Socrates' criticisms of poetry and his beautiful accounts of the philosophic inquiry into the truth. The story about Plato, however, is not entirely true, for Plato did not stop writing poetry after meeting Socrates, but discovered a form of poetry that was a tribute to his philosophic teacher. As Aristotle says, Plato's Socratic dialogues are forms of poetry (*Poetics*, i. 9). Neither did Allen turn away from art. Whatever he may have burned, it did not include his own notebooks that recount the burning.

Allen says that when he burned all his plays and poetry, "his room caught fire." Thus, his deed had surprising and dangerous consequences. Whatever reservations he may have had about poetry, there is no danger so great as an artist's trying to destroy poetry, for his doing so recoils on himself, even if the outcome is in this case more comic than tragic. Although the author of the "Allen Notebooks" does not die in the conflagration, he no longer has any place to live, and even becomes "the object of a lawsuit." Woody Allen, in contrast, like Plato, also perfected a form of poetry, his movies, which do not require burning. There need be neither tragic self-destruction nor his persona's comic ignorance of the effects of his action.

Because he grew up in America during "the time of the star system," when "there was not an emphasis on directors," Allen first thought of movies in terms of their stars. Later he realized "what the directors were doing," and that "certain directors were better than other directors."[34] Allen incorporates his reflections on directors, on movies, and on art in general into his films. *Stardust Memories* is about a movie director making a movie. A director directing a movie reflects Allen's own experience, even if Sandy, as Allen insists, should not be identified with Allen. *Purple Rose* is about a movie. The name of Allen's movie, in fact, is also the name of the Hollywood movie within his movie. Just as Allen invites us to compare *Stardust Memories* with the movie that Sandy is making in *Stardust Memories*, he also invites us to compare the two movies bearing the same name of *Purple Rose*. Allen's other movies also offer more or less explicitly Allen's reflections on art and artists.

In *Play It Again, Sam* Allen portrays the neuroses of modern life and raises the question of whether movies foster those neuroses.

Do they mislead us about life? Do they corrupt? Or can movies be of use in overcoming our neuroses? Is there hope for the modern, alienated individual, and what form might that hope take? While *Play It Again, Sam* explores the effects of art on the moviegoer and critic, *Annie Hall* and *Interiors* portray artists of various sorts—from playwrights and photographers to interior decorators and poets—whose artistic aspirations and achievements seem to be a cause of unhappiness—from Alvy's "anhedonia" in *Annie Hall* to Eve's suicide in *Interiors*. While Eve's art stifles life, her own and those of others, *Stardust Memories* portrays a movie director whose art comes to transcend the lifeless images of *Interiors*. *A Midsummer Night's Sex Comedy* juxtaposes an empiricist philosopher and the inventor of a spirit ball, which throws out images like a movie projector. The movie points to what the empiricist and the image maker must each learn from the other, which happens also to be what an artist must know to make movies like Sandy Bates's rather than "interiors" like Eve's.

Zelig is a fake documentary about a man who reflects the shape of everyone, or almost everyone, whom he encounters. He is like an artist whose eye—or camera—reflects the world for others to see. Zelig, however, is "a freak," a sick man who, while fascinating to society, indeed, "touching a nerve," must also be cured. And he is. The movie explores the possibility of a healthy relationship between the individual and the world with which he comes into contact—and how art can reflect and constitute such a relation.

The Purple Rose of Cairo most explicitly examines the relation between movies and reality, fantasy and life, when a character in a movie who walks off the screen and the actor who plays him compete for the affections of the star-crazed Cecilia. Which should Cecilia choose? How should she live, and what should be the place of movies in her life? Another woman, in Allen's movie bearing that title, is wrapped up in a book she is writing rather than the movies Cecilia craves, but while she seems equally distant from life, she is able to overcome that distance and understand herself by observing another. She is like a spectator at the movies who through the experience becomes able to play her own part in life.

In *Crimes and Misdemeanors*, a murderer escapes the law, while in

Manhattan Murder Mystery another murderer is brought to justice. In *Crimes* a marriage falls apart; in *Murder Mystery* another marriage is renewed. Is there anything but chance that causes one result or the other? Is *Crimes and Misdemeanors*, moreover, with its disjointed interweaving of tragedy and comedy in plot and subplot, an artistic tribute to the chaos—and immorality—of life itself? And is *Manhattan Murder Mystery*, where a housewife involves herself and her resisting husband in solving what she believes is a murder next door, an imitation of life by art that is as escapist as Cecilia's *Purple Rose*? Or does the movie show an imitation of art by life that demonstrates art's role in sustaining and elevating life itself?

Bullets over Broadway and *Mighty Aphrodite* offer explicit treatment of the relation between art and moral concerns about how we should live our lives. In *Bullets over Broadway*, the greatest artist turns out to be a murderer, one who will not compromise his art and suffers a tragic death. But Woody Allen's movie is a comedy, one in which the central character gives up his pretensions to be an artist. He cannot accept the morality of the decision to kill for art. He rejects the search for artistic integrity in favor of a conventional married life in Pittsburgh. Even if we cannot imagine Allen himself choosing married life in Pittsburgh, Allen the artist shows us his recognition of the limits of art. Allen understands that the limits of art ultimately reflect the limits of human choice and control. But the recognition of the limits of choice does not lead Allen to despair about the possibility of individual choice or morality. In *Mighty Aphrodite*, Allen transforms Greek tragedy into a comedy. His vision of the human condition is neither that of fated doom nor unlimited freedom. Virtue lies in making choices that will lead to a better life while avoiding the hubris of attempting absolute control of our lives and those of others. It is such an understanding of human life and virtue that makes possible a Woody Allen comedy—an understanding found in even as dark a movie as *Interiors*.

"Selections from Allen's Notebooks," mentioned above, is the first entry in his book *Without Feathers*. Allen derives his title, as he indicates by the epigraph at the beginning of his book, from a poem by Emily Dickinson in which she writes that "Hope is the thing with feathers." Something without feathers is therefore without hope. It can neither fly nor imagine itself flying. The "masterpiece" that Allen was burning when his room caught fire is entitled *Dark Penguin*.[35] A penguin is one of the few birds that does not fly. Although Allen burns *Dark Penguin*, he continues to write, and he continues to make movies. He does not forswear all art. He searches for a not-so-dark comedy that affirms the goodness of life; he searches for a reason to hope. If we thought we were going to either a Jazz Heaven or a garbage heap, hope would make no sense.

Allen, at times, especially in his early career, flirts with an existential despair. He wrote a play for the theater of the absurd, for example, in which the character who plays God dies on his way to save human events from disaster, and a writer is left with no ending for his play. The final lines of Allen's one-act *God* are identical to the lines with which the play opens, lines in which a writer and actor lament that their play has no ending.[36] But Sandy Bates finds an ending for his movie that does not reproduce the ending he filmed at the beginning. Sandy's vision develops, as does Allen's. Indeed, Allen seems drawn by the integrity of his art to affirm through his good artist's instinct more than he knows or at least thinks that he knows. While human beings are without feathers, Allen's movies show that they are not without hope. In fact, their ability to appreciate Allen's art allows them to soar in a way impossible for featherless bipeds.

2

The Hero and the Klutz

(Play It Again, Sam)

With *Play It Again, Sam* (1972), a more serious Woody Allen emerges. Where he was "zany and idiosyncratic," he now shows a "heightened sensitivity and moral complexity."[1] *Play It Again, Sam* is a film about film. It is also a film about *Casablanca*. At its opening, its hero, Allan Felix, played by Allen himself, watches the 1942 film *Casablanca* in a movie theater. As the credits pass across the screen, the camera moves back and forth from the last scene of *Casablanca* to Allan's face and reveals a man absorbed by what he is viewing. Bogart himself even appears from time to time in *Play It Again, Sam* as Allan Felix's advisor and confidant. Several elements from the plot of *Casablanca* appear in *Play It Again, Sam* as well: both Rick and Allan have been abandoned by the women they love, and *Play It Again, Sam* ends with the reenactment in Felix's life of the last scene of *Casablanca*. Woody Allen thus takes Ilsa's request to Sam not merely for his title but as an injunction to himself.

Play It Again, Sam is, in effect, a replay of *Casablanca*. But it is also a revision of *Casablanca*. Allan Felix may try to imitate Humphrey Bogart, but no one could confuse this insecure, clumsy, whining hypochondriac with Bogart. Allan Felix grows out of the *schlemiel*. A figure from Yiddish folklore, the *schlemiel* is a loser (especially in love) who is victimized whichever way he turns but nevertheless converts his weakness into strength by means of his wit, his intel-

19

lect, and his humor.[2] Thus, *schlemiel* Allan Felix, bemoaning that his wife left him, recalls that his wife was in the habit of watching television during sex with him and changing channels with a remote control. Whatever Bogart may be, he is not a *schlemiel*.

While *Casablanca* gives us Bogart for a hero, Allen gives us a klutz. Bogart is poised and debonair. Allan Felix is clumsy. Bogart is strong, tough, and self-reliant. Allan is constantly concerned with his health. He laments that his analyst is out of town in August, but given the quantity of pills in his dresser we may suppose he spends time with other physicians as well. He whines about everything, all the time. He is a world-class neurotic who when he goes to the beach worries about spiders and instead of a beautiful landscape sees "eagles flying over a cesspool." When his friends ask him what kind of women he would like to meet, he claims that he prefers "neurotics."

Allan Felix wants to be like Bogart in part because women find Bogart attractive. Although Ilsa mysteriously leaves Rick, it is only in spite of her great love for him. Allan's wife, Nancy, in contrast, tells him when she walks out: "I can't stand the marriage. I don't find you fun. I feel you suffocate me. I don't feel any rapport with you, and I don't dig you physically." Nancy generously advises him that he should not take her complaints personally, but of course this is not easy, especially when other women react to him in a similar way. When he tries to accompany a blind date up to her apartment, she slams the door in his face. When he asks a woman in a bar to dance, she utters a contemptuous "Get lost, creep." Allan clearly cannot "score" with women. As he laments, his "sex life is turning into the petrified forest" as he becomes "the strike-out king of San Francisco." Much of the "comedy" of the movie stems from Allan's attempt to imitate Bogart. Like a classic comic figure, Allan Felix overreaches and makes himself ridiculous.

Nor is Allan's wife, Nancy, any Ilsa Lund. Like her husband, she has more "modern" problems. While Ilsa leaves Rick to return to Victor and to support his work in the resistance against Hitler, Nancy wants to go skiing and dancing, she claims, she wants to laugh, she wants to swing. She wants adventure or excitement, which real life, or at least real life with Allan, does not provide. All she and Allan ever do together, she complains, is see movies. He is, she says, "one of the world's great watchers."

Nancy reproaches Allan for using movies as a substitute for life. Absorbed in the lives of those on the screen, he does not have one of his own. And yet movies are his livelihood, for he writes reviews for a small movie magazine. Does he provide for the necessities of life only in a way that fosters an escape from life? Or does his "occupation" hint that watching movies, at least in some cases, can be useful for life?

Allan's best friend, Dick (Tony Roberts), in contrast to both Allan and Nancy, serves as a parody of the American entrepreneur. He has time neither for "watching" movies nor for the "fun" that Nancy craves. His life is so consumed by his business that he constantly gives his office a string of phone numbers where he can be reached. He remains oblivious of the sarcasm in his wife's (Diane Keaton) suggestion that he give his office the number of the pay phone on the corner that he will pass on his way home. He too tries to comfort Allan about the loss of his wife: "A man makes an investment; it doesn't pay off," and since Allan has "invested his emotions on a losing stock," he must "reinvest."

While Allan Felix searches for the love of a woman, Dick does not notice the wife who loves him. And, although Allan tries to warn him, he remains unaware of how his neglect intensifies Linda's own insecurities.[3] Linda is, in fact, the neurotic of Allan's dreams. The situation is fraught with obvious dangers. As Dick goes about his business and his business trips, Linda becomes Allan's companion, attempting to give him the self-confidence he needs in his relations with women. But while Linda encourages him to drop the Bogart facade, Allan also gets advice from his immortal hero, who walks off the screen into Allan's life. As to Allan's rejection by his wife, Bogart tells him that this is "nothing a little bourbon and soda couldn't fix." There is no dame, he philosophizes to Felix, who doesn't "understand a slap in the mouth, or the slug from a forty-five." Be tough, and "dames" fall at your feet. The world is full of them, and they come when you whistle. In particular, try to seduce your best friend's wife when he is out of town and she is giddy from champagne, fond of you, and lonely due to

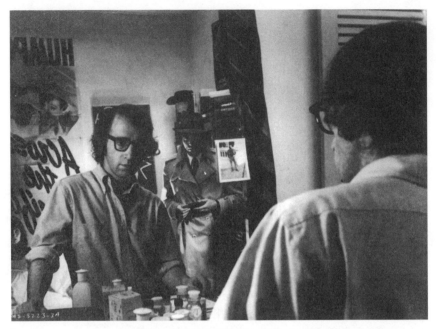

Jerry Lacey, as Bogart, offers advice to Woody Allen in *Play It Again, Sam*.
Credit: Paramount (courtesy Kobal).

her husband's inattention. This is his chance "to score." Allan finally acts and Linda responds. After they spend a night together,
Allan "manfully" decides that Linda should tell Dick she is leaving
him for Allan.

Meanwhile Dick has called from Cleveland and found his wife
away from home for the night. With whom could she be? He rushes
home to confide to Allan his suspicions as well as his new awareness of his love for her and his resolve that in the future he will take
her on all business trips. Far from blaming his wife for infidelity,
he admits that he had in effect abandoned her and must ask her to
forgive him before it's too late. He is determined to change. Allan,
for his part, is appalled by what he has been thinking of doing.
Dick loves Linda, more than Allan had known. To pursue his relation with her further would be to break up a marriage. Besides,
Dick is his friend. He cannot betray him. He and Linda must reconsider their decision before it is too late.

Linda too has had second thoughts. After initially rejecting Dick's declaration of love, she rushes to catch the plane he is taking back to Cleveland. Her cab follows his to the airport. Allan arrives only to find that Dick and Linda have left, and a third cab soon follows the other two. Bogart, it happens, is driving Allan's taxi, and while he had previously urged him to seduce Linda, he now lets him know that "there's other things in life besides dames and one of them is to know you did the right thing for a pal." When Allan overtakes Linda on the way to the runway, she tells him the wonderful thing that has happened—not merely to herself, for she sees the possibility of a better marriage with Dick, but to Allan as well, who has "scored" with a woman who knows him for what he is, who has even seen him in his underwear marked with the days of the week. He has "scored," in other words, without adopting the tough Bogart persona. Allan tells her that she must go with Dick, that if she is not on that plane, she'll "regret it, maybe not today, maybe not tomorrow, but soon, and for the rest of [her] life." He admits that he has been waiting all his life to utter these words from *Casablanca*.

When the two find Dick, Allan steps further into Rick's persona—not the cynic whom Rick pretends to be but the noble man whom we see by the end of *Casablanca* and whom we glimpsed in the taxi. Allan tells Dick, as Rick told Laszlo, that his wife was with him last night, and that although he tried to win her love she remained faithful to him. He may lie to his friend, but his lie is not a selfish one. Like Ilsa and Laszlo, Linda and Dick leave in the plane, and, like Rick, Allan walks off into the mist. Bogart, who has hovered over the movie, bids him farewell. From now on, he observes, Allan Felix will not be needing him. "Here's looking at you, kid," he says to him.

Casablanca ends with "the beginning of a beautiful friendship" as Rick walks off with Louie, while Allan Felix walks off alone. It is also the case that the original play that Allen wrote ended with Allan Felix meeting a new neighbor who seems to be the very woman he has been seeking. But the ending of the movie is not negative. Lee is correct, I believe, when he observes that "by removing this artificially happy ending of the [play] from the film, and by allowing Allan to walk alone into the airport fog, Allen implies that even though Allan is sufficiently mature to build a real relationship, that process is the stuff of a new and different movie."[4]

Because Allan discovers at the end that, as he says to Bogart, "the secret's not being you, it's being me," we might be tempted to conclude that the movie culminates in a choice of reality over image, of life over art. After all, Linda earlier tried to dissuade Allan from imitating Bogart, for "real life is not like that." She assures him that he doesn't "need an image." Such simple advice, however, is rendered problematic because it is the conclusion *of a movie*. A movie is itself an image. Girgus, for example, aware of this subtlety, argues that in the course of the movie Allen rejects one image in order to create another. He argues that in *Play It Again, Sam*, Bogart represents "sexual stereotypes, gender roles, and cultural archetypes" that Allen's movie subverts in order to reconstruct the American character. In particular, "in contrast to the classic Bogart myth of American manhood," with its ideal of "privileged detachment" and "immunity from commitment," Allen "contrives . . . a vulnerable hero . . . who articulates his fears and exposes his emotional dependence on others."[5]

Girgus's account of *Play It Again, Sam* thus rejects any simple dichotomy between life and art and preserves a constructive, educative role for the filmmaker. Girgus, however, argues not merely that art and life are inseparable, but also that they are indistinguishable. When Allan Felix watches *Casablanca* at the beginning of the movie and the camera shifts back and forth between his face and the movie screen, according to Girgus, "subjectivity and identity become largely ephemeral." The hero "floats from being the imaginary subject of the action of the movie to being simply a viewer who loses his identity and his ability to act through his total immersion in the interior film." And so the sequence of shots demonstrates "the fragmented and disjointed nature of subjectivity."[6] The ephemeral character of subjectivity and identity means that Allan Felix does not become his own person, or find himself, at the end of the movie. Rather, he comes to imitate a new kind of hero, the moviemaker's own construction of the American character. For Girgus, reconstruction becomes indistinguishable from "invention," as he imagines endless "destructions and reconstructions," as the human subject becomes whatever we, or perhaps artists, make of it.[7]

An obvious difficulty with Girgus's view is his too-simple distinction between the Bogart myth and Woody Allen's "new" American hero. Girgus views Bogart as the tough, independent, and selfish male, a stereotype that he argues *Play It Again, Sam* subverts. But there is another side to the Rick of *Casablanca*. While Rick may claim that he sticks his neck out for nobody, he does help a young married couple in need. Rick once was, after all, a romantic idealist, who loved and was loved and suffered greatly from Ilsa's disappearance. Not simply the tough cynic he pretended to be, Rick remained torn between the cynicism about life that developed in response to his hurt and the love that earlier characterized him and that he realizes again.

Girgus is no doubt right that Bogart often played hard-nosed, selfish characters, but the Bogart who most moves Allan Felix, at least first and last in the movie, is the noble Bogart who sacrifices his own happiness with Ilsa and who commits himself to the resistance against Hitler. Girgus himself observes that Rick's "external hardness and indifference . . . masks the inner yearnings and earnestness of the American hero."[8]

In the end it is still Bogart's advice that Allan follows, even though it differs from his earlier counsel. Moreover, Allan's final act in the movie is to imitate what Rick does in *Casablanca*. Other critics have therefore noted the "ironic nuances" in Allan Felix's choice at the end, for "the reality he chooses over romance is the opportunity to live out his fantasy of playing Bogart."[9] His choice to be himself, then, is not simply a rejection of Bogart. *Casablanca* remains a force in his life. If *Play It Again, Sam* is a reconstruction of the American character, as Girgus argues, it is not one that subverts an earlier archetype. Rather, it adapts—in a new form for a new era—the model in the earlier film.

Even critics who note that Bogart remains an important influence on Allan Felix, however, agree with Girgus that the movie questions the distinction of life from art. Nancy Pogel, for example, emphasizes the "unresolved problems" left "by the film's ending"—its "replication of *Casablanca*'s finale in the conclusion." "At the very moment," she points out, that Allan Felix "seems to choose reality over fiction, and the spectator decides that *Play It Again, Sam* demonstrates that film images can and should be distinguished from reality, the ending reemphasizes that real life remains more difficult to separate from fiction than we thought." She praises this "complicated vision" with which the movie leaves us, inasmuch as it "acknowledges that all resolutions are conditional in a world where fiction and reality have begun to merge." To her we are all—"filmmaker, audience, and characters . . . implicated . . . in a modern viewpoint that permits no comforting certainties about what constitutes fiction."[10]

While these critics correctly remind us of the subtleties and ambiguities in Allen's films, I believe that they neglect the way in which images actually function in the movie. We have seen a tension between two images of Bogart that Allan Felix holds—the hard-nosed cynic and the noble Rick who upholds moral integrity and personal loyalty. In *Play It Again, Sam* Bogart both encourages Allan to seduce Linda and speaks to him of doing the right thing and of being loyal to a pal. There is the Bogart who encourages the hot pursuit of "dames," and there is the Bogart who later advises that there is more to life than dames. The emergence of the latter Bogart out of the former is signaled in the movie when the cynical Bogart advises Allan what to say as he seduces Linda. The image of Nancy appears and shoots the image of Bogart. Just as Nancy earlier spoke up against the influence of movies on her former husband, she now takes dramatic action against them. With Bogart out of the way, Allan no longer treats Linda as "a dame." But although he drops the Bogart pose, he does commit adultery. The resurrected image of Bogart returns to uphold moral standards and friendship and to help Allan further find himself. However much she may have tried, Nancy cannot expel Bogart entirely from her former husband's life. Nor would it have been good had she succeeded. She does not understand the positive force of movies. There is more to life than dames, and movies convey this truth.

When Allan Felix learns to be himself, then, he does not simply reject Bogart or the heroism of old movies; rather, he filters the images of the past and models himself on what is appropriate to him. This does not mean that he is again acting out a role or a persona, but that one side of the Bogart image has helped him to see himself and to act according to the best that is in him. This is Felix's own potential, even from the beginning. While he is attracted to the tough-speaking Bogart, he is also extremely moved by the ending of *Casablanca*. He has been, after all, waiting "all his life" to utter those words. In the end Allan Felix affirms *Casablanca* and its ideals while rejecting other aspects of the Bogart image.

By rejecting one side of Bogart and accepting another, Allen achieves his own form with the help of a movie. He has not let movies form him. Viewing movies has not caused him to lose himself in imaginary worlds, but it has helped him to realize his own integrity. Allan Felix is "blessed," as his surname suggests, for he has discovered himself through his imitations of Bogart. The "re-

Diane Keaton and Woody Allen play Linda and Allan playing Ilsa and Rick at the airport. Credit: Paramount (courtesy Kobal).

play" of *Casablanca* is no mere replay, for Allen Felix has become an independent actor and has chosen the noble part of a friend.

Allan Felix is finally able to do what Linda would like him to do, that is, to be himself. What he is, however, is manifest not only in his present life but in the noblest images he holds of himself. Certain movies—and this is true of both *Casablanca* and *Play It Again, Sam*—remind us of our potentials by moving us to identify with their heroes. This means that they touch our souls, not that they distract us from our real lives. There is much truth in Girgus's observation that the beginning sequence of *Play It Again, Sam*, as its camera moves back and forth between *Casablanca* and Allan's face, does blur the man sitting in the audience with what he is viewing on the screen. But far from indicating merely the power of art to replace reality and consequently our inability to distinguish the two, it indicates the way in which movies speak to us by reflecting what is real. Otherwise, the scenes at the end of *Casablanca* could not move us. *Casablanca* would not have become the classic that it became. Some images resonate, others do not. *Casablanca* does. *Play It Again, Sam* reminds us of this.

There is one sense, however, in which Allen's movie *Play It Again, Sam* is not a replay of *Casablanca*. Something is missing. When Ilsa goes with Laszlo, she chooses not merely to preserve her marriage but to help the cause to which her husband is devoted. We cannot understand her choice without being aware of the political context in which it is made.[11] Nor can we understand Victor Laszlo if we do not know of the importance of the resistance. In the moving moment that Woody Allen produces for us in *Play It Again, Sam*, we must not forget that Linda is going to stand by her husband in his real estate deals, and that no letters of transit are needed in order to fly to Cleveland. The "same old story" of "As Time Goes By" is "a case of do or die." Rick risks his life when he shoots the German commander, who was trying to prevent Laszlo from leaving Casablanca. Allen's contemporary love triangle is not the story of a war-torn world. Even so, when Allan Felix walks away at the end of Allen's movie, his life, like Rick's, has changed. Like Rick, he will be able to love and be loved. Rick sheds his cynicism, and Allan Felix grows out of his neurotic approach to women. But Rick is going to join the resistance. Allen himself reminds us of the difference, when Allan Felix walks off to the strains of the French national anthem.

The point is not that Allen's movie falls short of *Casablanca*, or that Allan Felix is not as noble as Rick, but that heroism has a place in our ordinary lives. Linda comes to see the possibility of the marriage with Dick that she always wanted, and even Dick rises above his commercial self-interest. He wants to take Linda on his business trips because he realizes, he says, that life is not worth living without her. He is no Victor Laszlo, but he is capable of love and friendship. Contrary to Allan Felix's observation that "it's strictly the movies," and Linda's that "real life's not like that," we see that Rick's words at the end of *Casablanca* are not for Allan Felix "strictly the movies" and that his "real life is like that." Felix sacrifices his own happiness with Linda, both because it is the right thing to do and because Dick is his friend. Moral decency in our relations with others and friendship play the part of the political ideals that resound in *Casablanca*. These are demanded in all times and circumstances, not just in the extraordinary ones in which Rick, Ilsa, and Laszlo lived.

While such a vision is needed at all times, it is particularly needed in ours. Allan Felix's neurosis occurs in a culture in which "meaningful human relationships are difficult to establish and to maintain."[12] Nancy, at least as Allan Felix imagines her, would be satisfied by someone who had a leather jacket and a fast motorcycle. One of his blind dates is a nymphomaniac who, although she desires nothing but sex, finds Allan repulsive. Even his more promising date Julie goes off with one of the thugs who accost her and Allan in a bar. When he tries to speak to a girl looking at a Jackson Pollock painting in an art museum, she sees only "the negativeness of the universe" in the picture, "the hideous, lonely emptiness of existence, nothingness, the predicament of man forced to live in a barren, godless eternity like a tiny flame flickering in an immense void . . . in a black absurd cosmos." She declines Allan's invitation to go out Saturday night, for she will be busy committing suicide. As to the "happy" marriage of Allan's friends, Linda is initially so insecure in her relationship that she sees an analyst three times a week, while "security" means to Dick only something he can buy and sell.

The words of "As Time Goes By," which Ilsa asks Sam to play, do not change with time, but circumstances do. The "fundamental things" still apply, but the problems of contemporary America differ from those of a world at war. This is why, in fact, a "re-play" is necessary: we need to be reminded that in spite of the changes the fundamental things still apply, and a new artist must demonstrate how they apply to us. Allan Felix's imitations of Bogart's tough-guy stance only make him ridiculous. And what is worse, his adoption of Bogart's cynicism only feeds his neuroses. He must learn not only to be himself, but also how the fundamental things still apply, what imitation of Bogart is appropriate to him, just as we must learn what imitation of Bogart is appropriate to our times. We need *Casablanca* not to encourage the patriotism and self-sacrifice required of citizens during war but to show that only noble actions and moral standards make possible the "meaningful" human relationships we have such difficulty finding.

Moreover, in spite of changes in our circumstances, we are still able to appreciate the political struggles in *Casablanca*. *Play It Again, Sam* reminds us of these when it incorporates scenes and lines from *Casablanca*. Just as that movie can become part of Allan Felix's life, so too can it become part of ours. It is not that *Play It Again, Sam* reminds us of what is no more, when it reminds us of *Casablanca*. Rather it reminds us that *Casablanca* is still with us, if only because it can be replayed. Just as Ilsa and Rick "will always have Paris," we will always have *Casablanca*.

We have seen in "The Kugelmass Episode" how a magician injects a contemporary English professor into Flaubert's novel *Madame Bovary*. As a filmmaker Allen is also a kind of magician, who puts a character from the past into his contemporary movie and thus helps Allan Felix to put himself into *Casablanca*. Both Kugelmass and Allan Felix seek experiences they cannot easily find in their own worlds. Like the Jewish professor who desires a great lover, Allan Felix desires to be a great lover, and for this he models himself after a great hero. Kugelmass brings Madame Bovary back to New York City with him, encouraging adultery and temporarily disrupting the novel, while Allan Felix encourages a wife to stay with her husband and releases Bogart at the end of his movie. Bogart will continue to inspire others by his role in *Casablanca*, as he has Allan Felix. Kugelmass ends up lost among the verbs of a Spanish grammar, for his magician misfires, while Allan Felix "returns" to his own life, understanding himself better and more able to live well because of it. Woody Allen has become as early as 1972 a magician who does not misfire.

3

The Anhedonist and the Singer

(Annie Hall)

While *Play It Again, Sam* has its serious dimension, it is
clearly a comedy. So is Allen's 1977 movie *Annie Hall*.
But *Annie Hall* is different. As Allen admits, with *Annie
Hall* he had the courage to stop "just clowning around." Allen acknowledges that *Annie Hall* is not simply comedy, or at least not the
kind of clowning around for which he had become known. Allen is
still funny in *Annie Hall*, "but not funny in the same way." The
movie was, Allen believes, "a turning point" for him. And "it
worked out very well."[1] Even Hollywood had to admit that it
worked out very well, and gave the movie four Academy Awards,
including best director and best screenplay.

Annie Hall opens with Woody Allen doing a comedy monologue,
telling the audience jokes of the sort that he used in his real-life
comic routines. It thus begins with Allen's recollections of his own
past as a stand-up comic. As Maurice Yacowar notes, we do not
immediately know whether we are watching Woody Allen speaking to us or some character he is playing.[2] In the course of the
monologue, however, the speaker becomes Alvy Singer, comedian,
writer, and television star, who narrates the events of *Annie Hall*.[3]
Comic monologue blends into Alvy's story of himself, stand-up
comedy into film. The movie is not only a turning point for Allen,
but it records that turning point. Alvy Singer confides that "Annie
and I broke up," and "I still can't get my mind around that." *Annie*

Hall is about remembering the past, but also about "getting around it." Whether or not Alvy "gets around" his relation with Annie (Diane Keaton), however, Allen gets around stand-up comedy and makes movies.

In his opening monologue, however, Alvy reflects on his life situation, and it is not entirely a happy one. He illustrates it by two jokes. An elderly woman at a resort in the Catskills complains to another that the food is terrible. "Yeah, I know," says her companion, "and such small portions." That is "essentially how I feel about life," Alvy confides, "full of loneliness and misery and suffering and unhappiness, and it's all over much too quickly." His second joke, the key to his relationships with women, is no more upbeat: "I would never want to belong to a club that would have someone like me for a member." And he would not want the love of any woman who would love him. His life—and relationships—are no-win situations: either he loses, or his winning is losing. A loser can never be anything but a loser. Alvy attributes this latter joke to Freud in his *Wit and Its Relation to the Unconscious*.

Critics have pointed out the extent to which Freud and psychoanalysis are "a perennial theme" in *Annie Hall*.[4] While in *Play It Again, Sam* Allan Felix's therapist is out of town during August, in *Annie Hall* we see Alvy on his therapist's couch. As Annie later describes Alvy's problem, he is "incapable of enjoying [him]self." Allen originally intended to name this movie *Anhedonia*—a term that means "the inability to experience pleasure." "The program of becoming happy, which the pleasure principle imposes on us," Freud writes in *Civilization and Its Discontents*, "cannot be fulfilled," for "life as we find it is too hard for us," and "brings too many pains, disappointments, and impossible tasks." "In order to bear it, we cannot dispense with palliative measures" such as those which "cause us to make light of our misery."[5] Comedy, laughter, jokes, for Freud—and for Alvy at the beginning of *Annie Hall*—serve as lies that make life bearable, ways of "making light" of what is not light, a forgetting necessary for life. Life's miseries, presumably, are why anhedonist Alvy is a comedian.

While Alvy believes the joke about not belonging to a club that would have one for a member appeared originally in Freud, it is usually attributed, Alvy admits, to Groucho Marx. Allen later included Groucho Marx, one of his favorite comics, among the things cited by Isaac Davis in the film *Manhattan* that make life worth living.[6] Do jokes, and comedy more generally, simply help to make life livable, as Freud suggests, or is comedy among the things that make life worth living? That is, is life not so miserable after all, and is comedy an indication of this? Is comedy not only a forgetting of what we must forget in order to live but a reminder of why life is good? Comedy surely comes in a variety of forms, just as people laugh for different reasons. If one sort of comedy makes life livable by hiding its miseries, might there be another sort that expresses life's goodness? Is *Annie Hall*, in other words, not only about whether Alvy can "get around" Annie, but about whether Allen can "get around" Freud? Does *Annie Hall* come closer to a Marx Brothers movie or a New York City version of *Civilization and Its Discontents*? *Play It Again, Sam*, we might say, is what *Casablanca* would look like if Allen were magically transported into its frames. What would Freud's work look like if Allen appeared between its covers? What does Allen's magic do to Freud?[7]

Freud enters *Annie Hall*, however, not only alongside Groucho Marx, but through psychiatrist Ernest Becker's *The Denial of Death*, one of the first books Alvy buys for Annie.[8] Becker explicitly modifies Freud: it is not simply the necessary frustration of sexual instinct but dread of death that lies behind human discontent. We must "rework [Freud's] vision of man from that of primarily a pleasure-seeker of sex," Becker claims, "to that of the terrified, death-avoiding animal." Echoing Rousseau's account of natural man and the origin of civilization in his *Second Discourse*, Becker writes of "the fall into self-consciousness, the emergence from comfortable ignorance in nature" that "had one great penalty for man: it gave him *dread*, or anxiety." And it is finally a "consciousness of death," that is "the primary repression, not sexuality."[9]

It is no wonder, then, that Becker's book is a favorite of "hyperanxious" Alvy. Man, for Becker, at some point "is not helped by more knowing, but only by living and doing in a partly self-forgetful way."[10] Alvy's problem, even as a child, could be described as thinking too much. The first flashback of the movie shows us Alvy's

mother bringing him to a therapist when he stops doing his homework. The young Alvy sees no point in doing anything. "The universe is expanding," he tells the doctor, "someday it will break
apart and that would be the end of everything." "You're here in
Brooklyn!" his mother objects, "Brooklyn is not expanding!" As
Alvy grows up, he seems merely to take to heart his mother's advice to look closer to home. His own death, not that of the universe,
becomes a more immediate concern.

Death is a "big subject with me," he tells Annie soon after they
meet. "You should know this if we're going to go out." But if death
is the problem that no human being can "get around," seeing the
truth is hardly conducive to happiness, as Becker's own references
to the need for self-forgetting suggest. To what extent can therapy
be an answer? On one point Becker paraphrases Freud approv-
ingly, "psychoanalysis cure[s] neurotic misery in order to introduce
the patient to the common misery of life."[11] Alvy may be too reflective about life, and hence about death. His consciousness of death
underlies his anhedonia. As he tells Annie, "I have a very pessimistic view of life."

A stand-up comic, in fact, is one who is sufficiently reflective
about his own life—and his own problems—that he is able to articulate his reflections for others. And this is just what Alvy does in
the movie, whose events he narrates. Not only does he tell us that
he broke up with Annie, he also tells us about his talking to strangers on the street about his relationship with Annie. The very form
of the movie—inasmuch as it opens with Alvy's monologue and
proceeds by flashbacks—is simply Alvy's remembering. And while
he seems to be speaking to us, the audience, he also might be speaking to an invisible therapist.[12] Just as in analysis the memories of
one's past are not sequential, Alvy's memories are of bits and pieces
of his life out of sequence, for the order of his remembering of
events does not follow the order in which they occurred. Among
his memories is even a session with his therapist. He remembers
himself remembering.

Other flashbacks to his past with Annie remind him of other
events. In one of these, when Annie's thoughts about the next day
take her mind off sex with Alvy, Alvy remembers how his own

"obsessing" with a theory about Kennedy's assassination prevented him from paying attention to his first wife Allison. In another flashback his second wife's fascination with the "fake insights" of intellectuals at a cocktail party alienates her from Alvy. When Alvy wants to have sex with her in the bedroom, he thinks it would be great to be "quietly humping" while all the intellectuals in the next room discuss "models of alienation." He wants to use intimacy with his wife Robin to stage an ironic scenario, as he imagines what is going on in the bedroom with an eye to what is going on in the living room. When Robin is appalled that he uses sex to express hostility, Alvy objects to her reduction of his animal urges to psychoanalytic categories. Theorizing of all sorts, from Alvy's own conspiracy theories to Robin's analysis of Alvy, to say nothing of intellectual discussions at cocktail parties that involve "models" of alienation rather than the real thing, seems at odds with life and relationships. As Alvy observes during the cocktail party, "intellectuals . . . prove you can be absolutely brilliant and have no idea of what's going on."

Annie, at least before meeting Alvy, is not as self-reflective as he is. While Alvy theorizes that in photography "the medium enters in as the condition of the art form itself," when Annie takes pictures it is "all instinctive": she tries to get a sense of it without thinking about it too much. In contrast to Alvy, who has been in therapy for fifteen years, Annie goes to a therapist only after Alvy encourages her to do so. When Annie tells a story about death to Alvy, it is a death that happens as easily as falling asleep. Her Grammy Hall's narcoleptic brother George fell asleep in a grocery line as he waited for a free Christmas turkey, and never woke up. Annie laughs as she recounts the story. Annie's story recalls the "comfortable ignorance in nature" of which Becker spoke, as well as the unreflective condition of Rousseau's natural state where, like Annie's uncle, natural man "dies without noticing it." Allen highlights the difference between Annie and Alvy when Alvy clearly finds death and Annie's talk no laughing matter. Alvy says sarcastically, "great story," "it really made my day."

Critics have noted Annie's effect on Alvy. She is "a crazy, humanizing antitoxin for Alvy's seriousness," who "transfer[s her] optimism—at least for a while—to frustrated Alvy."[13] When the two reconcile after their first breakup, Annie pleads with him to let her help him have more fun. But Annie's battle for the pleasure principle is certainly uphill. When Annie wants to go to a party with West Coast recording artists, Alvy takes her instead to see *The Sorrow and the Pity*, although she's hardly "in the mood to sit through a four-hour documentary about Nazis." She suggests going away for the weekend with Alvy, but Alvy merely takes her to his old home in Brooklyn, where they have flashbacks to his childhood. They witness embarrassing arguments between his parents. Instead of a pleasant weekend outing, Alvy continues his analysis of an unhappy past. When Alvy proposed the visit to Brooklyn, he claimed that it would be fun for Annie—he does not mention himself. It is Annie who is able to laugh at some of the scenes from his childhood

Diane Keaton and Woody Allen, as Annie Hall and Alvy Singer, share a glass of wine on the balcony of her apartment. Credit: United Artists (courtesy Kobal).

that upset Alvy, and it is Annie who, as she tells him, "had a really good day."

While Annie tries to make Alvy more like herself, Alvy tries to make Annie more like himself. He may be attracted to Annie because of her spontaneity and vitality, but he nevertheless tries to impose on her his own self-consciousness. Not only does he pay for her to see a therapist and give her books on death to read, he encourages her to enroll in adult education courses (for example, "Existential Motifs in Russian Literature"). When Annie and Alvy break up, Annie leaves Becker's book with Alvy. The book is so much a part of him that when Annie comments "I feel like there's a great weight off my back," it is not clear whether she is referring to the book or Alvy himself. When Annie dreams that Frank Sinatra is suffocating her, her therapist reminds her that Alvy's surname is Singer.

Wernblad compares Annie and Alvy's relationship to the classic Jewish tale in which a Jew "falls in love with a young, beautiful, and relatively empty-headed WASP girl precisely because she is so very different from the world he grew up in." But as soon as he wins her, he tries to convert her to fit his world, and thus Alvy wants Annie to be "anhedonic, misanthropic, and obsessed with death."[14] This classic story suggests an impossible situation, for if the lover succeeded in making his beloved like himself, he would no longer love her. The story suggests that love has a tragic character, inasmuch as love is of the different but also wants to eliminate the difference. Love is self-destructive, and the lover is necessarily a loser. Either the lover fails to make the beloved like himself or herself, or the lover does so and no longer loves the beloved. Either the lover loses, or winning is losing.

Annie does not, however, represent a simply healthy spirit, a happy humanizing force, nor is Alvy's influence on her simply negative. Annie is a nightclub singer, for example, and singing may celebrate life and overcome anhedonia, but it may also foster illusions. The first song that we hear Annie sing is "It Had to Be You," words that capture the illusion of lovers that their love is necessary, fated in the order of things, and therefore a perfect fit. This illusion is the very one that Freud attributed to the pleasure principle, one "at loggerheads with the whole world," for "that man should be happy is not included in the order of Creation."[15] Annie's singing provides one of the "satisfactions through phantasy" of which Freud spoke when he explained how art induces in us "a mild narcosis" that brings about "a transient withdrawal" from life's misery.[16]

When Annie tells Alvy of her narcoleptic uncle, a veteran of the world war, she laughs at his death almost hysterically. Hysterical laughter hardly indicates, in Becker's words, being "comfortable in nature." Nor is Annie's singing a sign of her happiness.[17] Not only does it foster illusion, but it also serves as an excuse that keeps her from Alvy. Or at least Alvy thinks so when he wants to make love but Annie wants to "rest her voice" because she is singing the next night. Eventually her singing career takes her to California, and away from Alvy both physically and emotionally. That Annie is relieved of the "weight" of Alvy and his books on death suggests that there is something she wants to escape. Allen presents California as that escape.

The contrast that is shown between Los Angeles and New York City caricatures Annie's lack of reflection and Alvy's alienation. Early in the movie, a friend, Rob (Tony Roberts), suggests to Alvy that they move to sunny California, where they "could play outdoors every day, in the sun." When Rob eventually moves to L.A. at the call of show business, he is elated by the women who remind him of *Playboy* and by the "dynamite" machine that introduces canned laughter into his TV sitcoms. When Annie eventually goes as well, she finds it "perfectly fine" out in L.A. In contrast to L.A., New York, Rob thinks, is a "terribly worried" city. Similarly, Annie sees New York as "a dying city," like the city in Mann's *Death in Venice*, a book, Alvy points out, that Annie knows of only through him. Annie even associates Alvy's anhedonism with New York City itself: "You're incapable of enjoying life . . . your life is New York City. You're . . . like this island unto yourself."

Unlike Rob and Annie, Alvy loves New York, even if, as the self-righteous Californians claim, it has become such a dirty city. Alvy, after all, is "into garbage." Nor does he share Rob and Annie's infatuation with what he calls Munchkin Land, "where the only cultural advantage is being able to make a right turn on a red light." Rob should be doing Shakespeare in the Park, he urges, not Hollywood sitcoms. In California, he thinks, people simply watch movies all day, and eventually get old and die. It is a lifestyle that no thinking person could choose. The complete self-satisfaction that California represents to Alvy leaves no room for thought. Nor does it leave room for striving. "It's important to make a little effort once in a while," he tells Annie when she praises California "mellow." We begin to see "civilization and its discontents," even New York City garbage, in a different light, if canned laughter and thoughtless satisfaction is its alternative.

After Annie and Alvy break up, the distraught Alvy interviews people at random on the streets of Manhattan concerning their relationships. He finds a man and a woman who "look like a really happy couple," who claim they are happy because they are "shallow and empty," and "have no ideas, and nothing interesting to say." Could this possibly be happiness? Allen implicitly asks. Munchkin Lands, as Alvy well knows, fall short of their promise. There would be something good about alienation itself, and even a wholesomeness to discontent, if alienation were the condition for thought, and discontent the condition for striving.

The satisfaction represented by California is as illusory as Annie's hysterical laughter at her uncle's death. It is in California that Annie watches *Grand Illusion* when high. And in California, Rob supposes that you don't get old, as he guards against the sun's rays with helmets and goggles. Alvy well knows that if there is no crime in California ("no mugging," as Rob brags), there is something worse—"ritual, religious cult murders," even "wheat-germ killers."

Is there no middle ground, then, between Annie and Alvy, between L.A. and New York City? The Midwest, at least geographically, lies between the two coasts, and Annie and Alvy do visit her family at their home in Chippewa Falls, Wisconsin. But although Alvy does not experience the "chronic Los Angeles nausea" he gets in California, he is hardly less out of place. And if Alvy, the New York Jew, is out of place in Chippewa Falls, he is even more so at an Easter dinner there, with a traditional ham. So great is Alvy's discomfort that he imagines himself sitting at the table as an Orthodox Jew, with long black coat and hat, and even a full beard. His own quite different origins are in his mind, as we see when Allen splits the screen into two, with the Hall Easter dinner squeezed to the left and Alvy's family appearing to the right. The talk there is loud and boisterous, around a crowded kitchen table, in contrast to the staid and formal family dinner in Wisconsin. References to diabetes and coronaries, family quarrels, and sin and atonement take the place of the bland and meaningless pleasantries exchanged in Wisconsin.

Allen lets the two families converse—across space and time—from one side of the split screen to another. But speech only opens the gulf between them further, and the conversation drifts off into admission that they understand neither themselves nor each other. Wisconsin is no middle ground between L.A. and New York City, for Alvy's visit to Annie's family only accentuates the difference. As Allen's split screen visibly dramatizes Annie's and Alvy's different origins, we become aware of the distance between the two of them. This dinner, "exactly the half-point in the film," as Yacowar points out, is the beginning of the end of Alvy and Annie's relationship.[18] The divided screen literally divides the movie into two halves.

The split screen nevertheless does not represent a simple dichotomy. Annie's family, for example, at first seems to Alvy to be "very healthy" and "never sick," but Auntie Hall is a Jew-hater, and brother Duane confesses a desire to drive head-on into oncoming cars. Their healthy "American" wholesomeness is as illusory as Rob's supposing he will never get old in California. As to Alvy's louder, more raucous family, they speak of diabetes and coronaries, guilt and atonement with good-natured relish. Their complaints seem to bind them together. While the "healthy" Duane wants to die, this less "healthy" Jewish family wants to live. And while Annie's and Alvy's families can make no sense of each other, Annie and Alvy are not simply their families. They do love each other, at least for a while.

Later in the movie, Allen reproduces the split screen, with Annie on the left side of the screen talking to her therapist and Alvy doing the same thing on the right.[19] It is true that the two reveal their different perspectives: Annie and Alvy have sex three times a week, and to Alvy it is "hardly ever," but to Annie it is "constantly." But no more than in the split between Annie's and Alvy's families is there a simple split here between happiness and reflection, with Annie representing the one and Alvy the other. To the contrary, Annie as well as Alvy is talking to a therapist, and the self-reflective Alvy seeks greater closeness with Annie. The split screen itself thus suggests more of a split than there is in reality. In this case, as in his caricatures of Los Angeles and New York City, Allen's art both exaggerates and points to its own exaggeration. While the split screen foreshadows Annie's and Alvy's eventual split, the movie shows that each of them is better as a result of their relationship. *Annie Hall* is thus not as bleak as it might seem.

The complexity of *Annie Hall* appears in one of Alvy's arguments with Annie—over Annie's need to get high whenever she and Alvy make love. While grass relaxes Annie, Alvy is dismayed. To him, making love while high is like taking "a shot of sodium pentothal" so that one "can sleep through it." But when Alvy persuades Annie to forgo her customary joint, reflection prevents her from enjoying sex. She then seems distant to Alvy, who wonders whether she is just going through the motions. Allen uses another device to dramatize Annie's alienation—her ghostlike image departs her body and watches the two of them in bed.

No sooner does Annie's spirit get out of bed than Alvy also removes himself from the movie's dramatic illusion in order to address the audience. "That's what I call removed," he tells us. He wants not only Annie's body, but "the whole thing." Whereas in an earlier scene, Alvy's addressing the audience distracted him—and us—from an argument with Annie, he now removes himself from the movie to speak to us about Annie. The whole Annie he desires includes what can remove itself from the action, as Annie's spirit does. Just as Alvy wants more from Annie than her body, he wants to satisfy more than his body. How Annie "seems" to him in bed is important to him. His "imagination" suggests that she is only going through the motions. He is not simply having sex with Annie, but he is aware that he is doing so and is concerned about its character. That is why it "ruins" it for him when she has grass. Alvy mocks "the illusion that [grass] will make a white woman more like Billie Holiday." So too is Annie's unself-conscious wholeness an illusion, for it is artificially induced. Without the grass, Annie splits into two—she is both in bed with Alvy and watching from the bedside. The whole Annie that Alvy wants includes her spirit that looks on. Wholeness is incomplete without self-consciousness, just as Alvy's satisfaction cannot be complete if Annie gives him her body without her spirit. Although Annie's spirit escapes Alvy, Allen suggests that art can capture the complexity of a human being: it is his camera that captures Annie's spirit as well as her body, and it is to his camera that Alvy complains. When Annie removes herself from the lovemaking, she asks for her drawing pad. If she intends to draw herself and Alvy—if her art can capture only the immediately visible—Allen's art captures the spirit. He is a better drawer. He draws human beings whole—thinking, loving, desiring, even if their objects are in part elusive if only because they too are capable of thinking, loving, and desiring. The illusory wholeness from grass that Annie seeks gives way to the more elusive wholeness of life that Allen's art intimates.[20]

Alvy's memory of desiring "the whole thing" when Annie's ghost leaves her body in bed with him gives way to another of his being interviewed for a job writing a comedian's jokes. Alvy remembers wishing for the nerve to do his own jokes, and then his first appearance as a stand-up comic speaking about his own college experience before a college audience. In art, as well as life, he desires a kind of wholeness—not only to create a comic persona but also to be that persona himself. Only then, moreover, could he have a personal connection to the audience.[21] The college audience, as he remembers it, laughs, and, as the filmscript reports, "they're with him."[22] The show is at the University of Wisconsin, not in Chippewa Falls, but in Wisconsin nevertheless.

By the end of the movie, Alvy does more than the stand-up comedy that we see him doing at the beginning. He writes his first play—a dramatization of his and Annie's relationship. His art does not reproduce reality exactly, however, for in the play Annie returns with him from L.A. to New York City. Alvy apologizes to the audience: "You're always trying to get things to come out perfect in art because it's real difficult in life." Art for Alvy is still the creation of an illusory perfection, but one he clearly recognizes as an illusion. He is still the Alvy who deals with his annoyance at a loud-mouthed intellectual behind him in a ticket line by reaching behind a poster and magically pulling out Marshall McLuhan to put down the pontificating professor. "If only life were like this," Alvy sighs.

But Allen's movie is not like this, for it does not have the Holly-wood ending of Alvy's play. Either Allen's art does not try to capture the perfect or it has a different understanding of the perfect—one less difficult to square with real life. In Allen's movie Annie does return to New York from Los Angeles, but not with Alvy. She runs into Alvy, in fact, at a movie theater, where she is dragging her new lover to see *The Sorrow and the Pity*—which Alvy regards "as a personal triumph." Alvy and Annie later meet for lunch. While they "knock around old times," Alvy recounts, we see them "laughing and enjoying themselves." Alvy realizes, he tells the audience, "what a terrific person [Annie] was and how much fun it was just knowing her." While he regards Annie's going to see *The Sorrow and the Pity* as his personal triumph, we can regard this admission of his as a triumph for Annie. If he is able to appreciate a woman who could love him—like a club that would have him as a member—Freud's joke is no longer the "key" to his relationships.

Although Allen does not romanticize the ending of *Annie Hall*, as Alvy does his play, he does show that the former couple can meet as friends. They part after their lunch together, as the filmscript acknowledges, by kissing each other "in a friendly way."[23] Friendship is neither the self-forgetting hedonism of sunny California nor the self-reflective alienation of New York intellectualism. It is something more than either. As a turning point, *Annie Hall* intimates the maturer vision of Allen's later movies.

As Alvy recounts his meeting Annie for lunch, Allen replays a series of scenes from *Annie Hall*—those scenes in which Alvy and Annie were most happy together. Unlike Alvy's play, every happy episode Allen now shows us repeats one that did happen, even if

Allen's camera (and the couple's memories) obviously select them. Art can reflect happiness as well as sadness. The series of quick flashbacks that Allen gives us are accompanied by Annie's singing. Singing no longer signifies escape, for which Alvy feared Annie was using it, or repression, as when Alvy claimed that Annie's singing career was suffocating her, but reminds us of the bittersweet character of life. She does not sing "It Had to Be You" of her singing debut, but a song she sang soon after she and Alvy agreed to "never break up again"—"Seems Like Old Times." That song indicates a desire for the present to reproduce the past at the same time it acknowledges the impossibility of it doing so. It only "seems" like old times. And her singing it was the occasion of Annie's meeting Tony Lacey (Paul Simon), who eventually entices her to California.

Now, at the end, when we hear Annie sing in the background of Alvy's memories, it hardly "seems like old times" to Annie and Alvy, for they are no longer a couple, but their growth has made it possible for them to enjoy kicking around those old times. Alvy's first play, with its purely imaginary reunion of Alvy and Annie, unlike Allen's movie, is merely fiction. But then, as Alvy asks the audience, "What do you want? It was my first play." If Woody Allen, stand-up comic, merges at the beginning into Alvy Singer, who tells us about his relation to Annie, perhaps Alvy Singer in the end can develop into an artist who like Woody Allen discovers a new kind of comedy, whose vision of life permits him to be funny in a different way.

When Alvy visits Rob in California, he is disgusted that his friend injects canned laughter into his Hollywood sitcoms. Rob may suppose that the laughter-producing machine is dynamite, but Alvy thinks it is immoral. Earlier when Alvy objected to Annie's grass before sex, he had explained that he is a comedian, and if he "get[s] a laugh from a person who's high, it doesn't count . . . because they're always laughing." Laughter is not enough; Alvy is interested in laughter's conditions, its causes, its reasons. It is more than "happy" sounds; it must have a human dimension. It must be accompanied by awareness. Just as Alvy is able to distinguish "fake insights" of intellectuals from his own art, he is able to distinguish "fake laughter" from the kind of comedy he would like to produce.

Woody Allen, as uptight Alvy Singer, handles a lobster in *Annie Hall*. Credit: United Artists (courtesy Kobal).

As the pompous intellectual says in line outside the movie theater, "the most important thing of all is a comedian's vision."

Even Alvy's joke about the two elderly women who find their food at a Catskills resort both terrible and not enough is double-edged. They—and Alvy, who feels about life as they do about the food—are funny because they are inconsistent. If their complaint about the quality of food is correct, they are wrong to want more of it. If they are correct to want more of it, it cannot be all that bad. In either case, such a double complaint makes us ridiculous. Either we should be happy to die, or we should be happy and stop complaining. But we do neither. Alvy's joke rings true. We whine. Or, more positively, we love our lives and want them to be even better. *Annie Hall* begins with an explicit reference to Freud's work on jokes and their relation to the unconscious. In spite of Freud's influence on Allen, Allen has "gotten around" him.

One can "get around" Freud not so much by "getting around" death but by "getting around" an understanding of death that undermines one's ability to live. An awareness of death might make us anhedonic, as it did Alvy earlier, but it also might make us appreciate life's pleasures inasmuch as we do not have infinite time to experience them. The young Alvy's therapist implies as much when he tells Alvy that "we've got to try to enjoy ourselves while we're here." Contrary to Alvy's mother, "Brooklyn is expanding," and denying it may be no more conducive to getting on with one's homework than Alvy's reaction to this fact. Rob's "playing outdoors everyday, in the sun" is not exactly doing one's homework either. And there are health hazards to being in the sun too long, even if Rob recognizes this only through the words of a character he plays in a TV sitcom. Just as he abandons Shakespeare in the Park for California "mellow," he does not fully appreciate the bearing of art upon life, nor is he aware that he repeats his sitcom advice to lie down to Alvy himself when Alvy's L.A. nausea hits. He seems to forget completely what follows "mellow." It is Alvy who knows that if he "mellows" he also "ripen[s] and then rot[s]." The denial of death in the end undermines happiness rather than supports it, for it is only a grand illusion at loggerheads with life.

Alvy tells one last joke as *Annie Hall* draws to a close. A man reports to his therapist that his crazy brother thinks he is a chicken. He does not turn him in, he admits when the doctor inquires, because he "need[s] the eggs." And so our relationships, Alvy tells us, are "totally irrational and crazy and absurd . . . but I guess we keep going through it because most of us need the eggs." If others do provide us with eggs, however, their self-conceits are not entirely illusory. Allen's movie demonstrates that Alvy and Annie gave each other sustenance.

4

The Interior Decorator and the Vulgarian

(Interiors)

*I*nteriors, Allen says, is his first serious movie, a drama rather
than a comedy. For this reason he did not act in the movie.
Since he had created a certain role for himself as a comic figure
in his previous movies, the audience's expectation of a typically
comic Woody Allen, he thought, might detract from its appreciation
of the film's seriousness.[1] In spite of Allen's precaution, however,
Interiors received much negative press, and many critics thought
that Allen should not have strayed from the comedy that he did so
well.[2] *Interiors* was especially disappointing to the public and critics
in light of the popularity of *Annie Hall*, which Allen had made only
the year before. Expectations were up, and Allen did not meet
them.

Allen admitted that *Interiors* was not the kind of drama that
Americans like very much, but that he "wanted to go for the highest
kind of drama. And if I failed, I failed. That's OK. But what I was
aiming for, if I had made it, would have been very, very significant.
I'm not saying that I made it, but the ambition was good, the ambition was high."[3] Although there are things that Allen now claims
he would have done differently, he does not say that he failed or
that he did not achieve his goal. In fact, Allen admits that he is "not
unhappy" with *Interiors*.[4] What was Allen aiming at in this film,

and why did he desire to work in "dramatic" film as well as comedy?

More specifically, comedy is in some ways serious, if, as we have seen in *Play It Again, Sam*, to say nothing of *Annie Hall*, it raises questions about the value of art as well as issues of love, friendship, and loyalty. Does Allen's serious drama present a conception of life and its possibilities different from that of his comedies? Or are Allen's comedies and dramas different ways of presenting a single, although complex, understanding of life? *Interiors* is about a family and, in particular, the effect on the family of its matriarch, Eve (Geraldine Page). In the first words of the movie, her husband, Arthur (E. G. Marshall), describes her in a monologue to which Allen makes us privy: "She'd created a world around us that we existed in . . . where everything had its place . . . it was like an ice palace." The movie revolves around the effect of Eve's ordered world on her family, Arthur's request for "a trial separation" from Eve and that world, and the family's coping with that separation and its fallout, including Arthur's return from a holiday with Pearl (Maureen Stapleton), whom he intends to marry. It ends with Arthur's wedding and Eve's suicide and funeral. Eve is an interior decorator whose art suffocates and paralyzes both her and her family. In *Play It Again, Sam* Allen presents the positive potential of art to inspire noble action, while in *Interiors* he examines its more destructive side.

After her mother's suicide, one of the daughters, Joey (Mary Beth Hurt), recalls Eve's beauty and how her elder sister Renata (Diane Keaton) "looked up to her and her ideas about art." Renata, in fact, has been a successful, albeit unhappy, poet. She is married to Frederick (Richard Jordon), a less successful novelist who is plagued by self-doubts as well as feelings of inferiority to his wife. Their sister Flyn (Kristin Griffith) is an actress, who may have sold herself to Hollywood but at least Hollywood has bought her. While there may be some truth in Frederick's view of her as "form without content," Flyn has a certain self-knowledge that her sisters lack. She knows what she is, she admits, a good-looking actress who makes a living from television but who is passed over "when really classy parts come along." Disappointed with herself, she flirts with Frederick, and sneaks away from others for an occasional sniff of cocaine. Joey herself aspires to create, but it is not clear that she has any talent. She needs to express something, she tells her boyfriend, Mike (Sam Waterston), but she doesn't know what she wants to express or how to do it. She has tried acting and considers returning to it. She has also tried photography, and, while Mike tells her that this is where her talent lies, Renata does not think Joey's photographs are very good. Unfortunately, with Joey's aspiration to create comes a disdain for noncreative activities, such as the editing job in which she merely reads other people's work. The daughters are all artists or want to be, and none of them seems capable of living happily.

The first scenes in the movie are a series of almost still-life scenes.[5] In particular, we see first the living room of a beach house, then five vases on a mantel in the beach house, then the dining room of the beach house, followed by a painting on the wall with Joey's face reflected in the painting's glass. In the first two scenes, there is neither sound nor movement, and even in the third when we see Joey walking there is still no sound. Silent, and almost motionless, these scenes foreshadow the death we see at the end.

The scenes have been created by Eve, for as interior decorator of the beach house she has decorated its rooms. Eve has arranged five vases on the mantel, for example, just as she orders her and Arthur's lives and those of their three daughters. One of the other still-life scenes is Joey's face reflected in a painting's glass. Joey would like to be able to express herself in art of her own creation, but this painting in which she is reflected is not her own. Not only is Joey alienated from art, and hence from her own fulfillment as she understands it, but she is rendered motionless, part of a still life. Eve's interior decorating thus seems "to still" Joey herself. And, in truth, Joey is paralyzed at the beginning of the movie, for the notion of artistic perfection inherited from her mother makes her unable to act. Nor is she the only daughter who finds herself paralyzed when the movie opens. The more expressive Renata speaks into the camera of her "paralysis," and "impotence" that set in a year ago. Eve is an artist who stills the life around her.

We glimpse Eve's repressive art, her creation of interiors that shut out the external world with its motion and life, when early in the movie she enters Joey and Mike's apartment, which she has deco-rated. She desires to close the windows, she says, for "the street noises are just unnerving." Her closing her daughter's windows foreshadows the time when we see her seal the windows and doors of her own apartment with black tape before releasing the gas from the stove. Although her suicide attempt fails, the tightly closed-off interior that she creates as her death chamber reveals the character of her interior decorating and its effect on life.

Eve tries to create interiors that give the external world no point of access, no point of intrusion. Making life into still life, she can have absolute control over it, not only her own but the lives of oth-ers as well. It is the windows of Mike and Joey's apartment that she wants to close. She objects to Mike's aftershave, which permeates the house, and wonders if he would switch if she bought him some other kind of cologne. Nor is she pleased when she discovers that Mike has moved the lamp she placed in his bedroom into his

Woody Allen directs Geraldine Page, who plays an obsessive matriarch in *Interiors*. Credit: United Artists (courtesy Kobal).

kitchen, where it is of more use to him. For him, his apartment is not the still life that Eve has created but a place in which he can live and whose artifacts he uses. But Eve treats human beings themselves as artifacts to be placed in the still life she is creating. Renata indicates this quite explicitly when she describes how Eve put Arthur through law school: "It was like he was her creation." And Mike objects to Eve's plans to redo the floors of his apartment, "I never agreed about anything! I'm always being told."

Life, of course, is rarely still, as Mike reveals by moving the bedroom lamp to the kitchen. Life and its motion always get in the way of Eve's art. Eve must constantly recreate what she has created, otherwise she would relinquish control. And so she wants to continue redoing Mike and Joey's apartment, to Mike's consternation, if only because of their limited resources. Not surprisingly, Eve is constantly dissatisfied with her work and justifies her endless revisions because her art "is not an exact science." Renata, similarly, imagines revising a poem she has written, even though it has already been published in the *New Yorker* and is itself a revision of an earlier one. If mother and daughter try to keep open the possibility of revision, however, it is less from an acceptance of imperfection than from a rejection of it, from a desire to maintain control over what they have created, and from a desire to never let anything go that is less than perfect. Eve will not accept any decorating projects, for example, "until I'm sure that I can maintain the level that I expect of myself." In one scene where she is trying to compose, Renata keeps changing words, and finally crumples the piece of paper on which she is writing.

Similar concerns underlie Joey's reservations about having a child, although Mike clearly would like to have one. Having a child, she says, is "totally irrevocable," and thus seems to place a limit on her freedom. Ironically, she immediately mentions her unfulfilled desire to express herself. When she thinks that she is pregnant, she wants to have an abortion, for having a child would "be the end of the world." So too have all her jobs proven temporary. Nor has she married Mike. Like her mother and Renata, Joey in her own way wants to be able to always revoke or revise. Renata and Frederick do have a child, just as Renata does publish some poems. But in the former case as well as the latter, she interprets away any limit this places on her. Frederick accuses her, for example, of considering their child "great potential raw material." The one time Renata comments on her child, she finds her "cute" because "she sits and has conversations with the television set." Renata is her mother's daughter, for like Eve she "keep[s] everything going" in her house. But from what we see at the time of the movie, nothing there seems to be "going" anywhere. She and Frederick at any rate seem "stuck" in their own private obsessions and inadequacies. In their own ways, each is having conversations with the television set. Their lives together are standing still.

Joey claims that Eve is "really too perfect . . . to live in this world. I mean all the beautifully designed rooms, carefully designed interiors . . . everything so controlled." As a result "there wasn't any room for any real feelings." It is appropriate that when Arthur announces to Eve and his daughters that he wants a trial separation, he does so at the breakfast table, "just very nicely, and in a very gentlemanly way."[6] It is a scene that is so emotionally contained and deliberate that it is almost still life, but Arthur, part of that still life, declares that he is going to step out of the picture.[7] He is like a creature asserting his freedom from his creator, even if his staged announcement of that freedom to his family is as cold as Eve's interior decoration. We see a more positive expression of that freedom in his love for Pearl, who in more than one way creates havoc when she enters Eve's ordered world. She imagines redoing the beach house, for example, although she is no interior decorator. To the contrary, she is without taste and, as Joey calls her, "a vulgarian." And she has so many pictures and knickknacks, she admits, that they will turn the beach house into a warehouse.

One of Pearl's sons by an earlier marriage has found a career involved in art; he runs an art gallery. Pearl admits that it is "in the lobby of Caesar's Palace in Las Vegas," and that it is more a concession than an art gallery. Joey guesses correctly that the "art" involves paintings of clowns on black velvet, and while Pearl knows that it is "junk" it is also "what people like," and her son "does nicely." The humor in this movie—and there is humor in this "serious" movie—involves the contrast between Pearl and Arthur's family, with their more refined tastes, and their reaction to her. The red colors of her clothes contrast with Eve's beiges, pale earth tones, and ice-grays, as do her dark curls that hang loose contrast with Eve's tightly pulled-back hairstyle. Although Pearl prefers the beaches of Europe to closed buildings and cathedrals, she does like some art, at least the primitive statues from Trinidad "with the big hips and the big breasts."[8]

At the dinner party at which Arthur introduces Pearl to Renata, Frederick, Joey, and Mike, they discuss a new play that they have all seen. While the futility the play demonstrates may be fashionable, it is nevertheless difficult, Renata believes, to portray such a harsh truth. She therefore praises the playwright for arguing that "in the face of death, life loses real meaning." Earlier, Allen shows us Renata experiencing the meaningless of life in the face of death, when she admits paralysis and impotency: "I am preoccupied with my own mortality. . . . I can't seem to shake this . . . the real implication of dying. It's terrifying. The intimacy of it embarrasses me."

Renata shares many of Alvy's concerns without the relief of his Jewish humor. Her foil, and that of Eve and her other daughters, is Pearl. In discussing the play, Pearl shows little awareness of life's emptiness, for she has not read Socrates, or Buddha, or Schopenhauer, whom Renata mentions. But unlike Annie Hall, Pearl doesn't care. Intimacy with death—and she has buried two husbands—does not keep her from intimacy with others, as it does Renata. Nor is she embarrassed by intimacy, as when, to his daughters' dismay, she gets Arthur to lick cheesecake off her fingers.

Just as Renata praises the play for its futility, Joey admires its ambiguity, for "the writer argued both sides so brilliantly you didn't know who was right." Renata's and Joey's comments about the play are revealing: in life they see death, and in life's circumstances they see moral ambiguity. They consequently have trouble living and acting. They find nothing simply good that makes life worth living. One response to this void, as we see in Eve, is a kind of willful creativity, an imposition of order on the unordered world she perceives. The movie shows, however, that this response will work at best only for a time, as it did for Eve and Renata. It leads to inactivity or paralysis, as characterize Renata and Joey, and in a more extreme form, suicide, which Eve eventually commits. In the absence of anything good, there is no reason to live, and of course no reason to act, for action aims at some good.

Pearl, in contrast, does not doubt that life is good. She encourages Arthur to eat another piece of cheesecake, with the thought that "you'll live to be one hundred if you give up all the things that make you want to." Pearl understands that there are things that make one want to live to a hundred. It would be wrong, however, to see those things as exemplified simply by cheesecake, or Pearl as a narrow hedonist. Arthur tells his daughters that she is kind and affectionate. She loves Arthur and wants to make him happy. While she loves to dance—Arthur says she could go dancing every night— she encourages others to dance too, even Joey. She does care about Joey, as Arthur indicates when he asks Joey to talk to her. Joey's good wishes mean something to Pearl. Most importantly, she an-

Joey (Mary Beth Hurt) and Renata (Diane Keaton) visit their mother (Geraldine Page). Credit: United Artists (courtesy Kobal).

swers Joey's call for "mother" when Eve does not, and then brings
Joey back to life when she almost drowns trying to save Eve from
suicide. Here the physical touching, which repulsed Joey when her
father licked Pearl's fingers and when Pearl tried to get her to
dance, is life saving, as Pearl puts her lips on Joey's to breathe life
into her.

Joey is saved by the joint efforts of Pearl, who revives her, and
Mike, who rescues her from the waves. Mike is the only character
in the movie besides Pearl who is not a part of the family. Frederick,
Renata's husband, is not related by blood, but unlike Mike he fits
right in. He too desires to create and feels similar frustrations to
those felt by Eve's daughters. Like Joey, he feels inferior to conven-
tionally successful Renata. When he tries to rape Flyn, he tells her
that he has not for a long time made love to a woman he did not feel
inferior to. Frederick, not surprisingly, praises the play the family
discusses with Pearl as "pessimistic to the point of futility."

Nor is it surprising that Eve likes Frederick better than she does
Mike. Unlike Eve and her family, Mike is not absorbed in his own
inner world. He encourages Joey to have a child, for example. He
makes political films—and even suggests that Joey share his political activities with him, for they will "get you off yourself." Like
Pearl, Mike is awake when Joey needs him, in contrast to Renata,
Flyn, and Arthur, whom the camera shows asleep in their beds
(Frederick, we know, is drunk). Mike rushes into the ocean to save
the woman he loves. He does not suffer from the inactivity or paralysis that some of the others do.

Mike's politics are Marxist, as we see from the beginning when
Allen lets us hear some of the political speeches he is composing
into a tape recorder. When discussing the play with the others, he
finds none of the futility that Renata and Frederick see in it. What
impresses him most about the play is that the terrorists do not kill
wantonly, but only in the name of freedom, only when necessary.
He appears unmoved by Renata's objection that this is killing for
the sake of an abstraction. Nor does he see any of the moral ambiguity that Joey sees, for he thinks it is right to sacrifice the life of one
for the lives of thousands. His politics subordinate the individual to
a cause. While the self-absorption that plagues some of the individ-

uals in this movie isolates them from others in self-contained and self-created interiors, Mike's political convictions require that he sacrifice the individual to an abstraction, to the political end he serves.

Mike, however, is better than his politics; his practice is superior to his theory. When we first see him, he is commenting on Mao's appeal to the masses by his use of homilies. He quotes one of Mao's homilies, that "the hardest thing is to act properly throughout one's whole life," but wonders "what the hell does that mean?" His theories give him insufficient guidance in practice. In practice, his actions are less like the terrorists in the play than they are like Pearl's. He may speak of the lives of thousands, but he risks his life for the one woman he loves. And she is, as far as he has seen, not a "productive" member of society, and even too "self-centered" for political activity.

Pearl's reaction to the play, characteristically, differs from both that of Eve's family and that of Mike. She "didn't get" the moral ambiguity that Joey sees, for example, but found the play simpler: "one guy was a squealer, the other guy wasn't. I liked the guy that wasn't." Pearl's categorical imperative that "you don't squeal" demands loyalty to individuals and allows action for their sake, even if it does not provide standards for choosing those individuals. No sense of futility or ambivalence stands in the way of Pearl's acting to save Joey, no more than she could sacrifice those she loves for any abstract cause.

In the end, Joey and Renata, the two sisters who have been most at odds throughout the movie, cry and hug each other at their mother's funeral, and the "beautiful" Flyn is marred by "tears streaming down her face."[9] In the last scene of the movie, all three look out of the same window. They have come together in their grief, in their recognition, and in their acceptance. This last scene recalls earlier scenes where individual characters, Joey, Renata, and Arthur, stare out of windows alone.

Perhaps, then, Allen, leaves us simply with another still-life scene, doing to his characters, and to Eve's daughters in particular, what Eve has done to them. The ocean at which the three sisters stare might therefore reflect their own empty lives, while the silence at the end, recalling the silence at the beginning, frames the movie's speech and renders it soundless. Pauline Kael argues as much when she writes that "after the life-affirming stepmother has come into the three daughters' lives and their mother is gone, they still at the end close ranks in a frieze-like formation. Their life-negating mother has got them forever."[10]

Critics tend to see in Allen's portrayal of Eve a simple portrayal of art and to identify Allen's art with Eve's. They then attribute to Allen's art the negative aspects that he himself attributes to Eve's. Vernon Young, for example, writes, "periodically, having enshrined the creative personality in one context or another, [Allen] seems driven to follow up with a thumping self-accusation of the artist as charlatan or as detached and inhuman."[11] Pauline Kael, who does acknowledge that Eve may not represent art simply (she "represents art, or at least cultivation and pseudo-art"), nevertheless identifies her art and Allen's: "As a decorator her specialty, like Allen's, seems to be the achievement of a suffocating emptiness." She speaks of Allen's "repressive kind of control," and claims that *Interiors* is "so austere and studied that it might have been directed by that icy mother herself—from the grave."[12]

The "austere and studied" character of such direction, however, is appropriate to these characters whom Allen creates and directs, and is therefore a sign of Allen's flexibility as an artist, rather than of an Eve-like rigidity. Moreover, Kael's observations about the style of Allen's direction do not apply to his direction of Pearl. Pearl is the key to this movie, a key that many critics of Allen have not fully appreciated.[13] And Pearl is the single most obvious difference between Allen's art and Eve's. As Allen describes her to Bjorkman, Pearl is "alive"; she "represents vitality, and life and vibrancy."[14] While Pearl has a place in Allen's movie, she could never—since she is "alive"—have a place in Eve's still life. Indeed, Pearl belongs less in a still life than in a movie. As moviemaker, Allen offers a series of still-life scenes, but one quite different from Eve's, for a movie's quick succession of still-life scenes gives the illusion of motion and thus recaptures for its viewers the movement of life.

Critics note the extent to which Pearl resembles comic figures played by Allen himself in earlier movies, "warm, down-to-earth"

characters who act as foils to more conventional societies and values.[15] They nevertheless see Pearl as an ambiguous figure. Jacobs,
for example, claims that Pearl holds out no social and moral solu-
tions, but "is [t]here to complicate themes and relationships." She
hesitates to prefer Pearl to Eve, claiming, "our allegiances are
equally with both women."[16] And although Pogel admits that the
film "*appears* to make a commitment to the values embodied in
Pearl instead of Eve" (emphasis mine), she concludes that "any
commitment in *Interiors* is qualified by a series of dialogues, not
only within and between the characters, but between the reflexive
film and itself." As Joey does the play she discusses in *Interiors*,
Pogel finds the movie "ambivalent."[17] It is not surprising, then, that
Pogel sides with Joey's interpretation of the play against Pearl's.
As Pogel writes, "Joey's reactions to the play reflect greater self-
awareness and intellectual curiosity" than Pearl's, and Arthur's
family in general perceive "more complex sets of alternatives" than
Pearl does. Like Joey, Pogel finds Pearl a bit vulgar.[18] Ambivalence,
however, is not necessarily profound. Critics of *Interiors* do not give
sufficient weight to the more positive elements in the movie such
as Pearl. Pearl does answer Joey's call for mother and Joey is saved
by the joint efforts of Pearl and Mike, who love her. Allen says that
after Eve's suicide and Pearl's kiss, he felt that Joey "was reborn
and that there would be more hope for her in the future."[19] Allen's
movie thus ends not with death, even though it ends with a funeral,
but with the hope of life.

As Arthur and Pearl prepare for Eve's funeral, Pearl takes Arthur's hand, just as she helped him prepare for their wedding, clip-
ping his suspenders to his pants and touching his face tenderly.
Speech is necessary for communication—Pearl is, after all, somewhat loud—but it is not all there is to communication. When Arthur notes that the only problem he had in Greece, where he met
Pearl, was that no one spoke English, Pearl tells him that "it didn't
matter. Everybody understood what was important." Silence might
but does not necessarily mean emptiness and isolation, just as it
does not necessarily mean lack of understanding. When Pearl helps
Arthur with his suspenders and touches his cheek, there is "no
sound." The silence at the end among the three sisters differs from

the silence at the beginning of the movie, for it is informed by the speech and deeds that intervene. And that is why there is some ground for the hope that the sisters might finally arrive at a point where they could communicate.

A pessimistic interpretation of this movie, moreover, does not do justice to the scene previous to that of the sisters looking out of the window. In that scene, Joey writes in her notebook about their feelings after the funeral: "We all returned to the beach house. We couldn't help experiencing some very nostalgic memories . . . naturally of my mother . . . and pleasantly of the few warmer moments we'd known." The "warmer" images had hitherto been associated with Pearl, such as the sun, the "hot sand," and Florida, where Pearl is from, and the cold ones with Eve. Joey is now able to remember warm moments with Eve.

More important, in this scene Joey is writing something of her own, rather than comments on other people's manuscripts. She is also still able to say "I love you" to Eve, even after recognizing her mother's perverseness. And she demonstrates that love when she runs into the ocean to try to save her mother. Joey recognizes, in her words, in her deeds, and in what she writes in her notebook, her connections to others, to her mother and her sisters. This is no abstract creativity here, nor the artistic impulse that moves Eve and that produces only interiors. Joey's writing in her notebook, in fact, records past experiences with Eve and with her family, even if like Annie and Alvy's reminiscences of their past together, her memories are selective. In writing, Joey becomes less like her former paralyzed self and more like Pearl insisting that "you shouldn't squeal." Both acknowledge loyalty to particular human beings.

In *Interiors*, Allen presents a way of living and a kind of artistic impulse that produces still life and, in the case of Eve, death. In his image of "interiors," he inverts our usual way of looking at what is wrong with the modern world. The modern world, we think, produces "hollow men," to use T. S. Eliot's famous phrase, that is, people who have only surfaces, only exteriors, who are hollow inside. This resembles what Rousseau said of "civilized" beings, who live only "in the eyes of others," and it is what Frederick says of Flyn when he calls her "form without content" and tells her that she doesn't exist "except in somebody else's eyes." Frederick, intellectual that he is, applies Rousseau's criticism of modern life to Flyn.

The "artificial" human beings Rousseau saw resulting from the development of the sciences and the arts lack interiors. Rousseau's legacy has been our search for our inner selves and our attempts to give them expression. We are so much the heirs of Rousseau that it is hard to fathom an alternative way of looking at art, creativity, and the self. But the Flyn whom Frederick describes does not necessarily represent the deepest problem of modern life. That problem is less that we have no interiors, as we sometimes think, but that we have only interiors. Our need is less to turn "inward" than to turn "outward."

This does not necessarily mean "living in the eyes of others," or the artificiality that Rousseau criticized, but that our "interiors" can be humanized and deepened by our belonging to a world. We are not self-contained wholes, and when individuals use art as a means to create and protect such wholes, art becomes destructive of life. We become sealed-up interiors, as Eve sealed her apartment before attempting suicide and Renata isolates herself from others, especially Joey, in order to create. After tearing up a poem she is trying to write, Renata looks out of the window of her study: "It was like I . . . was here, and the world was out there, and I couldn't bring us together."[20] Allen had originally planned to entitle his movie *Windows*.[21] We might seal windows up, as does Eve, or look out of them, as do the sisters at the end. But if our windows are not sealed, we do not control what we might see or what might come in. If we love, we may be betrayed. However wrong it is to do so, others may squeal, whether they justify themselves by principles like the ones Mike espouses, or by the moral ambiguities of all action—both of which might serve as self-deluding excuses for cowardice.

There is only one shot of the exterior of the beach house in the movie. Although the camera focuses on the beach house, none of the characters in the movie is looking at it. We see the exterior only with Allen, who lets us see not merely the outside of the beach house but a world in which we belong beyond our own interior selves. Pearl breaks into this family with her energy, demonstrativeness, and openness. She is a force that foils the self-contained interiors that constitute the lives of its members and that isolate them from the world. Similarly, Allen breaks into modern thought and life with his movies. If most of the characters in *Interiors* could fit comfortably within an Ingmar Bergman movie, Pearl would not.[22] By putting Pearl among these "modern" characters, Allen has done something analogous to the magician's putting Kugelmass into *Madame Bovary*. Magic may have put him there, but this does not mean that he does not belong.

Pearl introduces comedy into this serious movie.[23] By means of Pearl Allen suggests the need for laughter. Indeed, his inclusion of Pearl in a serious drama serves as a mockery of attempts to make certain kinds of serious movies. His inclusion of Pearl, in other words, is analogous to Allen's laughing at himself when he makes serious movies. And he lets us share that laughter. It is a laughter that jars the laugher out of serious self-absorption, as Pearl does more or less for different members of Eve's family.

Allen's first "serious" drama in this way affirms the role for comedy in human life. Mike, as we saw, suggested that Joey might turn to political activity to "get her off herself." Allen's comedy, or laughter, functions in the same way, without the risk of the Marxist abstraction of Mike's politics. And only if we "get off ourselves" do we become open to the love and friendship that current theories of the self place outside our reach. Again, we see the possibility that laughter need not serve as an escape from life's harshness rather than as an access to life's pleasures.

Arthur's turning to Pearl, to be sure, is in part an attempt to escape Eve. But it is an escape not from truths of which Eve is aware but from Eve's own denial of life itself. And Pearl is not a sign of Arthur's forgetting, but of his remembering his own potential for happiness with another human being. In terms of *Annie Hall*, there is more to comedy than we meet on the pages of Freud.

Whereas in *Play It Again, Sam* much of the humor lies in the contrast between Allan Felix and his overblown and inappropriate "ideals," in *Interiors* the humor lies in the contrast between Pearl, with her vital exuberance, and Eve's family and their paralyzing self-consciousness. Overcoming both his whining self-absorption and his tough-guy Bogart stance, Allan Felix attains a self-awareness conducive to life and action. In the more serious *Interiors*, the experience of the vibrant Pearl gives Joey hope of a similar resolution. It is a possibility to which *Annie Hall* points as well. This is Woody Allen at his best, whether in comedy or serious drama. As Allen believes, his serious drama like *Interiors* is superior to comedy that is merely for laughs. By the same token, however, Allen's mature comedies are superior to dramas unlightened by the good humor of a Pearl.

5

The Director and the Fan

(Stardust Memories)

T he central characters of many of Allen's movies are artists or pursue careers related to art. In *Stardust Memories*, the protagonist Sandy Bates (Woody Allen) is a successful movie director, who like Allen both writes the scripts for the movies he directs and acts in them. He also resembles Allen in his desire to make serious dramas. Moreover, Sandy Bates is criticized by his public for not sticking to the comedy he does well, as Allen was criticized for doing the sober *Interiors*. It is no wonder, then, that Pauline Kael finds in *Stardust Memories* only "the merest wisp of a pretext that he is a playing a character; this is the most undisguised of his dodgy mock-autobiographical fantasies."[1]

Such identification of actor with a role, according to Allen, is "infantile," and unworthy of a sophisticated viewer. "Jerry Lewis was not the nutty character he impersonated," Allen observes, and "people tended to think that Humphrey Bogart was so tough when in fact he was a very educated man."[2] Of course, as we have seen, Allen himself brought Humphrey Bogart into *Play It Again, Sam* at least in part as such a tough character, and even when Bogart gives the protagonist less "tough" advice he does not speak as "a very educated man." And Allan Felix himself, although a movie critic, accepts this "infantile" identification of Bogart with his personas. Of course, to see this as any contradiction on Allen's part would be to forget that *Play It Again, Sam* is itself a movie and that Allan Felix is not Woody Allen. It would be to do the very thing that Allen insists that we should not do—to confuse life and art. While he admits that "all the characters are the author," he also insists "I've never been the character I've played."³

Stardust Memories warns against any complete blurring of art with life or film with reality. The movie begins on a dingy train. A character played by Allen sits on the train, surrounded by strange, ugly people—old, sickly, crying, and alone. As he looks around, greater and greater discomfort appears on his face. He glimpses through the train's window a group of happy, well-dressed people on another train partying, drinking champagne, and having a good time. One of the celebrities sees him on the other train, and sends him a kiss through the window. He looks at his ticket; he believes he is on the wrong train. He tries to get off but gets no help from the "pale and sinister-looking" conductor. The train moves; he pounds unsuccessfully on the window to be let off. Later the passengers arrive at a beach-lot junkyard strewn with wrecked cars and other garbage. The joyous passengers from the other train also arrive. Life holds the same destination for all. But then it turns out that this is not life at all. The scene ends, and the film cuts to a private screening room. This strong dose of "reality" is only a scene from a movie. Although Allen first presents this image as real, he immediately corrects this impression by showing us the studio and those who have been viewing the movie. Allen thus demonstrates that movies are able to deceive their audiences about image and reality, as well as to reveal their own dramatic illusions to be illusions.

The movie within the movie, we learn, is being made by actor-director Sandy Bates. While we thought we were seeing a character played by Allen in *Stardust Memories*, we were really seeing a character played by Sandy Bates, a character Allen plays, in a movie he is making. Indeed, this first scene of *Stardust Memories* is the last scene of Sandy's movie. His producers, however, will not accept such a bleak ending, since fans pay to see happy outcomes. The producers proceed to commission someone else to remake the final scene, in which the miserable occupants of the train Sandy is on wind up in a "Jazz Heaven," a "commercial," "upbeat" ending they believe appropriate to Easter, the time of the movie's scheduled release.

Sandy is appalled by the new ending. He plans to sue if he and the producers cannot reach some kind of accommodation, for "the whole point of the movie is that nobody is saved." He finds Jazz Heaven the stupidest thing he has ever heard. "You can't control life. It doesn't wind up perfectly. Only—only art you can control," he stutters, as if out of control. Art that is in control, paradoxically, must imitate life and its lack of control. Otherwise Jazz Heaven would be an acceptable ending for his movie. Sandy Bates has come a long way from Alvy Singer, who ended his play with his and Annie's reconciliation, for "you're always trying to get things to come out perfectly in art, because it's real difficult in life." However much Sandy agrees with Alvy about life's difficulties, he does not agree that art should provide an escape. Jazz Heaven is not appropriate, but what is? Is there an alternative to the garbage heap?

The rest of *Stardust Memories*, in effect, is about what the ending of this movie within the movie will be. To resolve the issue of the ending of his film, Sandy must resolve the question of what kinds of movies he wants to make, and therefore the question of what life is really like. "I don't want to make funny movies anymore," he protests. "I don't feel funny. I look around the world, and all I see is human suffering." His attempt to resolve the question of his movie's ending, however, leads him to examine his life too. A weekend festival of his own films, at which this celebrated filmmaker answers questions from his critics and fans, serves as the occasion for his self-examination, including memories from childhood, memories of past love affairs, and scenes from his own movies. This festival that forms the backdrop of Sandy's "stardust memories" takes place at the turn-of-the century Stardust Hotel on the Jersey Shore, itself a memory of the past, now frequented by the most avant-garde film culture. Sandy's examination of his life, on which his movie's ending depends, is inseparable from an examination of his art.

Allen raises the question of the "reality" of the images of art in *Stardust Memories* by the fact that the "life" that the movie imitates, whether it be Allen's or Sandy's movie, is often "surreal," or, in

Woody Allen, as movie director Sandy Bates, objects to dinner in *Stardust Memories*. Credit: United Artists (courtesy Kobal).

other words, projections of images from within the mind rather than from any external reality. Allen thus imitates Fellini's movies, which are known for their surrealism. Michael Dunne, for example, observes the movie's "surreal episodes involving U.F.O. freaks and Fellini-esque magic tricks."[4] Pauline Kael notes how Sandy's fans "have their features distorted by the camera lens and by Fellini-esque makeup; they become flat-lipped freaks wearing outsize thick goggles."[5] Allen thus imitates not only Sandy Bates's movie within his movie, which has more than its share of freaks, but Fellini's movies as well. So too, of course, does Sandy.

Allen's imitation of Fellini goes beyond his surreal characters and episodes, for in many ways *Stardust Memories* is an imitation or a replay of Fellini's *8½*.[6] That movie also is about a film director who is disillusioned with life and has difficulty in finding a satisfactory conclusion to a film he is making. Beyond the similarities between the situations of the protagonists, and the surreal episodes and people, there are also revealing structural parallels between the films.

The first scene of Allen's movie, for example, resembles the first scene of *8½*. Fellini's director, Guido Anselmi, is trapped in a tunnel in traffic, just as Sandy's protagonist is trapped on a train. In Allen's movie, however, there is a second entrapment reminiscent of Guido's—Sandy himself, sitting in the backseat of his Rolls-Royce, trapped in Manhattan traffic.[7]

In Fellini's film, Guido escapes traffic in a fantasy sequence in which he floats out of the tunnel, over the cars, and into the sky. Sandy is not treated to any such soaring over New York City traffic. Only later in a memory of his childhood does a young Sandy, dressed in a Superman costume, fly. We thus see from the outset that Allen's imitation of Fellini's movie leaves significant differences. Not only does the character in Sandy's film not escape the "wretched" train for the happier conveyance he spies, but Sandy does not escape his Rolls-Royce. Flying is only a childhood dream of his.[8] In these ways, Allen's replay of Fellini's movie corrects its surrealistic fantasy. *Casablanca*, with its upbeat heroism, proves to be a more realistic model for *Play It Again, Sam* than do Fellini's fantastic grotesques and Guido's ecstatic escapes for *Stardust Memories*.[9]

In contrast to Guido, Sandy reacts more practically to his entrapment—he uses his car phone to call his secretary and discuss upcoming arrangements. This is a more prosaic response than the one offered by Fellini. Allen certainly does not see a good car phone as the solution to modern problems of confinement and alienation. But in offering this more down-to-earth response, he pokes fun at Fellini's more romantic one. While Sandy definitely wants to make movies reflecting the suffering he sees everywhere, critics should not be misled about Allen's movie. On this point, I believe, Vincent Canby is correct when he says that *Stardust Memories* is one of Allen's funniest films.[10] This does not mean that it is not serious. One of Sandy's fans compliments him as "the master of despair." He probably means that Sandy captures despair in his movies better than anyone. But "a master" of something hardly succumbs to what he masters, and to revel in despair is to fail to "get off oneself," as Mike advised Joey to do in *Interiors*, and Annie encouraged Alvy to do in *Annie Hall*.

When studio executives see the original ending of Sandy's movie, they find incredible "self-indulgence" in Sandy's fobbing off his private suffering as art. Perhaps making a movie about Sandy Bates's search for an ending for his film is Allen's way of saying to himself what Mike said to Joey in *Interiors*.[11] But why might Fellini—whom the obnoxious professor in *Annie Hall* dubbed an indulgent filmmaker—be useful to Allen for this? If *Annie Hall* is Allen's "getting around" Freud, how is *Stardust Memories* his "getting around" Fellini? What happens to a Fellini movie when Allen enters it?

In addition to his comment on *8½*'s opening entrapment, Allen introduces other variations of Fellini's movie into *Stardust Memories*. As we shall see for Sandy Bates, so too for Guido, a woman plays a crucial role in the resolution of both movies. When Guido is caught between his wife and mistress, he escapes into fantasy by imagining an ideal woman, Claudia, a dreamlike figure in white who brings him peace and hope. She rekindles a childhood innocence and wholeness that makes it possible for him to live and act, reuniting past and present, image and reality in his art. At the end of the movie, Guido directs the entire cast of *8½*, characters from both his past and present, from his real life and his fantasies, as they move around a circus ring in a dance that he himself joins. The ending of Fellini's movie has been called "an epiphany," "an affirmation and celebration, however simple, of unity, of spontaneity, of freedom, of innocence. . . . The boy inside the man [Guido] has been freed and restored . . . by an act of grace."[12] Another critic calls Fellini's ending a "miraculous aesthetic equivalent to Catholic salvation."[13] In other words, Fellini's movie is just what Sandy's producers order—in spite of its grotesques it is a movie perfect for release around Easter time.

There are also three women in Sandy's life, but Allen collapses lover and wife into Isobel (Marie-Christine Barrault). She is Sandy's adulterous lover, but also takes the place of Guido's wife, for she represents family (she has two small children from a former marriage) and commitment (she and Sandy have discussed her leaving her husband and their living together, and even getting married). By this means, Allen suggests the possibility of reconciling the

forces that Fellini presents in conflict—love and marriage, fulfillment and convention, mistress and wife—without recourse to an
imaginary and elusive Claudia. Sandy is nevertheless at the outset
torn from Isobel by his attraction to another woman, a new interest
he meets at the hotel, the young and troubled Daisy (Jessica
Harper) who reminds him of a past love, Dorrie (Charlotte Ram-
pling). It is the unavailable Dorrie, not Daisy, who is the real threat
to Isobel, and whose image beckons Sandy, like Claudia's does for
Guido in *8½*, to escape the troubling present into a fantasy life.
Both Dorrie and Claudia represent some kind of ideal object of
longing.

Dorrie, however, is certainly less than ideal, even if Sandy tends
to remember her as "fabulous" and "wonderful" as Guido sees
Claudia. While Claudia brings peace to Guido, Dorrie, as she told
Sandy on their first meeting, is only "trouble." While for "two days
a month she was the most exciting woman in the world, . . . the rest

Sandy (Woody Allen) and Isobel (Marie-Christine Barrault) take her children
on an outing. Credit: United Artists (courtesy Kobal).

of the time she was a basket case." "Dorrie was a loonie," his friend Tony (Tony Roberts) tells him. In spite of the fact that the last time Sandy saw her was in a sanitarium, he still expresses surprise when a "superintelligent being" from outer space prefers Isobel to Dorrie. Sandy's haunting memories of an idealized Dorrie come between him and Isobel, and further alienate him from Isobel by causing his fascination with Daisy, whom he sees as Dorrie's image.

While Claudia is the ideal woman in *8½*, the perfect woman appears in *Stardust Memories* only in a scene shown from one of Sandy's early comic movies. Sandy plays a respected and well-known physician, who has put the brain of Doris, a "great personality," into the body of Rita, "nasty, mean, trouble," whom he "loves going to bed with." And so he makes Rita into "the perfect woman," who is "warm, wonderful, charming, sexy, sweet, giving, mature," and puts "all the badness" into Doris. "You're mad," his friend in the movie tells him.[14] One who seeks a perfect beauty at the expense of imperfect human life, Allen suggests, is a madman. Allen treats such a maniac by satirizing him, by showing him to be the comic dupe of his own delusion: in Sandy's comic film, the doctor whom Sandy plays succeeds in creating the completely perfect woman but then falls in love with the completely imperfect woman who was the side effect.

When Sandy's earlier comic movie about the lunatic doctor is shown at his film festival, the audience laughs. This laughter contains an important lesson. Neither the perfect woman the surgeon tries to create nor the one with "all the badness" is a human alternative. By the same token, neither is a Hollywood "Jazz Heaven" nor the dark ending Sandy initially prefers a good choice for his movie. A story with either ending would resemble the lunatic's tale, for both in his attempt to create a perfect beloved and in his final attraction to everything bad, the doctor "from Transylvania" has rejected human life. As Sandy approaches a fitting end for his own movie, Allen does as well. Neither is a tale told by a lunatic.

Near the end of the movie, Sandy again gets stuck in his car, not in New York City traffic but somewhere in the middle of nowhere in the New Jersey countryside. Since Sandy's chauffeur has been arrested for mail fraud, Sandy himself is driving back from a movie that he has gone to see with Daisy. His car breaks down. No car phone now connects him with the "real" world, from which he wants to escape anyway. He has just been reminded of death by running into an aging actress whom he had previously directed. She has had massive plastic surgery to preserve her youth. Moreover, he has just been remembering his offer to Dorrie that they go away and drop out for a while. And he will soon repeat this offer to Daisy.

As Sandy and Daisy abandon the stalled car to look for help, he observes that their situation is "absurd." But he hasn't seen "absurd" yet. At this point Allen contrives for him the most surrealistic scene of the movie, and one that in a way parallels the ending of Fellini's *8½*. The couple hear soulful jazz music as they come to a field "strung with lights," and we are reminded of the Jazz Heaven that was the producers' ending for Sandy's movie. Soon a host of people spring up, if not the miserable wretches on Sandy's first train ride, a group that is certainly as strange. There is an astrologer speaking of the three signs in the Earth's Trinity, weird twins defending modern science, and a "wild-haired man" arguing that life on other planets would have a Marxist economy. Science and astrology occupy the same field, except that it is science that requires the defense, albeit by twins reminiscent of Cartesian dualism. And a Marxist economy is more likely on another planet. Modern knowledge appears to have gone to seed in a field in New Jersey. Sandy and Daisy have happened upon, it seems, a convention of people waiting for the landing of UFOs, so religion appears in grotesque form as well. Very soon Sandy is talking to the Martians themselves, trying to pry from them the meaning of life and suffering.

Just as Guido's fantasy finale at the end of *8½* includes the various people seen hitherto in the movie, so too are the people at this UFO convention vaguely familiar, from the fans at the hotel and others from various roles in the movie. Those who have seen *8½* await the finale, Sandy's seizing control, finishing his movie by directing this strange motley of real and fantastic beings into an epiphany, a celebration of the oneness of life and art. But there is no such ending here, and Sandy feels only oppressed, when even here as at the hotel the crowd interrogates him about his films and seeks his autograph.

Neither the perfect escape Guido has at the beginning, as he flies out of his car into the heavens, nor the perfect control of his life and everyone in it that as director he has at the end is destined for Sandy. After all, when he asks Daisy to run away with him, he wants them "to get in his car and just give up everything." He can think of flying away with Daisy only in his car, and we know that his car is not at the moment running, and that if it were it could still get caught in traffic. Far from directing the assembly before him, he can't even detain the superintelligent Martians long enough to answer his questions. Meanwhile, the organizer of the film festival, Isobel herself, and Daisy's boyfriend Jack, have become so alarmed at Sandy and Daisy's prolonged absence that they have summoned two policemen. This search party now comes to rescue Sandy and Daisy and to take them back to the hotel. If we expected release, whether it is Sandy's flying away with Daisy, or his reconciling the conflicting elements in life, we are disappointed. Sandy insists that he doesn't want to go back, that he is tired of everything, and that he doesn't want to marry Isobel. He is asking for release when one of his fans steps out of the crowd, pulls out a gun, and shoots him. Release thus comes in another way, for the next thing we hear is his doctor pronouncing him dead on arrival in the emergency room.

The fan's motives, to say the least, are obscure. While no one has complained about Sandy's comedies, which have after all been the basis for his success and fame, there has been only frustration over Sandy's serious endings. Sandy's analyst speaks of Sandy's "faulty defense mechanism": "he saw reality too clearly," and "failed to block out the terrible truths of existence." Has Sandy given his fans "too much reality," which his producers know is not what the people want? Has Sandy become the victim of their revenge? Sandy's assassination suggests what happens to an artist who, like the philosopher Socrates, insists on what no one wants to hear.[15] So perhaps in a way "too much reality" has in fact caused Sandy's death. Since Sandy dies before conceiving an acceptable ending for his new movie, the movie itself will presumably end up in the garbage, just as Sandy ends up dead on a hospital table. Sandy's death thus replaces the UFO convention as a possible ending to *Stardust Memories*. Having teased us into expecting a Felliniesque Jazz Heaven, Allen has brought us to a garbage heap.

Allen, however, teases us again. The camera moves from the emergency room to what we again expect to be the last scene of the movie, for it is the last night of the film festival. Sandy's examination of his life, we suppose, will be completed by his critics' examination of his movies. Another of his films, *The Creation of the Universe*, is shown. Sandy was nominated for an Academy Award for his portrayal of God, the festival's organizer reports. The god-like control that Guido achieves at the end of his movie is only an early role of Sandy's, and while he presumably directed the film himself, he did not have the voice for God and it had to be dubbed. Sandy was a man who knew his own limits. His ghost appears to tell the audience that "this [role of God] was not easy, folks, because, uh, you know, I-I-I didn't know what the hell I was doing." Moreover, God did not stutter when he created the universe.

When the festival organizer comforts the deceased's fans with the thought that his films will survive him, and reminds them of his award-winning film, Sandy's ghost interjects that he "would trade that Oscar for one more second of life." Like Cloquet in Allen's sketch "The Condemned," he may "hate reality," but he "realizes it was still the only place to get a good steak."[16] And Sandy's ghost responds to the platitudes about his works' survival, "but what good is it if I can't pinch any women or hear any music?"

Indeed, the deceased Sandy has discovered a certain love of life, not in spite of his understanding its meaninglessness, but because of the moments that make life worth living. He shares with his fans one such moment: when looking at the beautiful Dorrie while listening to the jazz of Louis Armstrong, he became aware of how much he loved her. This "moment of contact" moved him "in a very, very profound way." The last time that he saw Dorrie may have been in the sanitarium, but the last memory he has of her in the movie is this happy one "of contact" that gives life meaning. Louis Armstrong's music sounds in the background. In contrast to Sandy's rejection of Jazz Heaven as an ending for his movie, Allen's movie about Sandy's life may end in a kind of Jazz Heaven after all.

Allen, however, surprises us again. Like Sandy, he refuses to let the producers have their way. Besides, the producers may be wrong about "what the people want," for the crowd objects to Sandy's memory as a "cop-out" and "a sentimental bore." And we hear the doctor's voice in the emergency room claim that Sandy has merely fainted from nervous tension. That he was shot by a fan was a hallucination. Unfortunately, as he awakes in the emergency room where Isobel waits for him, Sandy calls for Dorrie. Isobel has finally had enough. Sandy runs after her, and we again hope for a good ending, but a cop stops him. He has found an unregistered gun in Sandy's Rolls-Royce. The policeman is unimpressed by Sandy's claim of paranoia about Nazis. Just as in the opening sequence on the train when the panicked Sandy tells the conductor he belongs on the celebrities' train, he now asks the policeman to make an exception in his case, for he is "a celebrity." In neither case is there release. The character is stuck in the train, and Sandy is taken off to jail, where he sits opposite his former chauffeur. It looks like this pair, celebrity and his sinister employee, have ended up in the same place, and if it is not the garbage dump that the last scene of Sandy's movie pictured, it is closer to it than to Jazz Heaven.[17] They are as confined at the end as they were in the traffic at the beginning of the movie, and, of course, there is no car phone. Allen, ironically, has given Sandy a version of the end he wanted for his own movie. Sandy is not pleased.

The movie may vacillate between jazz heavens and garbage heaps, but it is still not over. We next see Sandy running toward the train station after Isobel and her two children. He has somehow flown the coop. He loves her and wants her to live with him. He is over Dorrie, and, even more significantly, he is over his attraction to those "dark women with all their problems." Isobel is still not persuaded, and Sandy follows her onto the train. It looks like it is going to be a train ending after all. She accepts him back only when he reports a new conclusion for his movie: there are still many sad people on the train, but he no longer knows where it is going. But it is not as terrible as he originally thought because "we like each other, . . . we have some laughs, and there's a lot of closeness, and the whole thing is a lot easier to take." He also imagines on the train with him a character based on Isobel, who's crazy about him, and who thinks he's the most wonderful thing in the world. While he does some foolish things and may be "ridiculous," he is not "evil," only "floundering." Isobel cannot stop laughing, even though she doesn't find it "realistic." And yet his new vision of an ending appears to have reconciled her to him: if he can embody his new conception of life in his art, then she is convinced that it is real. A "huge big wet kiss," Sandy believes, "would sell the idea," and she buys it. It would be "a big, big finish," he says, and the moving train with this kissing couple takes the place of both the sad and the joyous trains that we saw at the beginning, the one confining the unhappy Sandy, the other the woman who blew him a kiss. It may not be Jazz Heaven, but it is not a garbage dump either.[18]

Allen suggests not that Sandy's denial mechanism has been corrected but that he has come to see reality more clearly. At least Sandy tells Isobel that he has come to see things differently, for "I was thinking a lot of unusual things this weekend, and I feel much . . . lighter." His analyst may claim that he is plagued by "the terrible truths of existence," but he has not seen Sandy after his weekend in New Jersey.

While Sandy's love of life has been strengthened, it is not something completely novel for him. Sandy has never claimed not to love life. When Daisy finds it odd that "a guy who makes a lot of funny movies" is "a kind of a depressive," Sandy denies it. And he refers not to his intense but fleeting moments of happiness but to his daily existence. "I have a good time. I have laughs," he tells her. In fact "for laughs" he does "the usual . . . read, walk, communicate. All that stuff." Sandy associates himself more with life's ordinary pleasures than with the depressive musings he shares with Daisy. Unlike Guido in *8½*, Sandy never considers suicide.[19] If he can no longer make light comedies, it is because he is impressed by the suffering he sees in the world, and especially by the death of his friend Nat Bernstein.

Sandy is not a man who hates life or hates humanity. If anything, he cares too much. He supports his parents in Florida and visits his sister. And he has always had "the gift of laughter." While these words are spoken in the movie by a fool with little appreciation of Sandy's art, fools sometimes inadvertently speak the truth. When Sandy imagines that the people on the train "have some laughs" together, and when we see Isobel able to laugh at his description of himself, their reconciliation is therefore realistic. Sandy, after all, is not Eve trying to be reconciled with Arthur. He is not even Alvy Singer trying to be reconciled with Annie.

We have seen Sandy object to Jazz Heaven because it suggests that we have more control in life than we have, that it confuses life with art, where control is possible. Sandy's new ending does not do so, in that he does not know the train's destination. Life is open, and therefore subject to chance. It was by chance, he laments, that Nat Bernstein contracted a degenerative disease and died, while he became a successful moviemaker. The new ending of Sandy's movie accepts the lack of control that makes us vulnerable to chance without denying that "laughs" are possible or real. While the fan's assassination of Sandy was a hallucination, the truth that it recognizes is the lack of control that even as careful an artist as Woody Allen has over the effect of his films on others. Not even art escapes the limits of life, for art is part of life. But that Sandy is vulnerable to the ill will of fans, misfortune, and even death does not make life meaningless. Nor is the happiness of Sandy and Isobel merely imaginary just because it is in a movie. After all, even the imaginary Sandy imagines "a very warm and very giving" character for his movie, he tells Isobel, "based on you." Movies are a reflection of life.

Sandy is not, moreover, as hostile to his fans as he is accused of being. After all, in spite of all his remarks about the "hype" of the film festival in his honor, he does attend. He patiently signs autographs, feigns gratitude for gifts, and accepts invitations to countless benefits for humanitarian causes. When he is asked "hostile" questions from the audience about his work, he makes good-natured jokes at his own expense time after time. After all, his assassination by a fan was only an hallucination. Even in Allen's "Apology," the people reverse his sentence of execution before it is carried out. He is forced to drink the hemlock only by his own followers when he implies that he is not going to tell others the truth he sees "in all its clarity" outside the cave.[20] His execution comes from an intention to hide the truth, not from his revelation of it. The people at the festival, we have seen, do not want a "cop-out." Perhaps Allen has more faith than Plato that the truth can be presented "in all its clarity," even if it is the clarity of an image.[21]

While Sandy's movie may now have an ending, Allen's does not yet. The scene with Sandy and Isobel kissing on the train recalls the beginning scene, but with hope taking the place of despair. After we saw that first hopeless scene on a train, the camera surprised us by cutting to a studio to reveal that the scene was part of a movie. So now, too, the camera cuts to the studio. What we thought was the ending of Allen's movie—Sandy and Isobel kissing on the train—was the ending of Sandy's.

Again, as with the first scene of the movie, we have been watching a movie without knowing it. How long have we been watching this movie Sandy made and acted in, as opposed to the movie about Sandy that Allen made and acted in? It looks as if Allen's movie, which we thought we were watching, has merged into Sandy's, and as far as we know, we could have been watching Sandy's from the beginning. We now have no way of knowing, for example, that the scene with the two trains both ending in the garbage heap is not the scene of Sandy's movie rather than its intended last scene, or that the first scene in the studio in which the producers are displeased with Sandy's ending is not itself part of Sandy's movie. Perhaps now, for the first time, only at the very end, do we get outside of Sandy's movie to Allen's, as the projector is turned off and the viewers emerge from the studio discussing the movie they have just seen. Once again, Allen does not let us lose ourselves in an image without an awareness that it is an image. He places us outside, and allows us to see that we have been watching a movie, even if we are not sure when we began to do so.

Many of those who acted in Sandy's moving sat in the audience and watched themselves act. And now Allen lets them discuss the movie. Sandy's sister Debbie—or is it the woman who played Sandy's sister?—praises Sandy's work both as "funny" and "heavy." Her reaction may be merely incoherent, but she may also sense something about the movie. The actress playing Dorrie still seems to be playing Dorrie, for like Dorrie she is worried about her weight, and the actress playing the festival's organizer is complaining that her role was too thin. In some ways the characters in the movie are like those who play them, in other ways they are more complex. The actresses playing Isobel and Daisy, the two rivals for Sandy in the movie, discuss the scenes in which Sandy kissed them. They seem fast friends, and remind us of Guido's fantasy in *8½* when he imagined his wife and his mistress reconciled with each other, along with a whole harem of women whom he had known, now catering to his needs. In a less fantastic way, all of Sandy's actresses—and actors—have been guided by his vision as an artist. As in the scene at the UFO gathering, the various personages from the movie are assembled together, but watching Sandy's movie rather than waiting for UFOs. People from what we thought was his present life (like Isobel and the festival organizer), from his memories (like Dorrie and his sister), and from his movies are there, just as everyone is present at the end of Fellini's *8½*. And like Guido, Sandy has directed them all.

Unlike Guido, however, Sandy has no perfect control. They are not part of a circus that he commands by means his bullhorn. In fact, one of his actresses, as we have seen, complains about the role he has given her, and two of them, even worse, complain about the kisses he gives them when acting in the movie, which they find more "real" than they have to be. Even what they reveal, as well as the fact that they reveal it, suggests Sandy's lack of control. Nor does Sandy control his fans. Some praise the movie they have just viewed, but a skeptic has the last word, an elderly Jew who can't believe "From this he makes a living?" He would prefer "a musical comedy with a plot."

But while this is the last word we hear in the movie, the last person we see is Sandy himself.[22] He picks up his sunglasses from one of the first rows of chairs, looks at the movie screen, and walks out of the auditorium. Nancy Pogel views this ending of *Stardust Memories* as a sign that the movie is "inconclusive" and its "resolution" only "apparent." She contrasts Allen's ending with Fellini's. Unlike Guido, Sandy is alone: "Sandy does not join a circle. He is not reconciled with all his past. He does not recover childhood innocence. He does not achieve an epiphany where the world comes together through the magic of the artist's aesthetic ordering." Instead, "the single figure of the director who comes face-to-face only with himself," she argues, sets aside both Fellini's aesthetic satisfactions and Sandy's moments of contact. Pogel understands Sandy's "lingering" before "the empty white screen" before he walks out of the studio as a sign of his being "still puzzled before the indeterminate blankness." Moreover, she reminds us that "Guido's donning his sunglasses" in *8½* "typically signals that a fantasy scene will follow." Thus Sandy, she implies, will continue to confuse fantasy and reality. After all, he lives in "postmodern circumstances."[23]

Pogel's, however, is not the most plausible interpretation of the end of Allen's movie. Sandy may not join a circus like Guido, but he does become part of the audience watching his movie. While Fellini shows us Guido trying to direct and to be a part at the same time, just as his culminating fantasy blends together past and present, image and reality, Sandy merely joins his audience to watch the movie that he directed and in which he acted. There is nothing like this in *8½*. Sandy has a distance from his movie as he looks at its images on the screen, just as he examined his life in the movie itself. It was this possibility of self-reflection that had made it possible for him to improve his life—or at least find a good ending for his movie.

Nor is Sandy's walking out alone at the end necessarily a sign of his alienation from life, or from others, any more than is Allan Felix's walking off alone at the end of *Play It Again, Sam*. Distance is the condition for contact, as it is for reflection, neither of which Guido achieves in his mystical fantasy of oneness. At the end of *8½*, fantasy replaces reality, art replaces life. The characters dance around a circus ring and Guido himself is led in by clowns; it is only art. Sandy, in contrast, is able to find a middle ground between his initial ending and that proposed by the producers—there is only one train, not two, and Sandy is happy riding on it with Isobel and others, regardless of where it might be going. Allen has realized more fully in *Stardust Memories* what he attempted to achieve when he placed Pearl in *Interiors*.

Finally, it is Pogel who describes the movie screen as "empty" and "white," and "indeterminate blankness," not Allen. Sandy has just watched his movie on it, and he will presumably watch other movies not yet made, some of them his own. The screen is a sign of both past accomplishment and future achievement. A director might linger to look at a movie screen as an artist might look at any empty canvas, or a novelist at a pad of paper. The movie's close thus opens up the possibility of other movies. It is an appropriate ending for a movie in which a movie's ending is the opening issue, for it makes the movie a whole that points beyond itself, as does the series of successive endings that we have seen. And while Guido's donning his sunglasses signaled the onset of fantasies in *8½*, they have never so signaled in this movie. Sandy merely carries them with him out of his studio. We have no reason to think that they do more than help him to see in the sun.

One of the fans whom Sandy meets at the film festival declares to him, "I love you." Sandy merely laughs, for, it seems, his fan has identified Sandy with his films. When Sandy laughs, the fan corrects himself, "I mean, I love your work." Only then does Sandy thank him. Allen has dramatized in this brief exchange the theme of the movie—our tendency to confuse art with life, the necessity of correcting the confusion, and the possibility that we do so through laughter. But the point goes even deeper. It seems right that it is Sandy's work that the fan loves and not the actor or the director, for the actor is not his role, nor the director his film. Is a work of art, however, rather than a human being, a proper object of love? And does not the artist embody himself, perhaps his best self, in his work? After all, as we have seen, when Daisy is surprised that someone as "depressive" as Sandy can make funny movies, Sandy asserts not a distinction between himself and his films but his enjoyment of life. Perhaps Sandy laughs not because his fan is wrong when he says he loves Sandy, but because he is half right. When the fan retracts and admits that it is Sandy's work that he loves, he has expressed in turn both sides of the truth that Sandy is and is not his work. Only then does Sandy thank him. This exchange between the director and the fan, unlike the assassination, is not a hallucination. In contrast, it is real, at least from the perspective of Allen's movie.

6

The Empiricist and the Image Maker

(A Midsummer Night's Sex Comedy)

In *A Midsummer Night's Sex Comedy*, Woody Allen plays a comic figure who has a difficult time succeeding with women and who longs for a lost opportunity he once had with another woman. His wife, Adrian (Mary Steenburgen), has inexplicably lost interest in him. As happens in *Play It Again, Sam*, the character played by Allen finally straightens out his life, including his love life. And his doing so coincides with others, especially his best friend, doing so as well. In this sense, *Sex Comedy* plays again the earlier movie. But *Sex Comedy* is more complex in spite of the similarity of themes.

Just as *Play It Again, Sam* addresses *Casablanca*, *Sex Comedy* addresses Shakespeare. Its title is a modification of Shakespeare's *Midsummer Night's Dream*, which is itself something of a "sex comedy." Additionally, the woman whom all three of the male characters in Allen's *Sex Comedy* pursue is named Ariel, the name of the enigmatic spirit in Shakespeare's *Tempest*. As in *A Midsummer Night's Dream*, couples paired at the outset of the *Sex Comedy* switch their partners; some return in the end, their love renewed, while others find more appropriate matches. As in Shakespeare's play, references to the "spirit world" abound, and the poetic world of the imagination as well as the indifference of the natural world become explicit themes. In replaying Shakespeare's comedy, Allen follows Ingmar Bergman, who also portrayed a Shakespearean world of love and mystery in *Smiles of a Summer Night*.[1]

Shakespeare's play begins and ends in the city of Athens, ruled over by its duke Theseus. Theseus, we learn in the first scene, will celebrate in three days' time, at the full moon, his marriage to Hippolyta. Paralleling Shakespeare's play, Allen's *Sex Comedy* begins in an urban setting, a New York City university, where another prominent figure, philosophy professor and art critic Leopold Sturgis, "man of culture" and "human leader" (Jose Ferrer), also discusses his upcoming marriage.

We do not know whether Theseus believes in fairies, although they will soon play a prominent role in the lives of some of his citizens, but Allen's professor certainly does not. We first see Leopold discoursing to his students about reality. There are no "ghosts, little spirits, or pixies," he says contemptuously to students, but only the empirical world, "which can be touched, tasted, felt, or in some scientific fashion proven." The "civilized" setting of the university is one of confidence in the arts, the sciences, and the progress of human knowledge. It is guided by the professor's belief that "existence becomes more understandable every day."

The professor appears heir to the Enlightenment and disdainful of the romantic concerns encouraged by Rousseau.[2] A student raises a Rousseau-like doubt about the professor's world, for it "leaves many basic human needs unanswered." With little concern, the professor replies, "I did not create the cosmos, I merely explain it." After class, the professor's admirers follow him around a courtyard on campus, much as Socrates was followed around ancient Athens by young disciples. This modern-day philosopher, like his ancient precursor, upholds reason against those who "offer theories of the mysteries of life," for their theories are "nothing more than projections of their inner uneasiness." He himself should not be praised for his achievements, which amount to "merely . . . the accomplishment of being a civilized human."

Like Bottom in *A Midsummer Night's Dream*, the professor is indeed, as someone later calls him, "a pompous ass." Just as the ancient comedian Aristophanes mocked Socrates' "rationalistic" pretensions and scientific explanations of mysteries (see, e.g., *Clouds*, 368–423), Allen mocks those of this philosophy professor. Shakespeare's spirit world enters his life only in the name of his fiancee Ariel (Mia Farrow), who has the "face of an angel." He and Ariel met, the professor relates, in the Sistine Chapel, where he explained to her "exactly why Michelangelo's ceiling was indeed great." He supposes that he can reduce Michelangelo's "glorious images" to what can be explained, just as he reduces the universe to what can be sensed or scientifically proven. The professor may be an expert on Renaissance art, but he is an "art *critic*," just as he is a critic of those who believe in the spirit world. He looks forward to his lectures in Italy, for "it will be a pleasure to put Tintoretto in perspective for his innumerable sycophants." Similarly, he is a literary critic who recently published an argument that "Balzac is overrated." He is a cultured man who can sing a lordly rendition of the Lord's prayer as easily as a German lieder.

Allen mocks the professor, however, and his rationalistic reduction of art, poetry, religion, and love. His empiricism can explain neither his own attraction to Ariel, who has the "disposition" as well as the "face" of an angel, nor Ariel's attraction to him—which is based in part on his being a teacher. Leopold taught her, she says, "how to listen to Mozart." Someone sarcastically quips that one listens to Mozart with one's ears, but if ears were all that is required, teaching would not be necessary. The explanations of the world the professor gives can account for neither Ariel's appreciation of Mozart nor for Michelangelo's greatness. "Great" music and art, to say nothing of love itself, brings one into contact with what cannot be simply seen or touched. Whether there are more things in heaven and earth than Leopold supposes, there is more in Allen's movie than the university setting. The scene shifts quickly to a country estate in upstate New York, just as Shakespeare's comedy follows the young lovers in their attempt to escape from the laws and constraints of Athens to the woods outside the city. And in upstate New York we meet Andrew Hobbes (Woody Allen), who maintains that "there is more to life than what we perceive with our five senses."[3]

We first see Andrew trying to fly by means of a pair of wings that he has invented. As Nancy Pogel points out, Andrew's "attempts to fly with the help of parachute silk on his arms . . . resemble Oberon's fairy band waving their gauzy wings" in a 1935 film version of Shakespeare's play.⁴ Allen has transported us into his own turn-of-the-century American version of Shakespeare's woods. Andrew is by profession a broker on Wall Street, but we see very little in this movie of his mundane life.⁵ We do see his passion for inventions, which also include a flying bicycle and a "spirit ball" intended to give one access to the unseen world. Allen thus juxtaposes the country setting with the urban university, as he does Andrew's various attempts to fly with the professor's empiricism.

Allen's country setting, of course, is not simply the Athenian woods. It is more like an impressionistic painting. The colors and scenes of the countryside are those of French impressionism, and its activities are celebrations of nature, from hiking to bird watching and meetings by the brook. Its music is that of Mendelssohn. Allen reproduces Shakespeare's contrast between the Athenian city and what lies in the woods beyond its reach as a device for juxtaposing scientific reason and its romantic alternative. In the city in both Allen's movie and Shakespeare's play, we hear promises of an upcoming marriage celebration; in the country we meet its already wedded denizens, who are having marital difficulties. While Oberon and Titania fight for possession of a fairy boy, the cause of Andrew's and his wife's problems are not as clear. Adrian has been having "moods and odd feelings." What is clear, as Andrew laments, is that they have "a bad sex life," and "never sleep together anymore."

Andrew is at a loss, and suggests that his wife seek the help of some of the weekend guests whom they are now preparing to receive. There is Maxwell, who is both a friend and a doctor (Tony Roberts), as well as Adrian's cousin, who is a philosopher. Indeed, he turns out to be the very professor we have seen discoursing, who is coming with his fiancee to be married in the country. When Adrian resists getting advice, Andrew claims he is "only kidding," but as Maxwell will later claim, "no joke is ever completely untrue." Should not Adrian be able to turn to such "experts"? If the professor we have just seen and the doctor we are about to meet represent humanity's progress in "the arts and the sciences," as Rousseau would say, then perhaps Andrew has good reason to turn to his "spirit ball" and "parachute wings."

Andrew's marital problems are compounded when Adrian happens to mention the name of Leopold's fiancee. Andrew is so startled that he drops and breaks a glass. There is more here than meets the eye, as Andrew himself is fond of saying about the cosmos. Even Adrian is quick to suspect some old fling, although Andrew categorically denies that he has even heard the name of Ariel Weymouth. When Leopold and Ariel arrive, and introductions take place, Ariel innocently remarks that she and Andrew are "old friends." "Acquaintances," Andrew protests. His correction does not merely save face, however; it contains a grain of truth. While he and Ariel shared a pregnant opportunity many years ago—and at Andrew's country place no less—it was no more than that, to Andrew's, and, it turns out, Ariel's regret. The jealous Adrian offers to show Ariel to her room, unless she already "knows the way."

When Adrian asks Andrew whether his friend Maxwell will bring a guest for the weekend, Andrew cannot imagine Maxwell without "appropriate female companionship." Allen gives us a brief glimpse of Maxwell at work before he arrives. His medical practice is a cover for clandestine affairs, as we see when a patient uses her medical appointments as an excuse to meet him while her husband hovers in the waiting room. When the patient can't get away for a weekend in the country with him, Maxwell asks his new nurse whether she has weekend plans. As he quickly and effortlessly moves from one woman to the other, his invitation to his nurse almost seems part of the same conversation he has been having with his patient. Maxwell's pursuit "of dames" is one continuous affair, for it hardly matters to him whom he is with. Andrew thinks he acts "like one of those characters in Greek mythology who is half goat." His nurse, the "sweet" Dulcy (Julie Hagerty), is freer than his "patient," having plans no more exciting than Coney Island. She is free in more ways than one, for even though it is turn-of-the-century America, she informs Maxwell that "separate rooms" are unnecessary. When these guests, including Leopold and Ariel, arrive at Andrew's country home, the fun begins. It is no doubt more fun than Coney Island.

Maxwell and Leopold, to put it mildly, do not hit it off, just as certainly as Ariel and Maxwell do. Introduced to Leopold and Ariel, Maxwell surprises Ariel by recognizing her scent, "Blue Moon Glow," for it is a perfume they don't sell in this country. She, for her part, scents Maxwell's "Bay Rum," and Maxwell notes that in the animal kingdom, two who recognize each other's smells would be "married." Although their exchanges about their scents may all be in accord with Leopold's empiricism, the bridegroom is not pleased. Whereas Ariel and Maxwell speak of Paris, such "a romantic place" for two people in love, she and Leopold are planning a week in London for their honeymoon, where he will have "a long-awaited opportunity to show her Thomas Carlyle's grave." Allen thus lets us contrast Leopold's scientific realism with Maxwell's romanticism, as we watch their competition for Ariel. Not surprisingly, neither likes the other's professional work. Leopold claims that Maxwell's book about natural science "was poor." To Maxwell, the professor's work is "educated," but "narrow."

Leopold points out the poison ivy, the snakes, and the toadstools he sees everywhere. To him nature is something harmful, from which knowledge and civilization must and can protect us. He imagines that the woods in which they hike were once walked by some "long-haired Neanderthal, his primitive weapon in hand, stalking through the brush like an animal," not dreaming that he would eventually "be extinct" and "culture the order of the day." When archery becomes the order of the day at Andrew's estate, the professor explains to Dulcy that he gives vent to his aggressive impulses not with destructive weapons but on "the more socially-accepted chessboard." For the professor, nature must be conquered, including human nature itself, whether it is by science, knowledge, or the conventions of society. Nature represents the primitive, the barbaric, and the dangerous, which must be in some manner contained.

The professor has not been containing his passions, for he has led a life of sexual promiscuity, although he now plans to reform with his marriage to Ariel. That is why, in fact, he propositions

Philosophy professor Leopold (Jose Ferrer) overlooks a picnic in the woods.
Credit: Orion Pictures (courtesy Kobal).

Dulcy. Because he "hold[s] the marriage vows sacred and once wed would never be unfaithful," he must use well his "last hours of freedom." His fidelity to Ariel will follow less from his love for her than his respect for the convention of marriage. Thus, it is all right for him to meet Dulcy by the brook even on the eve of his wedding. He is attracted to her "raw energy" and "animal vibrations." When he teaches Dulcy that the "stallion" is called a knight in chess, he is recognizing not nobility but the conventional name for the chesspiece. Just as chess is socially accepted aggression, so marriage is socially accepted lust.

Throughout the movie, various characters raise the question of whether there is anything more to love than lust—which is a version of the issue of whether the professor's empiricism is a sufficient account of nature. If human beings are merely sophisticated versions of other animals, more sophisticated, for example, in their use of reason to satisfy their desires, as Thomas Hobbes taught, then love is nothing more than lust. Underlying the professor's rationalism is a seething passionate world that civilization and reason must contain. We should therefore be prepared for the professor's "metamorphosis," which takes Dulcy and the others by surprise.

Maxwell, although a man of science like the professor, proclaims that he "believe[s] in the spirit world." As Andrew quips, "you have to, it's where your patients go." Because Maxwell has seen "what goes on down at the hospital"—tumors, brain damage, and heart failure—he "seize[s] the moment" and "gather[s] rosebuds." He also becomes an incurable romantic, who "love[s] nature" and "could live in the woods." He does not hesitate to pop what Leopold regards as "poisonous fungi" in his mouth to prove nature's goodness. Although he has gathered rosebuds with one woman after another, he is also prepared to fall in love and to imagine it perfect. When he falls in love with Ariel, he claims, his "flirting days are over." He is ready to die if Ariel rejects him. His undying devotion to Ariel is therefore no more surprising than Leopold's seething lust for Dulcy.

When the professor and the physician meet unexpectedly by the brook before dinner, they might seem to be mirror images of each other. Both are attracted to Dulcy, and each wants to settle down with Ariel. Right at that moment, Leopold is expecting Dulcy for illicit sex in the woods, while Maxwell is waiting for Andrew to bring Ariel so that he can declare his love to her. Each is deceiving the other, as he is his female companion. But if they meet on the same path, they are going in different directions, the one toward the satisfaction of desires that he supposes marriage and civilization should restrict, the other toward a commitment unlike any he has ever made. Both Dulcy and Ariel are unexpectedly detained, and Leopold and Maxwell, both frustrated, go off together for a walk. Since they have both promised their "partners" to be back within half an hour, their meeting is short-lived.

On her way to meet Leopold, Dulcy is detained by performing another good deed. Adrian has come to her in what she describes as an emergency. She wants to "learn how to please her husband in bed." The compassionate Dulcy tries to put the embarrassed Adrian at ease and do whatever service she can. After all, she is a nurse.

Her natural compassion reminds us of Rousseau's description of man in the state of nature. Like Rousseau's natural man, Dulcy is oblivious of convention. She innocently tells the shocked Adrian about how she first "lost it," in a hammock, in spite of the delicate balance required. When she sees only "a stallion" in the chesspiece that resembles a horse, it is not that her vision focuses on the low rather than the high, but that she is not aware of the conventional names of things. As a natural being, she is unspoiled by conventions, but also untroubled by the primitive passions of which the professor is ashamed. She belongs in Rousseau's *Second Discourse* rather than in Hobbes's *Leviathan*. When Leopold describes the life of the Neanderthal, which has been replaced by culture, Dulcy sees only "the good old days" in his description of primitive times and would like "to try it for a night." When Leopold reports to her his dream that he "was a Neanderthal, hunting [his] enemies with primitive weapons, and loving [Dulcy] uninhibitedly," she wonders only what he had to eat before he went to sleep. She does well with the bow and arrow not because of any aggressive impulses but because it's a good use of her pectoral muscles. Her "expertise" in nursing, paradoxically, does not so much represent an acquisition of scientific knowledge as it makes her more of a natural being, for she has a wonderful sense of "how all the organs function." The simple goodness of her nature is clear: not only does she do her best to help Adrian, she is appalled when Leopold tries to kill Andrew, and of course she tries to please the professor.

When Andrew attempts to bring Ariel to a rendezvous with Maxwell on his flying bicycle, the pair reminisce about that weekend long ago, that "missed opportunity," that they have regretted ever since. Andrew held back, for Ariel was a diplomat's daughter raised by nuns in a convent, and he learned only later that she was no "shrinking mousy inhibited virgin," but had slept with everyone. When the flying bicycle turns out not to be built for two, they come crashing down into the lake. Like Dulcy's tryst with the professor, Maxwell's declarations to Ariel suffer delay.

After dinner, memories and hopes are encouraged by Andrew's spirit ball, which he demonstrates for his guests. As the group sit around a table as if at a seance, the ball projects an image of a couple in the woods in the distance. To some, the man seems like

Andrew (Woody Allen) introduces his guests to his spirit ball and the "unseen world" whose images it projects. Credit: Orion Pictures (courtesy Kobal).

Andrew, to others, like Maxwell. The woman in the projection, some of the group imagine, wants to be kissed, although the image is so far away it is difficult to see how they can tell. The man, on the other hand, is "too timid" and "misses his chance." Each seems to have a different interpretation of the picture the spirit ball produces, as they all sit around as if they were interpreting a movie. Leopold, of course, is skeptical, calling the image "an optical illusion," due to an effect produced on the retina by flickering lights. Like the disbelieving Theseus in Shakespeare's play, he attributes the visions of lovers to their "seething brains" that carry them beyond "cool reason" (*MND*, V. i.).

Whatever the character of the image projected by the spirit ball, however, it certainly has its effect. Ariel goes to Maxwell in the forest, and on no flying bicycle this time. Andrew leaves his wife asleep and goes to interrupt the rendezvous that Maxwell has confided to him, just as in Shakespeare's play Helena betrays her friend's confidence to Demetrius and he pursues the lovers into the Athenian woods. When Andrew and Maxwell meet, they argue over Ariel, much as Lysander and Demetrius argue over Helena.[6] Maxwell accuses Andrew of betraying their friendship, for he told Andrew how much Ariel meant to him. When Ariel arrives and chooses Andrew, moved by her memories of their lost opportunity and no doubt under the influence of the spirit ball's magic, Maxwell goes off to "anesthetize himself in meaningless lovemaking," which he now distinguishes from his love for Ariel. His newfound passion suggests a difference between love and lust, just as it has led him to articulate the obligations of friendship.

In the meantime, Leopold has found Dulcy alone, and comes to suspect that Maxwell is with Ariel, who has gone for a walk. He will not be "cuckolded by that medical dolt." But when Maxwell returns and the spirit ball projects an image of a man and a woman on the wall, the professor realizes that it is Andrew with Ariel. He recognizes him by his glasses, and takes off after that "third-rate inventor" with the bow and arrow he earlier rejected as primitive.

Andrew and Ariel, however, just as when they flew on Andrew's "wonderful" bicycle, have had another fall to the earth. Their love-making in the woods is disturbed by the croaking frogs, and Andrew gets a headache. They are not "the same people anymore," Ariel observes, and neither of them find the experience what they thought it would be. So much for the false hopes aroused by the misleading images of the spirit ball, the midsummer night, and the full moon. So much for romanticism.

Leopold too is deceived by what he sees, takes Maxwell for Andrew, and shoots him by mistake. He is less concerned by the mistake, however, than by his violence. "I've drawn blood," he muses, "Who am I?" and walks off, for all he knows leaving Maxwell to bleed to death. Andrew finds his friend, who believes that he is dying, and who confesses to Andrew that he once slept with Adrian near this very brook last summer. We now see that he too violated his friendship with Andrew, but he asks forgiveness. Maxwell has not only come to understand a love that goes beyond lust and learned that he was wrong to assert that "marriage is the death of hope," but he has come to recognize that he has wronged his friend.[7]

It is not Maxwell who dies, however. It is Leopold. The dazed professor recognizes that he is not the pacifist he is known to be, forgets about Ariel, and goes to Dulcy as the primitive savage from his dreams returning from the hunt. As Dulcy reports, "he was like an animal, he tore off my robe, it was wonderful. We did it, violently, like two savages. He was screaming with pleasure. At the highest moment of ecstasy, he keeled over with that smile on his face." Allen piles drama on top of drama, for the spirit ball explodes, and the spirit of Leopold dances out into the woods, becoming one of the "little glaring things" that Adrian had earlier claimed "enchanted the woods." Leopold's spirit acknowledges that Andrew and Adrian are right, "these woods are enchanted," as he joins "the lucky men and women of passion who have passed away in the height of lovemaking."

Sex Comedy mocks Andrew's attempts to fly, however, as much as the professor's empiricism. And like Leopold, Andrew has a lot to learn. Just as Andrew tries to overcome limits by "inventing" ways to transcend them, he also tries to transcend the limits of time, to go back as it were to what he might have had in the past with Ariel. But he discovers that it is "too late" for him to recover the past in the present and to relive that moment that his past hesitation lost him with Ariel. In this way, Allen replies to Bergman's *Smiles of a Summer Night*, which allows its principals to recapture the opportunity they once missed and its protagonist to leave his present wife to recover his past love.

Charming as that movie is, it is from the perspective of *Sex Comedy* as deceptive as Andrew's spirit ball. The spirit ball has deceived Andrew and Ariel into believing in a love that does not exist, just as Puck's magic potion misfires when he mistakenly lays it on Lysander's eyes. Andrew's infatuation with Ariel is due to as misleading an image as Lysander's with Helena. Like Lysander's, Andrew's love for the woman with whom he first contracted is restored. Not merely the reality of what happens—or fails to happen—with Ariel in the woods—but Maxwell's "dying" confession takes the place of Puck's "reversing" magic.

Knowledge of his wife's affair, for which he soon learns his partial responsibility, brings him again crashing to the earth. But this time it is a happy crash, and the reality to which he falls is his and Adrian's love. Seeing Andrew's knowledge of her affair, his acceptance, and his love helps Adrian overcome her paralysis. And Andrew finds with Adrian what he mistakenly thought he would find with Ariel. For Andrew and Ariel it is too late, but it is not too late for Andrew and Adrian. The real world to which he crashes in the end is therefore one informed by the spirit world, but one that he no longer needs a spirit ball to enter.

Pogel draws an interesting parallel between *Sex Comedy* and Jean Renoir's film *Picnic on the Grass*, to which she persuasively argues that Allen is indebted. Renoir also contrasts "modern empiricism" with "the joys of nature, spontaneity, and love." When its protagonist is intending to marry "a rigid, sophisticated woman," a Pan-like goatherd sweeps him away with a magical wind "into the arms of a sexy country woman, Nanette." In Renoir's film, unlike Allen's, the protagonist returns to this past on his wedding day, recovering his lost moment and marrying Nanette. For Renoir, Pogel thinks, "the magical and the natural are ultimately supreme," whereas Allen is more "inconclusive," and "sad," since for him lost moments are lost forever. Such "youthful moments" as Andrew and Ariel had, she writes, "cannot be relived once time has passed and we have gained enough sophistication to sense their importance."[8] As for Alvy Singer, reflection appears in tension with happiness.

Andrew's "loss" of Ariel, however, is his "gain" of Adrian, and his wife is not the "rigid, sophisticated woman" whom Renoir's protagonist rejects for Nanette but Andrew's true love. Allen thus presents a possibility not found in Renoir's movie.[9] *Sex Comedy*'s ending, at least for Andrew and Adrian, is a positive one. Although Andrew was once too timid to take action with Ariel, he is not too timid to seize the moment with Adrian when it comes. Moreover, when he failed to seize the moment with Ariel, he later admits to her, he was not in love with her, but moved by "pure animal lust." But Adrian he loves.[10] Andrew's surname may be Hobbes, the philosopher who depicted a brutal state of nature in which human beings are timid and fearful, but Andrew's first name means "courage." It is love, not lust, it seems, that is accompanied by the action that allows Andrew to be true to his own name. Thus, Allen presents an alternative beyond the two in Renoir's movie—neither the

rigid sophistication of a joyless civilization nor the simple spontaneity of nature, but the self-conscious love that Andrew and Adrian
achieve.

Pogel is in part correct in finding in the movie the impossibility
of recovering lost moments of happiness and a dose of reality ad-
ministered to Andrew's romantic expectations. But because she ne-
glects the movie's positive ending, she captures only one side of
Allen's movie. Neil Sinyard, on the other hand, who claims that
in this film "romance triumphs over realism and mysticism over
materialism," sees only the other side of this complex movie.[11]
Allen shows that the romantic aspirations of Andrew are as ridiculous as the materialism of the professor. Andrew's attempts to fly
indicate that he is not sufficiently tied to the earth. Just as his wings
cannot support the weight of his body, his spirit ball misleads. It
projects images that permit and indeed require interpretation, but
that provide no guidance for their interpretation. Are the lovers it
projects Andrew and Ariel, or Maxwell and Adrian, or Maxwell
and Ariel, or even Andrew and Adrian? Leopold and Dulcy? Each
interprets the meaning of the images according to his or her fears
and hopes. Because the images of the spirit ball provide no guidance to their meaning, the actions their interpretations encourage
lead as easily to the betrayal of love and friendship as to their support. While in the professor's philosophy Allen mocks and warns
against modern materialism, in Andrew's premier invention Allen
mocks, and points to the dangers of, modern—or perhaps postmodern—philosophies that deny any reality behind the images we
create. Imagination can become as dangerous as its lack. Just as
Leopold does not understand the implications of his loving, Andrew does not understand the dangers of his flying.

In Shakespeare's *A Midsummer Night's Dream*, what goes on in
the forest must find its place in the city, when the matches are sanc-
tified by the law or convention. We must return from the woods to
the city. In the last act of Shakespeare's play, the "natural" unions
are recognized at a marriage celebration presided over by Theseus,
the ruler of Athens. Similarly, in *Sex Comedy*, although the professor
receives the appropriate reward for his empiricist philosophy and
its implicit denial of love, the romantic vision of Andrew is also

corrected, and he returns to his marriage with renewed love. Like Demetrius in Shakespeare's play, Maxwell remains magically infatuated with his beloved, and his romantic love for Ariel is mysteriously grounded in their animal scents. But like Demetrius and Helena, these lovers also plan to marry.

Allen therefore does not merely favor romantic images over the professor's empiricism. Both are the object of his laughter and mockery. Rather it is his own movie's celebration of the connection between the seen and unseen worlds that he contrasts with both empiricism and ungrounded imagination. To point to the deficiencies of both the empiricism and imagination of modern thought, and the need to do justice to both in a more comprehensive vision, Shakespeare is useful. While Theseus does preside, in the last scene of *A Midsummer Night's Dream*, visible to all, Oberon and Titania look on and imagine their future actions in the lives they have already influenced. Seen and unseen worlds share rule, although we don't know their precise relation. Even if Allen used Shakespeare's play only as a convenient device to set up a contrast between the scientific rationalism of the university and the romantic images of the countryside, his movie points us back to Shakespeare in this deeper sense.

At the end of *Sex Comedy*, Andrew's spirit ball explodes.[12] Its explosion is as appropriate as the explosion of the illusions it has encouraged. It will no longer throw out projections, and its role can be taken over by Allen's movie camera, whose images and projections, like Shakespeare's, connect the seen and the unseen, nature and convention, earth and heaven.

7

The Changing Man
and the Psychiatrist

(Zelig)

Leonard Zelig, Woody Allen said, "wants so badly to be liked that he changes his personality to fit in with every group he's with." Zelig (Woody Allen) does more than merely change his personality, however. Zelig's very form changes. He does not simply act like an aristocrat among aristocrats and a member of the serving class among the kitchen help. He becomes Black when among Blacks, he turns into an Oriental when among Orientals, and his weight increases to over 250 pounds when in a group of obese men. Zelig does not merely become like whomever he encounters, he becomes what they are, or so it seems. "He becomes who he is with," Allen observes.[1]

Zelig is Allen's exploration of the openness of the self to the world. At first glance, there seems to be no limit to Zelig's ability to change. He seems to be as transparent as the film of a camera that is able to absorb anything that is placed before it. We can see an implicit parallel between Zelig and a camera when people at a carnival pay to see Zelig turn into themselves, just as they might buy a cheap snapshot. Zelig resembles the amorphous Clouds in Aristophanes' play of that name, which take the shape of whomever they meet, "becoming all things, whatever they wish" (*Clouds*, 348). And like Zelig, they reveal the character of individuals they en-

counter, taking the shape of a deer when they see a renowned cow-
ard and that of a wolf when they see a thief (*Clouds*, 351–53). Like
Aristophanes' Clouds, Zelig resembles both the poet, who is open
to and consequently able to reflect the world at large, and the
human soul, which is affected and even changed by the external
world it encounters. As Sam B. Girgus notes, in *Zelig*, "Allen analo-
gizes the way the mind perceives and deals with reality and the
way the camera operates to record reality."[2] *Zelig* is thus not only
about the self and its relation to the world but also about art or
poetry.

After conceiving of the "human chameleon" who blends in with
his surroundings in order to belong, Allen thought of presenting
him as a famous international figure in the form of a documentary.[3]
Zelig is a series of newsreels that documents the life of Zelig in the
1920s and 30s. Allen intersperses the newsreels with interviews
both with people who supposedly knew Zelig and with real-life
well-known authorities able to comment on the cultural, historical,
and psychological significance of the Zelig phenomenon. We see
Zelig not simply through Allen's newsreels but through the eyes of
such intellectuals as Susan Sontag, Irving Howe, and Saul Bellow.

As one of these authorities, psychiatrist Bruno Bettelheim, observes of Zelig, "he was the ultimate conformist." A conformist is
one who adopts the opinions of others or changes his behavior or
habits to resemble theirs. Literally, a conformist takes the "form"
of others. In creating Zelig, Allen takes a metaphor and makes it
real. Zelig literally changes his form, not just his opinions or habits
as a conformist ordinarily does. Allen gives the inner meaning of
conformist an outer manifestation. He lets us see into the conformist by, as it were, turning him inside out. One newspaper headline
proclaims of Zelig's malady that "IT'S ALL IN THE HEAD," but
Allen's comic device puts what's in Zelig's head in his physical
appearance as well. His film holds a mirror to a conformist only by
letting us see what is otherwise invisible to the naked eye. His
movie is thus based on the absurdity that what is "more than meets
the eye," as Andrew says in *Sex Comedy*, actually meets the eye.

To the extent that Zelig really is the ultimate conformist and simply takes the form of others, there is nothing inside to be seen. Zelig

has been characterized as the paradigm of an other-directed man, who derives his identity from others.[4] He is therefore "directed" by others; he lacks inner direction. He is all surface, with no depth, or, as Frederick said of Flyn in *Interiors*, he is "form without any content." He can therefore take on any form, as the flirtatious Flyn can sense what pleases others and act accordingly. As Flyn is said not to "exist except in somebody else's eyes," Zelig seems to exist only in somebody else's form. In contrast to Eve, he is the consummate exterior decorator. As the narrator of the documentary describes Zelig at one of his lowest points, he is "devoid of personality, his human qualities long since lost in the shuffle of life . . . a cipher, a non-person." If the task of Flyn's sisters is to discover themselves in their "exteriors," the task of Zelig is to discover an interior, to discover in effect that he cannot become all things.

One of the more intractable and enduring of Zelig's transformations occurs when he is first examined by a group of psychiatrists at Manhattan Hospital. The narrator's voice-over tells us that "with the doctors watching, Zelig becomes a perfect psychiatrist." In first

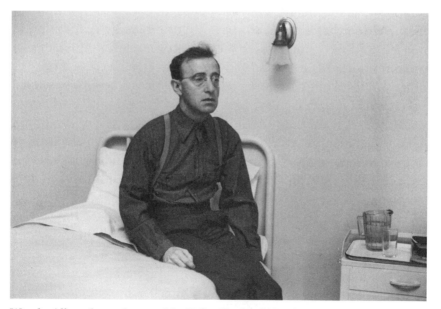

Woody Allen plays a lost soul in *Zelig*. Credit: Orion/Warner Brothers (courtesy Kobal).

laying eyes upon him, Dr. Eudora Fletcher (Mia Farrow) "took him—mistook him—for a doctor," for "he had a very professional demeanor about him." What happens to others in the presence of Zelig happens to these professionals as well, for they see Zelig turn into themselves. The joke is on the professionals, however, with their assumption of professional distance and objectivity. Their object disappears before them, and their "objective" examination of Zelig leaves only the subjects who are undertaking the examination. Zelig has become one of them. And like a "perfect psychiatrist," he reveals them to themselves. After all, just as patients pay psychiatrists to see themselves, so too do carnival goers pay Zelig for the same purpose.

However appropriate Zelig's transformation into a psychiatrist may be, it becomes a problem for Zelig, for it stands in the way of his own self-understanding. By posing as a doctor rather than a patient, Zelig examines others rather than himself, all the while projecting himself unawares onto his imagined patients. He has written on "delusional paranoia," for example, but does not see his own delusion. He is treating, he claims, "two sets of Siamese twins with split personalities," while he is as split as the patients he imagines. He does not see that in speaking of others he is speaking of himself, and what might make it easier to see himself—his external projection—makes it more difficult, inasmuch as he sees it only as other. He loses himself in the scientific objectivity of a professional psychiatrist, just as he loses himself in the various objects he imitates.

Eudora's first breakthrough with Zelig comes when she accepts Zelig's pretense that he is a psychiatrist and pretends that she is his patient suffering from the same symptoms she has observed in Zelig himself. Her breakthrough comes, then, when she throws off professional distance and identifies with her patient, no longer treating him as an object that she observes from the outside. By imitating or becoming like Zelig, she does for Zelig what Zelig himself has been doing for others. She can do this because she is in part like Zelig, as Zelig implies when speaking to her as a psychiatrist. He tells her that her desire "to be like other people," is "natural." Our ability to "conform" might become manifest in a cowardly

Speaking with psychiatrists, Zelig (Woody Allen) turns into one. Credit: Orion/Warner Brothers (courtesy Kobal).

other-directedness or group conformity, but it also makes possible a common humanity and mutual understanding.

By imitating Zelig, Eudora provides him with an image of himself. Her device brings to the surface not simply the inner meaning of the conformist, or what is natural or common to all human beings, but eventually Zelig himself. While it is natural that Zelig wants "to blend in," that he wants to do so implies that he does not simply blend in. There is something paradoxical about standing out as a chameleon, which Allen captures in Zelig's very notoriety for chameleon qualities. If Zelig were simply "the ultimate conformist," no one would ever see him, any more than one sees the chameleon who perfectly blends in with its surroundings. But Zelig certainly stands out. The narrator captures the irony, "He who wanted only to fit in—to belong, to go unseen by his enemies and be loved—neither fits in nor belongs."

For Zelig to maintain his role as a psychiatrist, he must stop mirroring, for his psychiatrist is pretending to be his patient. To mirror her, Zelig would become her patient, or what he in fact is. Not surprisingly, Zelig becomes "all mixed up and nervous," for he sees only himself when he looks at Eudora. Only then is she able to hypnotize him, and get him to talk about himself.

The popular press understands Zelig's uniqueness only in his possession of chameleon qualities, proclaiming that he suffers from a "UNIQUE MENTAL DISORDER." The popular media locates Zelig's uniqueness in his perfect embodiment of the human ability to imitate, in his having no identity of his own that cannot be perfectly assimilated to the outside. It is not all wrong in doing so, but Eudora discovers a unique human being who is not exhausted by mere chameleonlike qualities. Whom one imitates is as important to one's identity as one's ability to imitate. Eudora discovers that Zelig is more than meets the eye, and she falls in love with him.

The hypnosis Eudora employs resembles Allen's movie in bringing to the surface what does not ordinarily meet the eye. As Zelig reveals under hypnosis, he had a rather unique—and painful—childhood with which he has never come to terms. And he is able to express hatred—of his cruel stepmother—as well as love. As he says under hypnosis, "I love baseball. . . . It doesn't have to mean anything, it's just very beautiful to watch." Zelig not only becomes whomever he is with, but he also seeks out particular groups, particular people, with whom *he* wants to be. One of the first times in the documentary that we see Zelig get into trouble for his imitations of others is when he joins the Yankees at their spring practice in Florida. Zelig appears as "a strange new player [whom] no one on the team has heard of." Watching baseball, or experiencing beauty as a spectator, does not fully satisfy him. He must act, he must play a part, he must imitate what he loves. His dressing like a Yankee, of course, however much he may love baseball, does not work. The "strange new player" is eventually thrown out. He does not find what he is looking for until he finds Eudora.

Under hypnosis, Zelig reveals not merely that he hates his stepmother and loves baseball, but also that he loves Eudora. Zelig may change into a psychiatrist when Eudora approaches, but he does not change into Eudora, even though, or perhaps precisely because, he loves her. Far from assimilating himself to Eudora, he recognizes her weaknesses, for she is "not as clever" as she thinks, and her jokes are long and pointless. Instead of wanting to be Eudora, he wants to be himself for her sake. "I love you . . . I want to take care of you," he tells her. And while it is hypnosis that first permits Zelig to remember his childhood experiences, it is his love for Eudora that in the end leads Zelig to remember himself. When he loses himself for a final time under the pressure of widespread public disapproval, Eudora locates him in Berlin, in a mass of Hitler's followers. Catching sight of Eudora, Zelig becomes "like a man emerging from a dream," and "in a matter of seconds, everything comes back to him." Together they escape from Nazi Germany and live "full and happy years together."

Having disrupted Hitler's rally, the pair are chased by the SS and take off in a plane aided by Eudora's amateur flying skills. As the elderly Eudora remembers, "I was frightened. I lost control. We went into a dive. Leonard was so terrified that he changed his personality, and before my eyes, because I was a pilot he turned into one, too." Zelig, who had never flown a plane in his life, not only escapes the Germans, but "sets a record for flying non-stop across the Atlantic upside-down." And Saul Bellow comments, "what enabled him to perform this outstanding feat was his ability to transform himself. Therefore his sickness was also at the root of his salvation."

But neither Eudora nor Bellow is correct about the cause of Zelig's salvation from Hitler. It is not merely his ability to conform that explains his escape from Nazi Germany. After all, while Eudora may be an amateur pilot, she is merely a frightened woman who has lost control when Zelig takes over the pilot's seat. Becoming Eudora is hardly sufficient for the feat Zelig performs, for Eudora herself could not do it. Nor is it simply for the sake of being liked or fitting in, however much he earns the pride of the nation by doing so. Indeed, his feat represents an escape par excellence from such a desire, inasmuch as it is an escape from Nazi Germany, where he "could make something anonymous of himself by belonging to this vast movement."[5] And that feat includes saving Eudora as well as himself. He finally "takes care" of her, as his love earlier urged him to do.

Eudora's love for Zelig leads her to spot him in a faceless crowd of Nazi sympathizers. And Zelig stands out from that crowd even to Hitler when he remembers Eudora and his own love for her. It is a fitting touch on Allen's part that Zelig's remembering himself interrupts Hitler's speech. Neither Eudora nor Zelig could spot the other among Hitler's followers, nor could either love the other, if they perfectly fit in or belonged, if they simply lost themselves in an anonymous crowd. Formlessness, or the ability to become all things, then, is a false image of the soul's openness—at least of the soul that is able to love.

When Carter Dean pins a medal on Zelig and calls the couple "a great inspiration to the young of this nation, who will one day grow up and be great doctors and great patients," he is therefore right. Allen has shown that it is possible, paradoxically, for one to be "great" not only as a doctor but also as a patient. The greatness for both doctor and patient lies in becoming like the other, in simultaneously saving and being saved. Just as there is some truth in Zelig's pretense to be a psychiatrist, so is there in Eudora's assumption of the role of a patient before Zelig. She too had childhood problems: she "was a very moody . . . child . . . a very difficult girl," and her father "had problems, depression, he drank." But Eudora is able, her sister reports, to draw strength from Zelig. And the narrator observes that Eudora's life also changed because of Zelig, for she learned that fame and recognition "do not live up to the adolescent fantasies that prompted her ambition." She forsakes the upwardly mobile attorney to whom she is engaged and announces her intention to marry Zelig. Like Zelig, she too sought the approval of many, but the love of one man changes her life. It is appropriate that in the end, while Eudora continues practicing psychoanalysis, Zelig gives advice to others and lectures about his experiences.

Only by coming to reflect each other, then, do Eudora and Zelig come to live a full and happy life together. Each literally imitates the other, psychiatrist and patient, and the imitation becomes real. Zelig at least saves Eudora from her adolescent fantasies by giving her a love far superior to the fame she craved, just as he saves her from the Nazis. And Eudora becomes a patient, not primarily by pretending to be Zelig's patient for the sake of his cure, but in learning through him what she really wants and thus in allowing him to cure her. Although the human soul is not fluctuating form without content, amorphous as clouds that take every and all shapes, it is nevertheless open. That Zelig becomes able "to speak his own opinions" to Eudora means that he "open[s] up more and more" to her. His "being his own man" coincides with his expressing his love. It is Zelig's ability to change, after all, that makes possible his loving Eudora, his courage, and his transformation into himself.

Allen's newsreels of Zelig's life in the 1920s and 30s might have stood alone, his story being told by the film's narrator. Allen, however, adds both humor and depth to his story of Zelig by recording the reactions of others to Zelig. Like Allen himself, they tell Zelig's story. We are therefore able to compare their telling with Allen's telling. Because they tell their versions of Zelig's story within Allen's story, telling the story becomes part of the story. Because each of the authorities offers an interpretation of Zelig, Allen's movie about Zelig is also a movie about interpretation.

One of the authorities interviewed in the movie is the historian John Morton Blum. Allen credits him with writing the book *Interpreting Zelig*. While Blum's title might mean that he offers an interpretation of Zelig, he speaks most in his interview about the various interpretations to which Zelig gave rise. The title of his book, then, likely refers less to what he himself does than what others do, less about Zelig than "interpreting" Zelig. And, indeed, he finds Zelig less interesting than the interpretations given of him. To him, Zelig is only an ordinary man who preferred baseball to classical literature. Zelig's story is "a matter of symbolism," he claims.

The first voice we hear in the movie is a voice-over, which we soon learn is Susan Sontag being interviewed about Zelig from her home in Venice. "He was *the* phenomenon . . . of the twenties," she tells us. The first spoken word of the movie is thus a pronoun that has no antecedent, for we do not know who "he" is, just as at first we do not know whose voice we are hearing. In a way, it doesn't matter, for if "he" is merely the phenomenon of the twenties he signifies only the spirit of his times, formed by something external, and other directed. Throughout her interview, Sontag never uses Zelig's proper name.[6] For her he remains a pronoun without an antecedent. She has discovered not Zelig, but only a conformist.

Allen has a second authority, Irving Howe, immediately correct Sontag: Zelig's story "reflected the nature of our civilization, the character of our times . . . yet it was also one man's story."

Not only does Zelig himself in this movie take on a variety of shapes or forms, but the meaning of Zelig does so as well when he is interpreted by various intellectuals. We thus see Zelig lose himself not only in the forms of those whom he meets but also in the interpretations of the intellectuals. When Ruth Zelig and Martin Geist take Zelig to perform in France, "leading French intellectuals . . . see in him a symbol for everything." Historian Blum notes, "It was all symbolism—but there were no two intellectuals who agreed about what it meant." "To the Marxists," Blum notes, "he was one thing," while "of course, the Freudians had a ball."[7] Each, in other words, finds in Zelig confirmation of his own theories. Psychiatrist Bruno Bettelheim, for example, approves of Eudora's methods for establishing "a very strong personal relation between doctor and patient." And he sees Zelig as merely an extreme form of all of us, "not all that different from the normal, maybe, what one would call the well-adjusted normal person." Irving Howe, on the other hand, author of *World of Our Fathers*, Allen's caption tells us, claims that Zelig's story "reflected a lot of the Jewish experience in America—the great urge to . . . assimilate into the culture." Susan Sontag attributes Eudora's success to her aesthetic instinct rather than to psychotherapy. As Blum says, "they could interpret him in any way they pleased." As Ruth Perlmutter points out, the intellectuals in *Zelig* parody "their own scholarly predilections."[8]

Zelig is open to any and every interpretation, however, only if he has no identity that limits him, only if there is no Zelig by which we can measure interpretations. The movie lets us believe that Zelig has become his own man, but perhaps Allen's inclusion of these different interpretations of Zelig in his movie suggests our delusion, for we see that interpretations merely reflect the interpreter's predilections. And if Zelig is indeed "a symbol for everything," as the French intellectuals believe, the film *Zelig* may also be open to as many interpretations as Zelig himself.

When Sontag sees Zelig's cure as "a triumph of the aesthetic instincts," does she mean that Eudora was able to sense Zelig's integrity, or that she in fact created him, that Zelig is not really "his own man" but merely Eudora's? In spite of the promise of the title of her own work, *Against Interpretation*, she does not write against "interpretation in the broadest sense, the sense in which Nietzsche (rightly says) 'There are no facts, only interpretations.' "[9] She is "against interpretation," then, only in the sense that interpretation destroys the integrity of a work of art by trying to judge it from outside, by subordinating creativity to reason. Her attack on interpretation in no way contradicts the view that interpretation is all. It is actually premised on it. She criticizes interpretation insofar as it implies that there is something other than interpretation being interpreted, or that interpretation can reveal something that is more than mere interpretation. Is this Allen's view as well, and is this why he includes so many different interpretations of Zelig within his own?

This understanding of *Zelig* is found in the comments of many of the movie's critics. When Girgus points to Allen's analogy between the mind's perception of reality and the film's recording of it, he suggests that one is as elusive as the other. He views the mock documentary form of *Zelig* as a perfect vehicle for demonstrating this. We usually think of photographic images and films as "pure images or specific pieces of reality," Girgus points out. But since Zelig is a fictional character appearing in a documentary, Girgus argues, the movie "explodes this notion" and "undermines our complacency."[10] In other words, if even the "document" is fiction, all is fiction, or at least we have no way of distinguishing reality from fiction. As Sontag quotes Nietzsche, there are no facts, only interpretations.

Pogel, similarly, claims that because "illusions and reality" are so confused in *Zelig*, "truth always appears to be unreliable and self-contradictory." This "self-conscious film," according to Pogel, "deconstructs itself," just as "the contradictory personal perspectives" of the interpreters "question whether truth is ascertainable by any means."[11] The film, it seems, is everything and therefore nothing. And given the parallel between *Zelig* the film and Zelig its main character, so is Zelig. Accordingly, Girgus claims that "the film questions the possibility of even being 'your own man.' "[12] As

Girgus says, the mock documentary "immediately undermines any privileged perspective from which to document reality," and the film "becomes a visual extension of internal psychic instability and uncertainty."[13] Girgus understands such "increasing complexity" as a sign of Allen's "intellectual and moral maturity."[14]

"Psychic instability and uncertainty," however, does not necessarily indicate moral and intellectual maturity. It does not for Leonard Zelig, whose psychic instability makes him the plaything of chance and the dupe of others. And just as an amorphous self is a false image of the soul's openness, so too is a movie that condones any and all interpretations a false image of a film's complexity and maturity.

We have seen in other of Allen's films indications of the dangers of a view that interpretation or image is all. In *Play It Again, Sam* Allan Felix moves beyond total dependence on Bogart, sorting out the images he finds worthy of imitation. Sandy Bates in *Stardust Memories* insists that his movie must reflect life and dismisses the ending that his producers want. In *Sex Comedy*, Andrew Hobbes similarly rejects the false images projected by his spirit ball. And if in *Zelig* Allen mocks the French intellectuals who see in Zelig "a symbol of everything," so too does he mock the intellectuals he interviews and their self-confirming theories of Zelig. After all, Allen said that he used the intellectuals in the film because they added "the *patina* of intellectual weight and significance" (emphasis mine), just as Zelig has "the demeanor" of a psychiatrist. The intellectual authorities are not simply "outside" authorities who tell us the meaning of Zelig. They themselves are part of the intellectual milieu that fosters the problem of Zelig. It is in this sense that they do contribute to the film's "intellectual weight and significance."

Susan Sontag's opening reference to Zelig as a "phenomenon" of the twenties continues to echo in other uses of "phenomenon" in the movie. Ruth Zelig and her boyfriend Martin Geist, who exploit Zelig as a sideshow freak, advertise him as "THE PHENOMENON OF THE AGES." The sign on the building in which Zelig turns into other people for a dollar reads "A MARTIN GEIST PHENOMENON." Geist is an "ex-carnival promoter" and shady businessman, whose deals included selling the same piece of property to a lot of people. But the piece of property he sells so many times cannot be indefinitely appropriated, for it is "real" estate. Geist is jailed for fraud. He finds Zelig, the human chameleon, more indeterminate than real estate, for he and Ruth sell him to everyone who gives them the price of admission.

For Geist and Ruth, as for Sontag, Zelig is a phenomenon, or an appearance, with no interior, a pronoun without an antecedent. Nothing that he is prevents them from using him for their own purposes, just as the intellectuals interpret him as they please. It is one of the great ironies of the movie that there is a resemblance between intellectuals who see Zelig merely as symbol for everything and a man jailed for real estate fraud.[15] Allen's irony becomes more biting when he connects this interpretive use of Zelig with Hitler himself, who through his rhetoric and propaganda assimilates individuals to an anonymous mass, or treats them as pronouns without antecedents.

The intellectuals are like those who visit Geist's sideshow, for when they look at Zelig he turns into them, except that they don't know it. Like the professional psychiatrists who also examined Zelig, the intellectuals see in Zelig the confirmation of their economic, psychological, or cultural theories, just as others see their own obesity or brain tumor. Like Zelig and his contemporaries, they too are characters in Allen's movie, not simply reflecting on Zelig from outside but like the obese men in the hospital, reflected in Zelig as well.[16] If Zelig is Geist's sideshow, he is not Allen's. Allen calls his movie *Zelig*, not *Interpreting Zelig*, as Blum does his book. If there is a sideshow in *Zelig*, it is the intellectuals themselves, but only because their interpretations are beside the point, as they bypass Zelig when their reflections on him turn into reflections of themselves.

Zelig is a movie about the two senses of reflection. Reflection means deriving an identity or content from an object outside oneself, as a mirror reflects the person standing before it, and as Zelig reflects those who stand before him. And there is the sense in which one reflects on, or thinks about, an object from an apparently outside vantage point, just as the authorities reflect on Zelig. The movie moves back and forth between Zelig's reflections of others and others' reflections on Zelig. The movie as a whole also moves from Zelig's reflection in the first sense, as the changing man, whose troubles begin when he first pretends to have read *Moby Dick* among "very bright people," to his reflection in the second sense, when he is reading *Moby Dick* at the end of his life "to see how it came out." A movie throughout is reflective in both senses: its camera is directed by the world that it records, while it also has a director who reflects on what he records by selecting and arranging it.

We have seen that the intellectuals' reflections on Zelig are in part reflections of their own, albeit intellectual, milieu, whether Marxist, psychoanalytic, or existential. While Zelig is more free than he at first seems, in that he is able to stop reflecting others, the intellectuals are less so in that their reflections on Zelig are reflections of their own "intellectual" times. They are "phenomena" of their age. Paradoxically, they would be more free—and less confined to their solipsistic visions—to the extent that their reflections on Zelig were truly reflections of Zelig. Reflection in the sense of thinking must be grounded in reflection in the sense of mirroring if it is to have any meaning or truth, while reflection in the sense of mirroring must be grounded in thought about its object that comes from standing back in order to see from the outside, if it is to reveal more than exteriors. If Zelig must discover himself to be free of the other, or to escape conformity, the intellectuals must discover the other to be free of themselves. Zelig must come to reflect the world less, and intellectuals must come to reflect the world more. It is not surprising that a self-reflective movie is about the connection but not the identity of the two senses of reflection.

Allen has commented on the importance of opening scenes in his movies. In short stories or novels, he observes, "from that first sentence, everything spins out. The second sentence reflects the first sentence. . . . And it's the same thing in a film."[17] We have seen the significance of Sontag's opening comments about Zelig, followed by Howe's implicit correction of them. We have also noted opening scenes in the other movies we have discussed, Allan Felix's absorption in *Casablanca* in *Play It Again, Sam*, Alvy's monologue in *Annie Hall*, the ending of Sandy Bates's movie at the beginning of *Stardust Memories*, the professor's rejection of "ghosts, little spirits, and pixies" in *A Midsummer Night's Sex Comedy*, and the still-life scenes of *Interiors*. In one of *Interiors'* opening scenes, Joey's face is reflected in the glass of a painting Eve has arranged in their beach house. For Eve, Joey remains outside, because her domineering imposition of order tries to bring Joey totally within its sphere. Zelig, similarly, remains outside the interpretations of the intellectuals because they try to place him completely inside. It is Allen's art that brings Joey into his movie, where she is able to grow and develop. And it is Allen who is able to interpret Zelig, for he refuses to interpret him away. His reflection of Joey is truer than Eve's, as his interpretation of Zelig is truer than those the intellectuals offer, for he has reflected on Joey and Zelig in a way they have not. He sees the possibility of Joey's being "her own woman," and of Zelig's being "his own man." Unlike Eve's art, Allen's is not flawed by Sontag's "aesthetic instinct."

An art that understands and reflects a world finds a model in human love. Allen's art in fact reflects Eudora's love for Zelig, which permits him to stand out as the individual he is, and Zelig's love for Eudora, which gives her a more rewarding and solid happiness than that of the recognition she sought from her profession. Together, they can be famous without becoming other-directed. In the end, Zelig ceases amorphously changing: Allen tells us that "Zelig's episodes of character change grew less and less frequent and eventually his malady disappeared completely." And he too, like Joey, finds a source of love. To F. Scott Fitzgerald, who at the beginning keeps trying to get Zelig's name straight, Allen gives the last spoken words of the movie, for Fitzgerald is a poet whose efforts to identify Zelig have led to the truth about him. It was "the love of one woman" Fitzgerald notes, "that changed his life."

8

The Actor and the Character

(The Purple Rose of Cairo)

Richard Schickel says Allen's *The Purple Rose of Cairo* is "one of the best movies about movies ever made."[1] In Allen's movie, a character from a Hollywood movie, also called *The Purple Rose of Cairo*, walks off the screen and gets involved with one of the members of the audience.[2] Although something similar happens in *Play It Again, Sam, Purple Rose* is more fantastic. There is no question that the character can be seen by everyone. He gets in a fight with a real person. He is not just an image in someone's mind. He does not affect the world merely by giving advice to someone who admires him. At least from the point of view of the film's dramatic illusion, Tom Baxter (Jeff Daniels) comes off the movie screen to play a role in people's lives. Like some other Woody Allen characters, this one creates havoc in ordered worlds—a small town in New Jersey into which he descends from the movie screen, the film that he abandons, and the Hollywood world that produced the movie.

Tom walks off the screen in order to meet Cecilia (Mia Farrow), who has seen the movie five times. She is as impressed with *Purple Rose* as Allan Felix is with *Casablanca*. And like Felix, she has a pressing need to seek in movies what life does not offer her. Her prospects in life, however, are much more bleak. Allan Felix has been abandoned by his wife and uses movies for romantic inspiration in his search for female companionship. Cecilia, however, who lives during the Great Depression, expects very little from life. Her husband, Monk (Danny Aiello), is out of work and spends the little money Cecilia earns as a waitress on gambling, drinking, and other women. At the Jewel Theater, Cecilia is a regular, as we see when the manager addresses her by her first name to tell her the next attraction. She has seen almost everything and knows the personal lives of the stars as well. Their personal lives are as wonderful and as interesting to her as those of the characters they play. She speaks to her sister about both actors and movie characters in the same breath. She is ripe for a meeting with either or both. The movies— and Hollywood—offer her a glamour for which she longs even as it is well out of her reach.

Allen gives us a clear contrast between the world in which Cecilia lives and the world of the movies, especially that in the *Purple Rose*, which is the next attraction the manager announces to Cecilia. A playwright and his high-society friends, "bored with cocktail parties and opening nights . . . with evenings at the opera and weekends at the races," take off for adventures in exotic Cairo, since Paris is old hat to them. There, when visiting a pyramid, they pick

Socialites in the film within the film seek excitement in Cairo. Credit: Orion (courtesy Kobal).

up the man who will become Cecilia's love, "Tom Baxter—explorer, adventurer . . . doing a little archeological work." He is in fact looking for "the purple rose of Cairo," which, according to legend, a pharaoh planted near his deceased queen and which still grows wild around her tomb. The group from New York City is impressed. "A real-life explorer," one of them observes of Tom. Neither the actress who utters these words nor the scriptwriter who wrote them recognizes how prescient they are, for a "real-life explorer" is also one who explores real life. This is exactly what Tom comes to do. Writer has written and actress has spoken more than they know.

The group of travelers Tom meets in Cairo want to take him back to New York City to meet their friend the Countess, who will "love" the explorer exotically dressed in pith helmet and khaki. At their invitation, the explorer hesitates but decides to go, for "what's life without a little risk-taking?" He thus utters words in Cairo that within the Hollywood movie justify his flying back to New York but that also justify his walking off the screen into Cecilia's life. We should be prepared to expect trouble, for, after all, Tom is an explorer and adventurer, and the actor who plays him, Gil Shepherd, "worked so hard to make him real."

When Tom arrives in New York, his new friends take him to the Copacabana, where the words sung by glamorous Kitty Haynes foreshadow the love that according to the script will develop between her and Tom: "Ours could be a different sort of love affair/ Those busybodies couldn't help but stare/ Still we wouldn't care, dear/ Let's just take the dare, dear." Ironically, Kitty's words are much more relevant to her real-life rival for Tom, Cecilia. Surely Cecilia and Tom's is "a different sort" of love affair. One would be tempted to say it is unique except that we have heard of such a "mixed" marriage before, between the real-life Kugelmass and the "fictional" Madame Bovary. Again, Allen joins the real and the fictional in a loving embrace, even if in both cases the embrace is not lasting.[3]

The humor in the movie involves, in part, the fictional Tom's experiences of the real world. Tom, having had no life apart from the movie's script, knows only the movie world from which he came.

Thus he is surprised when after kissing Cecilia there is no fade-out to some "private, perfect place" in which they make love. He tries to pay for a real dinner with the stage money he has in his pocket; he tries to drive a car without a key as he does in the movies. Cecilia must explain to Tom how the real world works, specifically the need for money and jobs that earn it, or for the key that starts the car (and implies ownership). He has experiences of only what was "written into his character," just as he knows only what was written into the script. But since it was written into his character that he "take risks," it was "in character" if not "in the script" for him to step off the screen into real life. When he does so, the movie executives responsible for the film are surprised. But it is they, after all, who have produced Tom as a risk taker and a real-life explorer. They do not understand that the art they produce might have real-life significance.

When Tom asks Cecilia to show him the real world, she takes him by a Salvation Army soup kitchen, a group of bums begging for money (Tom kindly gives them some of his stage money), a shoe repair shop, a barbershop, and finally a church. While Tom finds the church beautiful, he doesn't know what it is. Cecilia tries to explain God to him, "the reason for everything, the world, the universe," but there was apparently nothing like this in the Hollywood *Purple Rose*. Tom supposes that Cecilia must be talking about someone like the writers of *Purple Rose*, Irving Sachs and R. H. Levine. The humor here is poignant. It works most immediately like the other incidents that contrast Tom's movie perspective with that of the real world: Tom does not know about car keys or real money, and he does not know about God or churches. But the situation here is more complex. While we again have the contrast between the perspectives of fictional Tom and real Cecilia, it is not as obvious in this case which understanding is real and which fictional. That is, Irving Sachs and R. H. Levine are real, at least in terms of Allen's *Purple Rose*, but is God real, or is God as fictional as Tom Baxter? Could the fictional character believe in something real, while the real character believe in something fictional? Or does Tom, in this instance as well, have much to learn about the world outside his movie?

The church provides a fitting setting for the discussion about God, but the discussion would have been possible without it. Allen puts this exchange in a church, empty except for Cecilia and Tom. The relatively empty church stands in contrast to the crowded movie theater. During a time of economic depression, distressed individuals such as Cecilia find solace in Hollywood movies rather than in church, however much the ardent moviegoer Cecilia may be surprised that Tom has never heard of God. That he has never heard of God highlights the fact that God was not written into the script of the Hollywood movie that gave birth to Tom. In contrast to his ignorance of what goes on in a church, Tom "know[s] exactly what an amusement park is, and what goes on" there. Hollywood movies tell us more about amusement parks than churches. They do not write God into the script. Indeed, as Allen suggests, the movie theater has taken the place of church. The first scene of Al-

The crowd flocks to the Jewel to see *The Purple Rose of Cairo*. Credit: Orion (courtesy Kobal).

len's *Purple Rose,* as the credits appear on the screen, is from a movie in which Fred Astaire is singing "Heaven, I'm in heaven . . . And I seem to find the happiness I seek/ When we're out together dancing cheek to cheek."

As a movie character, Tom is "perfect" in a way that no human being is. In the world of the movies, from which Tom comes, he tells Cecilia, "people, they don't disappoint. They're consistent. They're always reliable." Like a perfectly consistent movie character, Tom remains true to Cecilia; unlike the "real" men she knows, he does not disappoint her. When the movie Tom leaves cannot go on without him, one of the movie patrons becomes indignant. She "want[s] what happened in the movie last week to happen this week, otherwise what's life all about anyway?" Only the consistency, or perfection, of art, she supposes, can give life meaning. For the same reason that Cecilia wants Tom to descend from the screen, the moviegoer wants him to stay in the movie.

Reality seeks the perfection of fiction. It is no wonder then that churches are empty, for while religion may hold out the promise of heaven, it is not now, not here. Religion often teaches, moreover, an inevitable gap between the perfect and the imperfect, the divine and the human. The movies—or at least the kind that Cecilia watches or the kind that Sandy's producers want him to create in *Stardust Memories*—foster the illusion that "heaven" is "dancing cheek to cheek," that after the kiss comes a fade-out to "some private, perfect place," and that we all end up in a Jazz Heaven.

Although Tom wants to be free, when he recognizes that he does not have the financial resources to take Cecilia for a night on the town, he takes her back into the movie with him. The socialites whom he has left on the screen, after all, are about to go to the Copacabana. Cecilia enters the Hollywood *Purple Rose,* just as Kugelmass enters *Madame Bovary.* For her it is a dream come true, not simply because it is dancing cheek to cheek at the Copacabana, but because she has wondered for her whole life what it would be like on the other side of the screen.

Even if cinema could create a perfect world, however, it is not real. Can it be perfection if it does not exist? "Perfect" implies "having everything," but this "perfect" world does not have reality. Tom is said to be "perfect," but as someone asks, "what good is 'perfect' if the man's not real?" To some, Cecilia is "wast[ing] her time with a fictional character," and "deserve[s] an actual human." Cecilia herself inadvertently points to the difficulty, "I just met a wonderful new man. He's fictional, but you can't have everything." Fictional characters, however perfect, do not have everything, no more than do those who have them for lovers.

In particular, fictional characters do not know or experience what it is to be human. Cecilia must explain to Tom what a pregnant woman is. As Tom begins to wonder about "the finality of death" and "the miracle of birth," it seems to him "almost magical [to be] in the real world" as opposed to "the world of . . . celluloid and flickering shadows." Tom wants to "learn to be real," just as the real world attracted him from the screen. Human beings, who experience the miracle of birth and the finality of death, are also free to make choices, which is what Tom wants. They can therefore escape the endless repetition that we find in a work of art.

Tom rejoices in his freedom, "Cecilia, I'm free. After two thousand performances of the same monotonous routine, I'm free." He wants the freedom and also the spontaneity of life, where "just because a thing never happened before doesn't mean it can't happen for the first time." He is the perfect antithesis to the movie patron who wants the movie to be the same from one week to another, without concern for the miracle of birth, the finality of death, or the magic of reality. But then she has been sitting around in a movie theater, whereas Tom has visited a church with Cecilia.

It might seem to us, as it does at times to Sandy Bates, that because there is so much suffering there can be no God, at least no God that has any connection to human life.[4] But if there would be more order and consistency in life—and thus less suffering—there would also be less freedom and thus less humanity. We may desire perfection and consistency, but we would not want a script from which we couldn't deviate.

This is why Tom is wrong to try to understand God in terms of the collaborators who wrote *Purple Rose*.[5] Unless life becomes art, its creator must assume less control than an artist. Unlike art, life manifests no inevitable repetition. When his producers want to end his movie with Jazz Heaven, Sandy Bates objects that while there is perfect control in art, there is not in life. He therefore will not let his art—since it is one thing he can control—give an imperfect description of life. If art imitated life perfectly, however, it would not have the control possible for art. It would suffer the fate of the Hollywood *Purple Rose*, for in Allen's movie, Irving Sachs and H. R. Levine have written something they are unable to control. And that is the irony in Tom's supposing that God must be like these scriptwriters. It is not true as Tom means it. It is true only in the exception, for the movie out of which Tom comes. The scriptwriters have in their art come up against life's lack of control. Their art imitates life so much that it is not art, and to this extent they are like God. God is not an artist. While an imperfect world is obviously no evidence for God's existence, it is also no evidence against it. This may be why Sandy Bates objects to his critic's calling him an atheist: "To you—I'm an atheist," he says, "to God I'm the loyal opposition."

Tom wants to learn to be real and supposes that "there's nothing to it." But as a skeptic points out, one "can't learn to be real. It's like learning to be a midget. . . . Some of us are real, some are not." When Tom gets in a fight with Cecilia's brutal husband, Cecilia is surprised to find that Tom is "not even marked" and his "hair is in place." "I don't get hurt or bleed," he tells her, my "hair doesn't muss"—it's "one of the advantages of being imaginary." But if his hair doesn't muss, does it grow? Does he need the barbershop that Cecilia showed him on his tour of the real world? More important, can an imaginary being, who cannot get hurt or bleed, manifest courage, or merit praise for standing up to Cecilia's husband? And can such a being face the finality of death?

Cecilia's attempt to find happiness with a movie character is derailed by a further problem that Allen places in his movie, the actor who plays Tom Baxter. Allen explains the difficulty he had completing the script, until he thought about the actor who played the character who walked off the screen. Then it occurred to him that Tom Baxter "would be part of his problem, too." With "a totally fictional character and an identical real character," Allen has "enough substance to do a film that . . . would be entertaining and also about something: the difference between fantasy and reality."[6] And when the identical real character, actor Gil Shepherd, appears, Cecilia must choose between him and Tom.

Gil is horrified that his "creation" Tom Baxter has walked off the screen and ruined the movie. Even more alarming, Gil fears that this will also ruin his career. Not only is his double running around loose, maybe robbing banks or raping women, but if Gil is an actor who "can't control [his] own creation, nobody's going to risk a picture on [him]." He takes off from Hollywood for the small New Jersey town where Tom is courting Cecilia in order to coax Tom to back into the movie. And, of course, he meets Cecilia, who at first mistakes him for Tom. It is not clear, however, whether Cecilia is more amazed by a character's walking off the screen into her life or Gil Shepherd's doing so. When Cecilia introduces actor and character to each other, and Gil pleads with Tom to return to the movie, Tom refuses to budge. He loves Cecilia and wants his freedom, and it seems more important to him than Gil's career. He recognizes no obligation to his creator and even claims responsibility for the critical acclaim Gil received for playing him.

Actor and character are in an irresolvable deadlock, at least momentarily. But Gil makes a play for the star-struck Cecilia. He offers her a less one-dimensional existence. She believes that Gil "is deep and probably complicated." And he knows the script not only of the Hollywood *Purple Rose*, as does Tom, but of the many movies in which he has acted. Gil and Cecilia enact together the last scene of another of Gil's movies, whose lines Cecilia knows by heart. They also visit a music shop, where Gil buys her a ukulele and sings songs that she is able to play, songs that Tom would presumably not know. After Gil gives her "a long lingering kiss," with no expectation of fading out, it is no wonder that poor Cecilia is "confused." When she next meets Tom, she has come to doubt her love for him, for he is "some kind of phantom," and moreover, they are "broke" together. We are ready for Cecilia's choice, even if she is not.

Gil enters the theater and sees the now-running movie, for Tom has returned to it with Cecilia for their fling around Manhattan. Gil calls her down from the screen, as she had in effect originally called Tom. Gil declares his love for her, admits his jealousy of his own creation, and offers to take Cecilia back to Hollywood with him. Tom, in turn, urges that he is "honest, dependable, courageous, romantic, and a great kisser," while Gil urges merely that he's real. He holds out life, and Cecilia goes with him. She explains to Tom that she is "a real person," and that "no matter how . . . tempted I am, I have to choose the real world." The "devastated" Tom returns to the movie, although his tears call into question how imaginary he really is. His tears were not written into his script, nor his pain at losing Cecilia. While Cecilia's husband cannot hurt this "perfect" being, Cecilia evidently can. It seems that the creature is more than a creature, just as it will turn out that his creator Gil is less than he appears to Cecilia.

As Cecilia packs her suitcase for Hollywood, her husband warns her that the life to which she is going "ain't the movies! . . . It's real life, and you'll be back." There is irony in Monk's supposing that Cecilia's harsh life with him constitutes a superior alternative to the harshness of real life in Hollywood. But he is right that Cecilia has much to learn about her choice. While she supposed that choosing Gil over Tom was choosing the real world over fiction, Hollywood is for her only a version of the glamorous world of the movies. We have seen how she spoke of what went on in movies and what went on in the lives of actors as if it were all part of the same alluring world.

Faced with a choice between Tom and Gil, Cecilia does not face a "real" choice. Indeed, her decision for Gil over Tom might be viewed as a choice of the more utopian alternative, for in choosing Gil she opts for romance plus the money to pay for it. Tom has only stage money and no job. It is the Depression and "explorers" are not in great demand. She chooses everything. Her rejection of Tom, therefore, is not simply a rejection of romantic perfection.

Cecilia's choice of "reality" turns out to be of "fiction" in another sense, for Gil's offer is only fiction, whereas Tom really loved her. As her husband warns her, she experiences the "reality" of Hollywood, but she does so without leaving the theater, where Gil leaves her waiting, suitcase in hand. This man who is attractive because he has played more roles than Tom was only playing another role. Eudora may have found Zelig behind his roles, but for Cecilia, Gil has disappeared. The warning of Cecilia's husband is therefore prescient, for she chooses a harsh reality indeed in choosing Gil, precisely because she has chosen a phantom.

Cecilia not surprisingly returns to the movie theater for solace. The *Purple Rose* is no longer running; presumably the producers have destroyed the film, as they threatened to do. The current movie is with Fred Astaire and Ginger Rogers, and now we watch with Cecilia as Astaire sings the same "Cheek to Cheek" he sang in the opening scene. Since Astaire sings about being "in heaven," it might seem that Allen has given us a version of the Jazz Heaven with which Sandy's producers wanted him to conclude his movie.

The last thing we see is Cecilia's face as she watches the movie, with a smile finally replacing her tears. This repeats a sequence that we saw earlier when, fired from her job in the diner and watching *Purple Rose*, Cecilia's tears give way, if not to an actual smile, at least to an absorption in the movie. Allen's *Purple Rose* thus seems to affirm the repetition and routine that Tom Baxter claimed characterized movies rather than life, so that Cecilia has achieved a version of "movie" life after all. And it resembles Eve's "still-life."

But Cecilia is not the same Cecilia that she was at the beginning of the movie. Her last few days can hardly be called routine. Hasn't she, as she told Tom on parting, "loved every minute" with him? Her smile in the end at Astaire's singing and dancing could be a recollection of that time with Tom, and therewith a recognition of how movies and the heroes they create remind us of our own potential for happiness.[7] Although Allen claims that movies serve as a narcotic for Cecilia, he admits that her return to the movies at the end is ambiguous and that "the ambiguity may be good luck, something that came from the healthy growth of that film."[8] Like Sachs and Levine's *Purple Rose*, Allen's film has a life of its own. But because he is a better artist, that life shows itself as good luck rather than bad. His *Purple Rose* dispenses to Cecilia a mix of reality and fantasy—although different from the one on which she bargained—not the real life of Gil and his fantastic Hollywood existence, but an experience of Gil's betrayal and another romantic movie. Her tears and her smile suggest that she has learned from her experience and that she has achieved a combination of real life and image more realistic than romantic.

Tom's grasp at freedom turned topsy-turvy not only Cecilia's and Gil's worlds, but also that of the Hollywood movie from which he came. Without Tom, the other characters become "stuck," and the movie comes to a standstill. One of them is "bored with sitting around." Being "a dramatic character," he "need[s] forward motion." A woman in the audience complains that there is "no action." In a way, however, there is "action" for the first time for these characters, for without Tom, on whom the movie turns, they must abandon the script. They speak for themselves, to one another, and even to the theater manager and the members of the audience. They argue, not unlike the actors or actresses who play them might do, about their relative importance to the movie, as well as about the movie's purpose or meaning. When the characters come alive, they offer interpretations and look for meanings, thus demonstrating that such activities are as essential to life as the "action" the complaining patron wants when she sees the characters do nothing but "sit around and talk." They try to interpret the movie that has given them birth, just as Tom tries to understand the church to which Cecilia brings him. It is in this sense that all these "characters," especially Tom, are more "real" than the real Gil.

The characters within the movie are torn between a desire to become free too and a desire for Tom to return, so that they can "continue with the story." They are more ambivalent—and therefore more human—than the slave in Allen's early one-act play *God*, who responds to the promise of freedom: "I don't want to be free. I like it this way. I know what's expected of me. . . . I don't have to make any choices."[9]

But while the characters are more desirous of freedom than the slave, it is not clear that they have the option inasmuch as they are characters in a movie. Indeed, if they choose freedom and the movie does not go forward, they fear, the projector might be turned off; they will disappear and become nothing. They have a self-interest in coaxing Tom to return.[10] When Gil and Tom present their cases to Cecilia, the movie characters get involved in the discussion, for the most part on Gil's side. Their fear inadvertently points to the fact that insofar as they are only characters in a movie, they too are without a "real" option. If the story goes forward, they will be "stuck" in the story just as they are at a standstill when their script is suspended.

When Cecilia pronounces her moving choice of "real life," one of the movie characters, Rita, stares offscreen, absorbed in Cecilia's words. Critics have pointed to the similarity between Cecilia's watching Astaire at the end of *Purple Rose* and Allan Felix's watching Bogart at the beginning of *Play It Again, Sam*. Both scenes show the power of film to affect the moviegoer. But here in *Purple Rose*, we see as well a real-life scene, at least from the perspective of Allen's movie, affect a movie character. Or more accurately, Allen's ability to reflect something real in his movies is so powerful that it can move even the fictional characters within it.

The fictional characters of the Hollywood movie are not long for this life, nor is their film. The producers, understandably, do not trust their characters to remain in the movie. After all, Tom has walked out once, and other characters have expressed a desire for similar freedom. If all movie characters followed Tom's example and started walking off the screen in the middle of their movies, the producers foresee, it would be the death of movies, and art and life would blur into each other. It would be the end of art and its service to life. So, prints of the film and its original are destroyed.[11] The Hollywood *Purple Rose* continues to exist, although in part, only in Allen's film of the same name due to the part it plays there. Allen places it in the service of life by showing that the pull of life's freedom can move even fictional characters, even if it means giving up their seemingly "perfect" lives.

The "flawless" Tom in the end is more open to change than the less-perfect real-life jerk Gil. Tom cries as he returns to the movie, while Gil sits expressionless on a plane flying back to Hollywood. It is Tom, not Gil, who acknowledges that he has much to learn and who asks for Cecilia's help. And it is Tom who thinks "some very deep things" about the human life he wants to possess. While there may be more perfection in the Tom of Hollywood's heavenly movie, there is more humanity in the Tom who leaves that role for the less consistent real world because of his love of Cecilia. Even the

"heavenly" life of the characters in the movie, we see from the outset, gets "boring," and if Paris is old hat, what happens after they
have been to Cairo and Tangiers? In Egypt, they see the "divine"
and "perfectly preserved" pyramids, but it is Tom they want to
bring home with them. Their visit to Cairo, the most exotic place
they can think of, is not enough, for they need the real-life explorer
Tom for future amusement. Their boredom with their playboy lives,
their search for relief, and their discovery of Tom all foreshadow
what they do find as their movie progresses and what Tom actually
brings to them, if only momentarily. The order or consistency of
still life, however divine it may appear, does not represent human
fulfillment. If earth were like heaven, it would be as little desirable
as the lives of the characters at the beginning of the Hollywood
Purple Rose, which are surely free from suffering in any ordinary
sense.

Cecilia is "a real person," and no matter how tempted she may be
by Tom and the perfection of art, she must choose "the real world."
Cecilia's words, however ironic as support for Gil over Tom, do
state what the movie demonstrates. The "most human of all attributes," one of the movie characters says to her, "is your ability to
choose." These words are spoken by the character who most
wanted to follow Tom's lead and to have the freedom of life, even
if as a movie character he does not have the ability to choose that
Cecilia has.

By affirming the goodness of imperfect human life, Allen's movies steer a middle course between the heavens of saccharine Hollywood movies and the hells of pessimistic European films. That
middle course leaves room for God, albeit one whose imperfect
world leaves room for us. Allen's *Purple Rose*, unlike Hollywood's,
does include a church, as well as Cecilia's belief in and Tom's won-
dering about God. In the Hollywood *Purple Rose*, in contrast, a
priest is called in only when Tom leaves, only when the characters
cannot follow the script, only when they become more than they
were created to be, only when they become real. God plays a role
in life, not art, and Allen's art, like Sandy's, strives to be true to
life. Thus, it is not "celluloid and flickering shadows" but real life,

especially birth and death, that leads Tom to speak of magic and miracles.

When Gil is outraged at Tom's defection from the movie, he wonders whether he made him "too real." I said earlier that Gil made Tom more real and, in that sense, more fit for human life, than Gil himself. But there is also one way Gil did not make Tom real enough. Tom did not become real for Gil himself, for the actor was not improved by his character. Had Gil become more like Tom, Tom would have become real for him in the way Bogart's Rick did for Allan Felix, and as Tom became for Cecilia when he inspired her to imitate his courage. While Allan Felix's leaving Linda is a sign that Rick lives in Allan Felix, Gil's leaving Cecilia is a sign that Tom does not live in Gil. Tom's returning to the Hollywood movie, however, is not simply his death, for he has lived in Allen's movie as the character who wants to experience life and its miracles. Should any viewer be moved, as Rita was by Cecilia and as Allan Felix was by Bogart, Tom would live again, just as he lives to some extent in Cecilia's smile at the end of *Purple Rose*.

9

The Eavesdropper and the Patient

(Another Woman)

Woody Allen recounts that many years before he wrote *Another Woman* he had thought of making a comedy in which he played a man who overheard a woman talking to her therapist, sharing "her most intimate secrets." He discovers that she is beautiful when he sees her leave the building. Since he knows from what he heard through his heating vent "what she dreams of in a man," he contrives to meet her and to make himself into her ideal.[1] We can understand why this idea appeals to Allen. Like Allan Felix in *Play It Again, Sam*, the protagonist would have an image of what he thinks a woman wants and would try to act accordingly. And just as Allan Felix gets his image from the movies, this protagonist would get his image from, as it were, "looking" at a scene between others who did not know they were being watched. And like an actor, he would, in effect, play a character out of a script, which the beautiful patient did not know she was writing.

Allen delayed creating this comedy—which he eventually made in *Everyone Says I Love You*.[2] But he used the idea in a different way, he recalls, in *Another Woman*.[3] In this movie, it is a woman who overhears through a heating vent another woman talking with her psychiatrist. Like the man in the original sketch, she becomes fascinated with the woman, follows her from the building, and eventually meets her. And like the protagonists of many of Allen's movies, eavesdropper Marion Post (Gena Rowlands) comes to understand herself and improve her life with the help of an image.

That image is the image of another woman, the woman (Mia Farrow) whose voice she overhears through the vent in her apartment. And it is an image through which she comes to see herself. Allen has observed that this other woman serves as an incarnation of Marion's inner self.[4] Through listening to this woman describe herself to her therapist, Marion understands the ways in which she herself is like this other woman, and this knowledge frees her from a quite different image that she has of herself. She comes to understand herself only through an image of another woman, only when she sees herself reflected in another. The name of this other woman is Hope.

Another Woman constitutes an implicit defense of art, for art can consciously create such images for us—images of ourselves—that Marion encountered by accident, because she chanced to rent an apartment next to a psychiatrist, because he happened to have a patient who revealed problems that reminded Marion of her own, and because the repairs of a heating vent that would prevent such private disclosures had not yet taken place. Art can do deliberately what life does only by chance, if at all. And that is one reason art is useful to life. *Another Woman* suggests how art can help someone to understand and be herself.

Marion does not appear to be a woman interested in the private lives of strangers. Why does she eavesdrop? When she first becomes aware of the voice coming through the vent, she covers the vent with a pillow. She acts not for any moral reasons, but because she is not interested. She has other things to do. She is in fact a professor on leave from the university, where she runs an undergraduate program in philosophy, to write a new book. She has rented this apartment in Manhattan as an office in order to have a quiet place to work during the day. So although "eavesdropping may be fascinating to some people," she observes, "it was not what I had in mind when I rented the place." We see immediately, however, that she is fooling herself, for when the pillow drops away and she overhears a woman's voice, she was, she reports, "arrested by its anguish." That she thinks that she has no interest in what she might hear through the vent is only one example of Marion's self-deception, although it is the first that we discover. We proceed to discover others along with Marion.

She is arrested because Hope's anguish is her own anguish. When the first voice she hears from the therapist's office through the vent is that of a man talking of his bisexuality, she has no difficulty in blocking it out with pillows. She continues listening to Hope because Hope reminds her of herself. She is no disinterested spectator of another's suffering. And she eventually learns more about herself than about Hope from eavesdropping. What she has done may be morally questionable, but we do not simply condemn her, for she is in a way listening to herself.

The movie is a narration by Marion of this period in her life. It begins with her speaking directly to the camera about herself—of her recently having turned fifty, of her having achieved "a decent measure of success, both personally and professionally." She tells us, in passing, of her family—her mother, recently deceased; her father (John Housman), who is still alive and healthy; a married brother, Paul (Harris Yulin); her husband, Ken (Ian Holmes), a cardiologist who "examined [her] heart, liked what he saw, and proposed"; and her teenage stepdaughter, Laura (Martha Plimpton), whom she takes under her wing. But beyond that, she claims, she does not choose to delve, for "if something seems to be working leave it alone." But shortly Marion comes to reassess her relationship with each of these people in her life and also comes to understand her professional success in a different light.

We learn something of Marion's past when she looks at old photographs with her stepdaughter, and Allen provides flashbacks for the stories Marion tells. Marion and Laura see pictures of Marion's mother, who "loved strolling around the grounds," Marion says. "She loved all beautiful things; she loved nature, music, poetry, that was her whole existence." They see a picture of Marion's brother Paul, with whom Marion claims she has always been very close. And finally they look at a picture of Claire (Sandy Dennis), who used to be Marion's best friend. Marion's memories, however, are incomplete. She sees the photographs without seeing the full reality from which they are drawn. In the course of the movie, Marion comes to see that reality more fully. Only from more complete memories, however painful, can she have hope for the future.

While Marion sees only her mother's love of beauty, for example, and in particular her love of Ranier Maria Rilke's poems (to which she had introduced Marion), Paul reveals the harsh results of their mother's living in her own beautiful world. She neglected him, she did not understand him, and he is filled with resentment. One of their mother's favorite poems is Rilke's "The Torso of Apollo." Marion reads the lines from the tear-stained page in her mother's book of poetry, "here there is no place that does not see you. You must change your life." But Allen gives us no sign that Marion's mother changed her life. We know only of Paul's resentment of her and her own tears when she read Rilke's poem.

Although Marion believes that she and Paul have a close relationship, Paul's wife, Lynn, tells her frankly that while Paul may idolize Marion he also hates her. All of the things Paul said about their mother's living in her own world and its effect on him he might have said of Marion as well. And this revelation is followed by others. When she asks Paul to be honest with her, he tells her that he stopped pursuing her when he realized how uncomfortable it made her feel. He remembers once giving Marion something he had written to read, and her response. She found it "overblown," "emotional," "maudlin," and told him that while his dreams may be meaningful to him, to the objective observer they're embarrassing. Marion does not remember the incident, but it obviously meant more to Paul than it did to her. She may have been trying "to be truthful," but now Paul is being truthful to her. By quoting words she once spoke to him, he lets her see herself. Another revelation, equally difficult for Marion, comes from her stepdaughter Laura.

It may be, as Ken tells Marion, that Laura is closer to her than either to him or to her mother, and that Laura listens to Marion because she looks up to her. But Marion now remembers overhearing an exchange between Laura and her boyfriend, Scott, when they realize that Marion saw them making love by the fireplace. Scott does not understand why Laura is upset, for she had told him how "hip" Marion was. But knowing that Marion saw them turned what was romantic into something cheap for Laura, who explains that Marion is judgmental: "She stands above people and evaluates them." Laura has heard Marion talk about her brother Paul and fears that "she'll judge me that way."

Marion receives yet another shock from her old friend Claire, whom she has not seen for a long time. Marion meets Claire unexpectedly coming out of a theater, where she has been acting in a play. Marion goes for a drink with Claire and her husband, Jack (Jacques Levy), who converses at length with Marion about her work in Amnesty International and in the ACLU. The somewhat intoxicated Claire relives the experience that separated her from Marion. And she now shares it with Marion, whom she believes lured from her a man she once loved—by "conversations full of subtle flirtations, meaningful little looks [and] little gambits designed to seduce." Marion avers that she had not the slightest interest in him, but this actually makes her case worse. Marion may have never accepted his overtures, as she claims, but Claire tells her "by that time you had what you wanted." It is after a series of such revelations that a former student of Marion's approaches her in a restaurant to tell her that her class "Ethics and Moral Responsibility" changed her life. While Ken and their friends look proud of Marion, Marion herself has become perceptive enough of the irony to cringe.

It is not clear that Marion would have been open to any of these revelations, to say nothing of her seeking them out as she does from her brother, had it not been for the anguished Hope. The words of Hope that Marion overhears resonate with what Marion is afraid to utter about herself. Hope admits that there is something unreal about her life. She reports "a curtain parting" that lets her see herself, while her own voice coming through the heating vent functions as just such "a curtain parting" for Marion. After overhearing Hope's imagining her husband "as a stranger," Marion asks herself whether her own husband is a stranger too. That evening at a party after their friend Lydia (Blythe Danner) mentions she and her husband passionately made love on the living room floor, Marion asks Ken whether he would ever want to do that very thing with her. She is just not the hardwood floor type, he tells her, with unintended irony, for the very lack of passion that keeps her off the floor does make her hard as wood to many who know her. Later in the movie, Marion discovers her husband's interest in Lydia, clearly "the hardwood floor type," for she claims that it's "not unpleasant, if you don't get splinters."

Marion's lack of feeling contributes to her loss of Ken, although it seems clear that he was not much to lose in the first place. When she eavesdrops for a second time, she overhears Hope questioning whether her marriage was the right choice. Hope even remembers someone else she might have married, and wonders about "real love," something "more intense" than she has experienced, and which she keeps herself from thinking about. Her words remind Marion of her and Ken's engagement party, which we see in a flashback. There a friend of Ken's, novelist Larry Lewis (Gene Hackman), tries to persuade Marion that she loves him rather than her fiance, who he tells her is "cold," "a prig," and "a snob." Marion resists, but Larry insists that their conversation frightens her. When she escapes into the crowded living room, a guest praises her work on Heidegger, who "definitely got what he deserved." Like Leopold in *Sex Comedy*, who explains how the revered are overrated, Marion is a philosophy professor whose work is primarily criticism. She is particularly critical of Heidegger—as we learn at her inauthentic engagement party—a philosopher popularly known for his theory of authentic engagement, something that becomes possible for a human being only after confronting her own mortality.[5]

Whether or not Marion's criticism of Heidegger represents an unwillingness to face death, her high school essay on Rilke's poem "The Panther" argued that the caged animal is frightened by a vision of death. Marion not only remembers her teenage essay, but also seems haunted by her own vision of a caged panther.[6] And although she ran away from Larry at her engagement party, she does not run away from Hope, or at least from that vent through which she overhears Hope's sessions with her therapist. Although she did not see herself in Larry's words when he first uttered them to her, she now sees herself in her memory of them. Her image of Hope has allowed her to look at herself more directly, not only in her memories but also in what others such as Lynn and Paul tell her. Marion comes back to hear more and more of what Hope has to say, as if she were looking in a mirror she cannot put down.

Exhausted one afternoon, she falls asleep and has a long dream. In the first scene of her dream, Marion overhears another session between Hope and her psychiatrist. This time, Marion herself walks into the psychiatrist's office. Now not only hearing but also observing the session, Marion, if we might interpret her dream, comes closer to Hope and to Hope's situation. What makes you afraid to speak, the psychiatrist asks Hope, although Hope had not been afraid to speak before. It is Marion, we may presume, who is afraid to speak, and whose dream blurs herself with Hope. Hope answers, "the universe, life, the cruelty, the injustice, the suffering of humanity, illness, aging, death." She sounds like Sandy Bates when he refuses to write comedies.

Since it is Marion dreaming, it is Marion attributing such concerns to Hope. It is thus Marion who thinks of them, who projects them onto someone else, just as a playwright, for example, must have had the thoughts that he attributes to his characters. Marion

Marion (Gena Rowlands) muses about her life in *Another Woman*. Credit: Orion Pictures (courtesy Kobal); photographer Brian Hamill.

also dreams of the psychiatrist's response to Hope, as a playwright composes the various parts of the dialogue. "All very abstract, don't worry about humanity, but get your own life in order," she dreams that he advises Hope, and in this indirect way speaks to herself. Marion, we recall from her discussion with Claire and Jack, is involved in Amnesty International and the ACLU and, as Claire said, "always had the urge to save humanity." Such urges may be diversions from her own problems, Marion suspects, attempts on her part to get the world in order that distract her from her own disorder.

Hope leaves, and the psychiatrist turns to Marion and asks her what she thinks Hope is suffering from. He draws Marion into the conversation, which becomes about Marion as well. Hope is suffering from "self-deception," Marion responds, "but I don't think that she can part with her lies . . . not that she doesn't want to." Marion could not know what Hope wants or doesn't want. Ostensibly describing Hope, she is describing herself. The psychiatrist of the dream proceeds to tell her that Hope does not give up her lies precisely because she does not want to, but that "when she wants to she will." He holds out hope, but he has to hurry, he says, for he must prevent her from killing herself, something that she has been doing "slowly and methodically" since she was young.

The psychiatrist then brings in another patient, Marion's father. Letting Marion eavesdrop on her father is one way he might prevent Marion's own slow and methodical suicide. Her father is full of regrets, regrets that echo Marion's own, for he regrets that while he achieved some eminence in his field (as has Marion), he has asked too little of himself (as is true of Marion). He regrets that there is little love left between him and Paul (which applies to Marion and Paul as well). He regrets that he has been too severe and too demanding of Marion (which Marion has also been of herself) and, most tellingly, that "the woman I shared my life with was not the one I loved most deeply." Whether this is true of Marion's father we have no basis of knowing, nor any reason to think that Marion does. But what her father says of himself in Marion's dream may be true of Marion herself. Larry Lewis, at any rate, once insisted that Marion loved him more deeply than the man with whom she is now sharing her life.

The dream shifts from the therapist's office to a theater that Hope invites Marion to enter. Again, Hope beckons her to further self-knowledge.[7] When her dream carried her to the therapist's office, Marion saw her problems reflected first in Hope and then in her father. She now sees herself more directly, as a character on stage.

In the first scene of the play, Claire plays Marion. The scene is of a conversation we have already heard between Ken and Marion, when Marion asks Ken whether he would ever want to make love with her on the living room floor. Although the first several exchanges are exact repetitions of lines that we heard Marion and Ken utter earlier, in the dream play there is a further discussion, much more frank than any Marion and Ken have actually had. Marion observes to her husband that there is not much passion left in their marriage, but Ken had not noticed. Marion observes that their marriage is not very erotic anymore, but Ken asks if it ever was. Before he goes to sleep, for he is tired, he mentions that Marion spoke the name of Larry Lewis in her sleep. At the mention of Larry's name, Marion is filled "with melancholy and longing."

In the next scene of the dream play, Marion plays herself, and Claire plays Larry's new wife, to whom Larry introduces her. Larry also tells Marion of his daughter, who is "the greatest, most beautiful experience" of his life. Marion is a spectator in more senses than one, both watching herself with Larry on stage, and looking at Larry's life, in which she might have played a part but did not. Claire's husband Jack, who presents the program to Marion, tells her not to cry, although he is pleased that she is moved by their performance. He asks her to stay for the "second act finale," her first husband's suicide scene.

Marion next hears her first husband, Sam, also her philosophy professor (Philip Bosco), tell her that she was "a dazzling pupil" for whose seduction he paid the price. There comes a time when a pupil inevitably absorbs all she can from a teacher, he explains, and his joy of imparting knowledge turns into frustrating suffocation. Suffocation, his dream image concludes, was the very thing written on his death certificate. It is he who has died slowly and methodically, although it appears that Marion bears some responsibility. When Jack asks Marion to wait for another important scene between her and Sam, Marion pleads "no more." Her dream ends before it is complete, but she will later complete it when awake by remembering another scene with Sam.

The play that Marion dreams serves as a documentary of her life and becomes a turning point for her. Soon afterward, when Marion and Ken return from a dinner with friends interested in ESP and parapsychology, Ken points out that Marion put down the couple's beliefs unequivocally and rather cruelly. Marion acknowledges her foul mood, as well as the possibility that the couple may be right and that there might be "more to life than meets the eye." Her language recalls the disagreement between Andrew and another philosophy professor in *Sex Comedy*, but Marion is a philosophy professor who does not have to die before recognizing that the "woods *are* enchanted." Like Leopold, although in a less comic vein, Marion will also admit that her life has been a self-deception. She is well on her way to becoming "another woman," one whom Larry Lewis loved long before.

Marion finally meets Hope in person in an antique store, finding her crying at the sight of Gustav Klimt's painting of a pregnant woman. Marion, however, thinks it "a very optimistic" painting, "the most positive" of all the paintings Klimt did during that period. Allen noted that it was pure coincidence that this painting, which "had the right feel for the movie" was named *Hope*.[8] Art, of course, makes good use of such coincidences. Hope, herself pregnant, has hope from her child. And Marion finds hope for a new life in other ways.

When Marion and Hope go to lunch, Marion intends to get to know her better without seeming pushy, but nevertheless ends up doing most of the talking. She tells Hope how she was traumatized when she recently turned fifty and has not regained her balance since. She thus corrects the first words of the movie that she herself uttered, how at fifty had she been asked to assess her life, she would have noted that her life was working well, and delved no further. She is now more truthful in talking to Hope than she had been to herself. Her life is not working.

She talks to Hope of lost opportunities she cannot have back, in particular the opportunity of having a child, something she admits she has never said before. Her conversation with Hope about wishing to have a child leads her to remember another episode with Sam, possibly the final scene of the play that she refused to watch earlier in her dream. In that episode, Sam discovers that she has aborted their child and angrily accuses her of caring only for *her* career, for *her* life of the mind. She hears her own words to Sam: "It's my life that gets derailed" by a baby, "you've accomplished your book, I'm just starting, I'm trying to make something of myself." We hear words similar to those spoken by Joey to Mike in *Interiors* when she thought she was pregnant, but for Joey it may not be too late. When Marion admits to Sam that she loves "the idea" of children, "but not now," her husband, older than she, tells her that his future is "not stretched out indefinitely in front of him." Marion had insisted to Jack that Sam had not committed suicide, but Jack pointed out that when a man, alone in a hotel room and depressed, dies of pills mixed with alcohol, "there's always a grey area."

Later that afternoon, Marion again overhears Hope through the heating vent. This time she hears Hope's description of the "really sad woman" with whom she had lunch, a woman who one would think has everything but who "has nothing," who "can't allow herself to feel, [who has] lived this cold, cerebral life and has alienated everyone around her." Instead of seeing herself merely in Hope's account of her own life, Marion now overhears Hope talking about Marion herself. Marion can no longer suppose it is Hope that she is hearing about, even if this image of herself she now sees is filtered through Hope's understanding of her. There is no longer any place where she does not see herself, and so she must change her life.

Hope, for her part, is frightened that if she doesn't stop herself she will wind up like Marion. Hope admits that she is like Marion—embarrassed by emotions and running from men who threaten her because of the intensity of their passions. But she does not, she tells her therapist, want to look up when she is Marion's age and find that her life is empty. Hope terminates her therapy, having learned what she needed to learn, not through psychiatry, but through seeing herself in another woman. Marion is the very medicine she needed.

Just as Marion sees herself first in hearing Hope speak of herself, so Hope sees herself in hearing Marion speak of herself. Without intending it, Marion has returned Hope's unintended favor. She has given her the hope for a better life that Hope has given to her. Each finds another woman who is also an image of herself, and becomes able to see herself as she had not been able to before. This reflection of herself in another person lets her see herself as other and helps her to become the woman she is capable of becoming. Each is able to transform herself into another woman who is not simply another woman with the help of another woman who is not simply another woman. These are the deepest ironies in the movie's title.

Marion, however, has to contend with another "other woman" in the more ordinary sense, one with whom she has seen Ken in a restaurant, none other than their good friend Lydia, the "hardwood floor type." Indeed, we do not learn of Ken's affair until we overhear Hope reporting her lunch with Marion to her therapist, including the upsetting moment when Marion saw her husband and good friend together. Again, Hope inadvertently leads Marion—and now us—to see her own situation more fully. Marion sobs when she hears Hope's words. And, again, Marion says "no more," but it is no longer to seeing the truth about her life, but to the lies and deceptions she has lived. As the therapist advised Hope to do in Marion's dream, she attempts to get her own life in order. And that requires leaving Ken.

Marion now reads a passage from Larry Lewis's novel about a character rumored to be based on her, a passage that she had hitherto resisted reading. It is about a woman who, while capable of intense passion, screens out such feelings and the people for whom she might have them. Marion just heard Hope say something like this of Marion herself. While Marion had claimed that she aborted her baby to get on with her career, Hope reported to her therapist that her sad lunch companion feared "the feelings she would have for [the] baby" she aborted.

After reading the passage from Larry's book about the woman

like herself, Marion feels "a strange mixture of wistfulness and hope" and wonders "if a memory is something you have or something you've lost." Throughout the movie, Marion, with help from others as well as from chance, recovered memories that had been lost of events and people who had therefore also been lost. But although remembering is recovering what has been lost, it is still experience at a distance, however real memories may seem. Memories both connect us to and separate us from experience. And so too do hopes, which are as much a part of this movie as are memories. But neither memory nor hope is a satisfactory substitute for experience.

After she leaves Ken, we see Marion talking with Laura, admitting her own responsibility for her failed marriage with Laura's father, and hoping that their divorce will have no bearing on her and Laura's relationship. They both acknowledge their friendship and its value to them. Marion also visits her brother Paul, with whom she wants to do things differently, including spending more time with him and his family. Paul accepts her overtures. We also see her visit the therapist next door to report the broken vent. Any further revelations of another that Marion hears will have to be intentional. The therapist tells her that the heating vent has been fixed. That is the way Marion wants it.

Marion also asks the therapist for Hope's address. She wants to pursue Hope further, as she had earlier pursued her through the streets of the city. She learns that Hope has terminated her therapy, moved, and left no address. While the movie looks forward to Marion's continued growth in her relationships with others, it also suggests that it is unlikely that Marion and Hope will meet again. Roger Ebert observes that when Marion and Hope meet "we expect more to come of that meeting than ever does." But he defends the fact that the women "did not interact more deeply." "The whole point," he argues, is that Marion "has suppressed everything inside of her that could connect her to that weeping, pregnant other woman."[9] But while that is true of Marion during the early part of the movie, when she meets Hope she has already had the dream that documents her life. She already feels connected to the weeping pregnant woman. In fact, that is why Marion follows her. Moreover, she does admit to Hope the difficult fact that she regrets not having had a child. She reveals enough to Hope for Hope to know that she is "a very sad woman" who "has nothing" when she should have everything.

Perhaps Allen does not show us the two women "interact[ing] more deeply" in the way Ebert expects, because they have already interacted deeply in another sense—for each has acted as an image of the other. Marion has learned what she needed to learn about herself by listening to Hope, just as Hope did in turn by listening to her. Further interaction therefore runs a greater than ordinary risk that the pursuit of each by the other would be a pursuit only of herself. The movie is not about friendship between Marion and Hope. Rather it is about attaining self-knowledge and growth by seeing oneself in another, which is also the effect of art at its best. While the movie holds out no hope that the two women will meet in the future, it does suggest each will pursue others who do not

Gena Rowlands, as Marion Post, meets Hope, played by Mia Farrow in *Another Woman*. Credit: Orion Pictures (courtesy Kobal); photographer Brian Hamill.

serve merely as images of themselves. Each has now become more capable, in the words of Larry Lewis, of intense love.

In an interview with Allen, Bjorkman observes that Allen uses close-ups only sparsely in his films. Allen agrees, for close-ups create a certain heaviness and are therefore inappropriate for films of movement as many of Allen's are. Allen's description of close-ups as "very long, long, long static" images recalls the still-life interiors of Eve's art. They might give the impression of in-depth revelations of character, but the camera's narrow and intense focus on a character's face abstracts from the living whole that she is and to which her actions and words give us access. Allen nevertheless admits that close-ups, if in the hands of an expert like Bergman, might reveal inner movement and conflict. But for most directors, from whom he does not except himself, they are only a heavy-handed and ineffectual attempt to be dramatic and powerful, which Allen places in the category of suicides, foul language, or showing blood. The overuse of close-up, Allen observes, "can be barbaric."[10] Close-ups bring us too close to the privacy of others. They are like eavesdropping, both in their violation of others and in the illusions of intimacy they provide.

In spite of his sparse use of close-ups in general, Bjorkman points out, Allen does employ a couple of very sudden close-ups of Marion listening by the heating vent. Allen skillfully allows his own violation of Marion through close-up to occur simultaneously with her violation of Hope. His movie in these various ways raises questions about movies, and what we as spectators are doing in watching movies, just as it raises questions about what Marion is doing listening to private conversations through a heating vent.

As members of the audience watching the movie, we too are eavesdropping on Hope along with Marion. But Allen not only lets us listen with Marion to Hope, thereby implicating us in Marion's eavesdropping, but he also lets us see Marion eavesdropping. Surely Marion does not choose to make her eavesdropping known. When in the middle of one of Hope's sessions Marion's doorbell rings, she quickly replaces the pillow over the vent to hide what she is doing from her visitor. She does not want her stepdaughter to see her eavesdropping. Allen thus reveals to us what Marion would hide. And we do not see Marion merely eavesdropping and hiding it; we see her coming to understand awful truths about herself and her life.

Together with Marion, we violate Hope; together with Allen, we violate Marion. It is no accident that this movie, which is about eavesdropping, makes us feel like eavesdroppers. Roger Ebert's reaction to this movie, I believe, is what ours should also be. "Film is the most voyeuristic medium," he writes, "but rarely have I experienced this fact more sharply than while watching Woody Allen's *Another Woman*. This is a film almost entirely composed of moments that should be private." Ebert points out that not only is privacy violated by characters in the film, Marion's eavesdropping on Hope being the prime example, but "at times we invade the privacy of the characters."[11]

It might be objected that Marion chooses to reveal herself to us, inasmuch as Allen's movie is a running commentary by Marion on her inner feelings at the moment she is experiencing them. Perhaps Marion is reading to us from a book that she is finally writing—one about herself rather than the one about German philosophy that she had originally intended to write, and that Allen's movie is a visual presentation of Marion's book.[12] But it is not entirely clear to whom Marion is speaking. She may be speaking to herself, and Allen's movie lets us hear her private conversation. Or perhaps Marion is speaking to her own therapist. We, in effect, are listening through some kind of vent that Allen's movie represents.

We would feel no violation of Marion, however, if Marion were not at least in part like ourselves. If there were nothing of ourselves in Marion, we would have no interest in the movie, and we would leave the theater—or watch only half-heartedly—just as Marion covered the vent with a pillow when a patient spoke of his bisexuality. We too, perhaps unawares, are eavesdropping on ourselves. And this is what *Another Woman* reveals about movies and perhaps about art more generally. Art is most justified when it leads us back to ourselves and to our lives. Thus, the "barbaric" close-up, which brings us so close as to be a violation, itself calls attention to the drama's illusion. As Allen observes, close-ups bring us so close there is "almost an artificial quality about them," and they make us "suddenly aware of being in a movie."[13] The close-up, by bringing us closer to a character's face than we ordinarily come in real life, thus breaks the dramatic illusion of the movie. Close-ups bring us back to ourselves, the spectators, who look at others and feel the violation, for we resemble those whom we are watching— something we would never know if movies were nothing but close-ups.

The self-knowledge we can gain through art is nevertheless imperfect, just as Marion's seeing herself in Hope goes only so far. Marion's memories of her past, similarly, are essential, but so are her present choices and deeds. Marion does not merely look back at her life, but she ends her marriage with Ken, visits her brother and discusses improving things between them, and makes efforts to preserve her friendship with Laura. She also reports the broken heating vent. Understanding is completed by action; we should not be mere spectators or moviegoers. The best movies serve life by pointing to their own limitations.

Moreover, while movies may help us see ourselves, they do not see us in turn. In a movie theater, more generally, one cannot be seen. One cannot say to a movie spectator the words of Rilke's poem "here there is no place that does not see you." If two individuals, in the words of Ebert, "interact more deeply," they would see close-ups and hear private conversations, as moviegoers do. But they would differ from moviegoers, for their seeing would not be voyeurism, nor would their hearing be overhearing. What they see and hear would be given by another rather than merely taken. Although art fosters friendship by letting us share the experience of someone like Marion Post, it is no substitute for it. We need close-ups of a kind that art cannot give us. And that is why *Another Woman* ends with hope as well as memory. It is correct for the film.

10

The Ophthalmologist and the Filmmaker

(Crimes and Misdemeanors)

I n *Crimes and Misdemeanors*, Allen turns up in another old book, this time Dostoyevsky's *Crime and Punishment*. When he turns up in *Crime and Punishment*, however, something happens to it, just as *Madame Bovary* is not the same with Kugelmass playing a role, and *Play It Again, Sam* is not *Casablanca*, nor is *A Midsummer Night's Sex Comedy* Shakespeare's play. The two most obvious differences between Allen's movie and the Russian novel are suggested by the changes Allen made in the title.

In the first place, the punishment drops out, just as it drops out of Allen's story. In Dostoyevsky's work, a murderer suffers remorse for his crime, terrible pangs of conscience, even physical illness. He is tormented by having to hide his crime from others. He finally confesses, goes to prison, and expiates his crime. Punishment follows the crime, but so does redemption. In *Crimes and Misdemeanors*, in contrast, a financially successful and cultured ophthalmologist, gets away with the murder of his mistress Dolores.

When Dolores (Anjelica Huston) threatens to reveal their affair to his wife, Judah Rosenthal (Martin Landau) confides his adultery to Ben, his rabbi, old friend, and patient (Sam Waterston). Ben advises Judah to confess his affair to his wife, ask her forgiveness, and hope that a maturer and richer love will develop between them. The rabbi insists on a moral universe and a higher power that give life meaning. But his advice to Judah is ineffectual, and Judah proceeds instead to ask his gangster brother to have his mistress murdered. Like Dostoyevsky's Raskolnikov after the murder, Judah at first suffers from pangs of conscience. He is haunted by words from his childhood—God "sees the righteous and he sees the wicked, and the righteous will be rewarded, but the wicked will be punished for eternity." He returns to the home of his childhood and witnesses a flashback of a Seder where his pious father and nihilist Aunt May discuss crime and punishment. But he finally heeds his brother's advice to "put this behind him." A version of Dostoyevsky's detective appears, but he merely asks a few polite questions and is heard from no more. By the end of the movie, Judah seems happy with his family, his wife and children, and is looking forward to his daughter's wedding.[1]

The good rabbi, moreover, goes blind in the course of the movie. Whereas Ben fails to persuade Judah to confess his adultery, ophthalmologist Judah cannot save Ben's eyes. The unjust man prospers, and the just one suffers. No wonder critics have claimed that in this movie Allen is "more pessimistic than ever" in his presentation of the universe as "morally neutral and coldly indifferent."[2] James Nuechterlein says it well: "Bad things regularly happen to good people and good things to bad. The cosmic order of reward and punishment operates apparently at random—or worse, it favors the evil, who are ruthless or single-minded enough to take what they want and protect themselves against loss."[3]

Moreover, Allen does not merely drop something from *Crime and Punishment*, he adds something as well—misdemeanors. This addition has several effects. Because both crimes and misdemeanors are in the plural, the particulars to which they refer are not as clear as what Dostoyevsky refers to in his title—even if Raskolnikov commits a second murder to protect himself from the discovery of the first. Is Judah's adultery, for example, a crime as well as his murder of Dolores? Are the lies that he tells his mistress, his wife, and even Ben crimes or merely misdemeanors? When Judah's conversation with Ben moves from his adultery to the existence of a higher power, Ben comments that "we went from a small infidelity to the meaning of existence." Judah insists, however, that his wife Miriam will not "see two years of scheming and dishonesty as a small infidelity." Paradoxically, it is the good rabbi who in his belief in forgiveness can imagine adultery as "a small infidelity," while the adulterer, too aware of his wife's perspective, points out its larger significance. It is thus not merely the omission of punishment, but the addition of misdemeanors that suggests a moral ambiguity lacking in Dostoyevsky's title. As Richard Combs suggests, "in a modern, relativistic world, you can plea bargain for a lesser offense, a misdemeanor."[4] In one way or another, crimes and misdemeanors appear to merge into each other.

Moreover, the possibility of misdemeanors not only confounds our understanding of Judah's situation, it also blossoms into a subplot involving pretentious television producer Lester (Alan Alda). While Judah is the one who commits a crime, Lester, we assume, is guilty of misdemeanors. But the movie draws our attention to similarities between them. Like Judah, Lester is affluent, successful, sophisticated, at home in high society, knowledgeable about art and culture. We do not know whether Lester has committed adultery, but we do see him hit on numerous women in the course of the film and use his position as a television producer to entice aspiring starlets into his bed. Like Judah, he makes promises he has no intention of keeping. Judah chooses to have Dolores murdered with considerable anguish and is then tormented with guilt, while Lester hurts others without a second thought, as when he dismisses his comic writer who has cancer when his jokes are not funny enough.

The subplot, like the main plot, not only has its villain, it also has its lovable loser, documentary filmmaker Cliff Stern (Woody Allen). Cliff has difficulty finding employment. His idealistic, public-awareness documentaries (about such things as toxic waste, leukemia, and starving children) do not seem to be in public demand. The film most important to Cliff, his documentary about life-affirming philosophy professor Louis Levy, is cut short when he hears that Levy has committed suicide. As Cliff's friend Halley (Mia Farrow) observes, "this will put a damper on the show." Cliff is shattered. Not only has his film become useless, but Cliff's role model—one who said "yes to life" in spite of his inability to imagine "a really and entirely loving" God—has now gone "out the window," as his suicide note reports. Moreover, Cliff ends up getting a divorce from his wife, Wendy (Joanna Gleason), and also losing Halley, whom he loves, to Lester.

Comedy nevertheless dominates the subplot. There are losers, and there are losers, and when Woody Allen plays loser Cliff, we cannot help laughing. There are echoes of other Allen figures in Cliff, who comes to a lavish wedding in rented clothes—including his underwear—and whose one love letter to Halley is a plagiarism of James Joyce with irrelevant references to Dublin. Like many of the earlier Allen figures, Cliff remains an outsider, unhappy in his own life but also aware of the pretensions of the world he would not want to share. And he reveals those pretensions in Lester by the documentary he makes of him for public television's "creative mind" series. Cliff's juxtaposition of Lester's playing a crowd with Mussolini's doing so and of Lester's seemingly profound ideas about tragedy and comedy with the braying of an ass does not simply make a comedy of Lester; it makes one of *Crimes and Misdemeanors* as well. To a serious story of murder Allen grafts a comedy. It is not surprising that Denby found *Crimes and Misdemeanors* Allen's "most ambitious and complexly organized film yet."[5]

Allen has made many comedies, as we have seen, as well as serious dramas, however many comic elements are interwoven into their stories. But *Crimes and Misdemeanors* has two separate plots, one a serious story of crime, guilt, and forgetting, the other comic. Indeed, reviewers have criticized the movie for its disjointed structure. While Hilary Mantel, for example, recognizes that in *Crimes and Misdemeanors* Allen "displays his two talents, the tragic and the comic, in a plot with two strands," she believes that "the comedy is not integrated with the rest of the film": "the two plots are loosely connected."[6] Others have noted that Allen gives both plots a single theme, and find the cohesiveness in the film's message that they find lacking in its structure. Denby observes that "what holds the two disparate stories together is not the occasionally overlapping characters but Woody Allen's fascination with the drama of winners and losers."[7] And according to Schickel, this "somewhat bifur-

Alan Alda, as TV producer Lester, pronounces on art, love, and life in *Crimes and Misdemeanors*. Credit: Orion Pictures (courtesy Kobal).

cated movie" is "thematically unified"—both plots "bear witnesses to the inequities of his careless time" and of a world in which "if the deity is not dead, he must be suffering from seriously impaired vision."[8]

To add a comedy to a serious drama, however, is not simply to repeat the serious drama, for the subplot functions as comic relief. Girgus explains how the "comic countermovement to the dark and sinister story of Judah" functions: "Humor provides a dramatic mechanism to avoid direct and immediate confrontation with the very issues, fears, and conflicts that such humor implies and presents."[9] Girgus thus understands laughter in the Freudian sense that arose in *Annie Hall* and in *Stardust Memories* of a self-protective mechanism that clouds our view of harsh realities so that we can live with them. But if "such humor" lets us avoid "immediate" confrontation with such realities, Girgus argues, it also confronts us with those realities on another level. Relief is only necessary if there is something from which one needs relief.

In *Crimes and Misdemeanors*, Lester in fact adheres to a version of this theory of comedy, and tries to give people that "something funny" he believes they need. "You got to get back from the pain," Lester claims, and laughter helps to do it. Laughter causes beneficial blindness, or at least momentary dimming of vision, that makes life acceptable. Louis Levy, who commits suicide, presumably had what the therapist attributed to Sandy Bates—a faulty defense mechanism. Lester does more than explain the function of comedy, moreover. He also explains the way in which Judah's story avoids tragedy: "If it bends it's funny, if it breaks it's not funny." Judah is at first pained by the murder of Dolores, but he gets over it in time. He bends, giving up his father's pious views, and in time his pangs of conscience disappear. As Roche observes, "The film appears to fulfill Lester's insight that 'comedy is tragedy, plus time.' "[10] Time, like laughter, eases the pain and in fact makes laughter easier. As Lester says, "the night Lincoln was shot, you couldn't joke about it; now time has gone by, and it's fair game."

Allen appears to have allowed the pretentious Lester to voice the theories that explain Allen's own work. Everything, even Ben's piety, seems fair game for Allen in this movie, which mocks the rabbi's moral vision by making him go blind.[11] When Lester pontificates about *Oedipus* he interprets it as a comedy, just as Allen himself converted *Oedipus Rex* into *Oedipus Wrecks*. Is Lester Allen's spokesman? Allen has worked other parallels between himself and Lester into his movie. Like Allen, Lester "loves New York." And like Allen, Lester never finished college. And yet "that same school now offers a course in the existential motifs in [Lester's] situation comedies."

If Allen parodies himself in Lester, however, Allen is laughing at himself. Lester, in contrast, cannot tolerate being laughed at. The parody Cliff makes of Lester is not "the real me," Lester proclaims as he fires Cliff. Insofar as Allen compares himself to Lester—a comic producer who treats himself with the pretentious seriousness that many of Allen's most vociferous critics attribute to him—he does something of which Lester himself would be incapable.[12] Laughter is not merely a way to get back from the pain, a kind of forgetting and blindness, but a recognition of our own foibles that lets us rise above them.[13]

Seeing is as important an element of *Crimes and Misdemeanors* as blindness. In the first scene of the movie, a black-tie dinner celebrates the hospital's new ophthalmology wing, and also the man who according to the master of ceremonies made it possible through endless hours of fund raising, Dr. Judah Rosenthal. Judah, however, does not take all the credit and attributes his good deeds to the spirit of community, to generosity, and to answered prayers. Although Judah is "a man of science" and "a skeptic," he remembers the words of his father: "The eyes of God are on us always." I wonder, Judah goes on to admit, whether "it was just a coincidence that I made my specialty ophthalmology." But while Judah publicly "remembers" these words of his father, he is also remembering, as the movie's flashback indicates, the more recent events of the day—a letter from his mistress to his wife that he intercepted and burned. His public memories are quite at odds with his private ones, as are his father's words with his own deeds.

While we do not know if the eyes of God are on the latter, Woody Allen's camera is. The theme of seeing—who sees, what can be seen, and how—is so prominent in the movie that critics have claimed Allen's use of vision is heavy-handed.[14] God sees everything, or so Judah's pious father believes; Judah himself examines eyes, which his mistress claims are the windows of the soul; Cliff's documentary about his brother-in-law intends to let us see the real Lester; and Allen's flashback lets us see what is going on in Judah's mind. Seeing is important, whether in the form of religion, science, or art, but so is seeing into the heart of things. If there is more than meets the eye, as Andrew claims in *A Midsummer Night's Sex Comedy*, Ben's failing eyesight does not necessarily affect the clarity of his vision of life. And Judah's seeing only a "black void" behind the eyes of Dolores's corpse may tell us more about the man who sees it than what he sees. The specter of death haunts the movie, both plot and subplot, as do the "staring" eyes of Dolores's corpse. In the main plot, we have a murder; in the subplot, Levy's suicide. Judah, clearly, is conscious of aging. As he jogs along the beach with his mistress, who is, as he tells Ben when he confides in him, "young," she tells him, "you're in such wonderful shape." When Judah insists only "for a man my age," her rejoinder "for any age" suggests a timelessness that is surely music to his ears.[15] Similarly, she tells him, "you still make love like a youngster." Consistent with her denial of time and its effects is her inability to keep straight the difference between Schumann, "the flowery one," and Schubert, "the sad one."[16] Judah's words echo ironically, as he promises to teach her about classical music, for "someday we'll have a lot of time."

Judah and Dolores do not have "a lot of time." His promise to teach her the distinction between Schumann and Schubert, between flowery and sad music, is not realized—unless it be by having her murdered, an act accompanied by the foreboding and sad music of Schubert. But it is a music that Allen's audience, and not Dolores, hears. Hers is no kind death.

Allen brings lines from Emily Dickinson's poem about death into his movie: "Because I could not stop for Death/ he kindly stopped for me/ The carriage held but just ourselves and Immortality." When Cliff recites one of the lines, he emphasizes the way in which death waits: "kindly, the word kindly, right?" While death waits,

Judah (Martin Landau) and his mistress Dolores (Anjelica Huston) enjoy a moment together. Credit: Orion Pictures (courtesy Kobal).

he waits "kindly," not simply because death is our passage to immortality in the religious sense, as Dolores's mother taught her, but also because our own mortality makes our deeds significant. Death is kind if it makes us aware that our time is limited and that, in the words of Louis Levy, the moral choices we face "throughout our lives" define us. "Some [of our choices] are on a grand scale, most . . . are on lesser points," but regardless, "we are in fact the sum total of our choices." The suspenseful music—by which we know that Dolores does not have much time left—reminds us of a more universal lack of time, for Judah as well as Dolores, and for those who view movies as well as those who make them.

Allen's two plots come together at the end of the movie when Judah and Cliff meet at Ben's daughter's wedding. Cliff and Wendy are planning to divorce. When Lester and Halley announce their engagement, Cliff is even further left in the cold. He is "off by [him] self" when Judah finds him, "plotting the perfect murder," as he tells Judah. A "movie plot?" Judah wonders, for Ben has told him that Cliff makes films. Cliff is not actually plotting a movie, but a real-life murder, of Lester, even if not seriously. Judah, who has himself plotted a real-life murder, nevertheless expects art from Cliff, but Cliff is thinking about life. So too is Judah, even though he proceeds to present his own life to Cliff as art, by telling him of "a great murder story" with a "strange twist."

The murderer, Judah tells Cliff, is at first plagued by guilt, and "little sparks from his religious background" demonstrate it is "not an empty universe at all, but a moral one." Then one morning he awakens, the sun is shining, he takes his family on a vacation to Europe, he prospers, the killing is attributed to another. The murderer's awakening echoes the story that Judah earlier confided to Ben, when he himself "awakened as from a dream" from his adulterous affair. The awakening to guilt is now replaced by an awakening from guilt. Ben saw "wisdom" in Judah's awakening to guilt, and the possibility of a deeper relationship with his wife. But in Judah's story, the murderer awakens "scot-free," his life "back to his world of comfort and privilege." When Cliff and Judah discuss the moral implications of the story and various alternative endings, they, in effect, discuss the movie Allen has made of Judah's life and has not yet brought to an end. Allen thus incorporates criticism of his movie into the movie itself.[17]

Cliff does not see the "freedom" in the ending that Judah presents, for he thinks that the murderer's "worst beliefs are realized" if he succeeds in putting his crime behind him. He may not be punished in the ordinary sense, but he is punished by having to face an empty universe that does not punish. Either way he is punished. Cliff thus suggests that the murderer Judah describes would be unhappy even if he is not caught—whether he is plagued by his moral scruples or by the meaningless of life in the absence of them. Contrary to Judah, there is no putting murder behind one. Roche's more theological interpretation of the movie substantiates this point—the suffering of the wicked "consists not in God's punishment, but in God's withdrawal."[18]

If Cliff were writing Judah's story, he continues, he would have the murderer turn himself in, "because in the absence of a God or something he is forced to assume that responsibility himself." This, Cliff supposes, would give the story "tragic proportions." Judah, however, claims that Cliff's solution is "fiction" and that he has "seen too many movies." For a happy ending, he advises Cliff, "you should go see a Hollywood movie." He sees a happy ending—presumably because a crime is in one way or another punished, and because responsibility implies a moral structure to the universe. In seeing a happy ending in the murderer's turning himself in, however, he inadvertently confirms Cliff's notion that with his crime unpunished and forgotten, the murderer's worst beliefs are realized.[19] His is a deeper unhappiness than suffering from the just punishment of the law. It was Judah, after all, who called his own story "chilling," and when he insists that "people carry awful deeds around with them," he inadvertently admits the deeds at issue are awful.

Although Judah tells the story of a murderer who escapes his feelings of guilt, it is therefore arguable whether Judah himself has.[20] While others are celebrating, Judah is, as he admits, "off by [him]self, like [Cliff]." As Lee asks, if Judah has escaped from his deep sense of guilt, "why would he have indiscreetly told Cliff, a virtual stranger, so accurate a version of his story?"[21] Like Coleridge's Ancient Mariner, he finds a stranger—also a wedding guest—to whom he tells his tale, even if he does not admit that the tale is about himself. And like the Ancient Mariner, presumably, he will continue to repeat the tale to others.[22] And when someone sees Judah at the party "celebrating enough for two," we must wonder if Judah is trying just a little too hard. Regardless of Judah's state of mind, however, he does not have what he once wanted when he desired to free himself from "a double life" by breaking off his affair with Dolores, for now, with her murder, he has much more to hide from his wife and family.[23]

Allen concludes the movie with the words spoken by Louis Levy, as if from the grave. Levy speaks of our capacity not only for moral choice, but also for love, which gives meaning to an indifferent universe, and of our capacity for finding joy in simple things—in our families, in our work, and in the possibility of further understanding. Girgus understands Levy's concluding voice-over simply as "optimistic moral assurance" and therewith "a kind of Hollywood ending" constituting "a self-reflective parody on Allen's part."[24] But is it "optimistic moral assurance" to insist as Levy also does at the end that "events unfold so unpredictably, so unfairly, human happiness does not seem to have been included in the design of creation"?[25] For Girgus there is no middle ground between Ben's pieties and Aunt May's "realities." Girgus to the contrary, Levy himself articulates a middle ground, for while he acknowledges that human happiness is not included "in the design of creation," he does not claim that it is precluded by it. An "indifferent universe" is not a hostile one.[26] Nor is an indifferent universe a fated one. Whatever is implied in the Greek story of Oedipus, Levy was not fated to commit suicide. Whatever horrors this survivor of the Holocaust suffered at the hands of others, he is responsible for his own death.

Lee's position comes closer to my own, for he does find a middle ground of sorts in the Sartrean existentialism he finds in Allen's work and in *Crimes and Misdemeanors* in particular. He refers us to Levy's words to support our constructing moral principles for ourselves, and exercising our freedom by creating meaning for our lives. He argues further that Cliff maintains his moral integrity and thereby preserves the opportunity for authentic moral commitment. He finally endorses, in Allen's name, the assertion of Judah's father Sol at the seder, "If necessary, I will always choose God over truth!"[27] The difficulty with his position, I believe, is that truth does not support that choice, and that authenticity cannot be had at the cost of denying the truth about the world. Lee writes that we "have no reason for choosing a truth that destroys life's joy over the fulfilling of subjective values we can create for ourselves,"[28] but by the same token do we have reason for avoiding Levy's path? A sustainable middle ground must involve a moral foundation for human relations rather than merely a subjective will to morality. That middle ground emerges not primarily from Cliff's moral integrity, however suggestive that may be, but from Allen's movie as a whole.

Cliff was attracted to Levy because the philosopher maintained a positive attitude toward life in spite of his awareness of life's tragic, even nihilistic, dimensions. While Lester clearly enjoys life, in contrast, he has no appreciation for tragedy and interprets Oedipus's story as "the structure of funny." He could look upon Oedipus's self-discovery as a good joke only if he were looking at it completely from outside, as if his own life could never resonate with Oedipus's life. His lack of compassion for the comic writer with cancer suggests his distance from human suffering. Whereas Lester's theories of drama turn Oedipus's story into a comedy, Cliff, who is devastated by Levy's suicide, turns Judah's story of successful crime into one of "tragic proportion." This maker of documentaries about the suffering of the innocent accepts his loser status, just as Levy kills himself. Although Cliff says "yes to life" in that he does not follow Levy out the window, his documentary does not live beyond Levy's suicide.

It is Allen who includes not only Levy's suicide but his life-affirming words in his movie. Allen assumes the responsibility for the movie Cliff fails to make. But Allen's movie is not the documentary Cliff would have made. He puts some of Cliff's footage into a story of Cliff himself, as well as one of Lester and Judah. Levy's words—but also his suicide—take a place in a more diverse whole that includes comedy. Allen laughs, but his laughter is neither callous nor unreflective like Lester's, for it mocks those very characteristics. Nor is his laughter inconsistent with concern for the suffering of the innocent. But this concern, which plagues Cliff and almost causes Sandy in *Stardust Memories* to leave his movie unfinished, leads Allen to make *Crimes and Misdemeanors*. Allen can join a comedy to a serious drama precisely because human happiness is not clearly the design of creation. If it were, there would be less room for human responsibility and freedom. A necessary coincidence between goodness and success therefore leaves little room for moral action. If the unjust and wicked were always punished, and the just and good always rewarded, moral integrity would be indistinguishable from the basest of calculations.

Cliff's proposal of an ending for Judah's story—that in the absence of a God who punishes, the murderer accept that responsibility himself—is therefore correct for the film. But Judah's sense that this is a happy ending is also correct, even if he is wrong to attribute it to Hollywood. Allen's 1972 play *God* confirms what *Crimes and Misdemeanors* suggests. In that play, characters discuss the pros and cons of staging a deus ex machina. While the slave implores Zeus to "come forward with your thunderbolt and save me," the writer claims to be "a free man" and not in "need of God flying in to save his play."[29] Refusing to accept Hollywood endings—or dei ex machina—does not necessarily affirm the emptiness of the universe; it might constitute a more solid version of Levy's "yes to life." There is a middle ground between a God who punishes every crime or misdemeanor and nihilism,[30] as there is between the "really and entirely loving" God that Levy sought and suicide.[31] Indeed, a God with too much respect for human life to arrive in a machine is such a middle ground. The writer in *God*, who wants no such machine in his play, resembles the "real-life adventurer" Tom Baxter, who wants to leave his Hollywood movie to experience human life, while the slave resembles those in the audience eager to take Tom's place in the Hollywood *Purple Rose*. To omit the punishment, as Allen does in the title of his movie, is to leave out the deus ex machina. It is a tribute to Tom Baxter, who is more than a character in the Hollywood *Purple Rose*. He is also a character in Allen's.

Only the rabbi Ben plays parts in both plot and subplot—for he is Judah's confidant and foil and also Lester's brother—and it is at his daughter's wedding that Judah and Cliff meet. Ben connects the serious drama with the comedy, but he does not know that he is doing so. If Ben is the link between the two, that link seems tenuous. Ben surely does not see what Allen allows us to see, if only because he never knows of Judah's role in murdering Dolores. The two plots of Allen's movie, however, are connected not simply by the rabbi but by the series of Hollywood movies that Cliff watches and that reflect the main plot. He is as blind to that connection as Ben is to the extent of Judah's guilt. Cliff does not know Judah and Dolores and sees no connections between the movies he watches and the real world.

The representative of religion, even one of unquestioning piety, and the representative of art, even one as crass as Hollywood can be, serve as alternative forces that unify Allen's admittedly "bifurcated" film. Both the rabbi and Hollywood believe in happy endings, the former in spite of his going blind in the physical sense, the latter too often deserving its reputation for shallowness. Allen's juxtaposition of his plot and subplot, and of the Hollywood movies Cliff watches and the events in Judah's life, shows us what Ben and Cliff do not see. The former's pieties and the latter's Hollywood movies are simplistic versions of Allen's own more complex "happy" ending.

The one Hollywood video Cliff owns is *Singin' in the Rain*, a movie that he "watch[es] every few months to get [his] spirits up." Like Lester, he finds a need for comic relief. And when he watches less happy Hollywood movies with his niece—stories, for example, of adultery and betrayal—he nevertheless reacts as if he were Cecilia watching a romantic *Purple Rose*: it is great—"tuxedos and evening gowns and everything" and "it would be wonderful to live like this." Allen's juxtaposition of the events on the screen with those of his own movie, however, indicates that he finds more "reality" in movies than Cliff sees. Conversely, if human life has a moral structure not in spite of our uncertainty of divine control but actually made possible by that uncertainty, life itself permits a kind of "singing in the rain." Just as Allen's substituting "misdemeanors" for "punishment" may signal human responsibility rather than the triumph of evil, Allen's addition of a comic plot to a serious one is appropriate. It is not that singing distracts us from the rain, but that rain does not fall in the way of singing.

None of the characters in *Crimes and Misdemeanors* fully understands that they are acting in a world where singing in the rain makes sense. Judah instead either sees the almost blinding rain in which he meets the distraught and angry Dolores and in which he decides to murder her, or speaks of the sun to which his fictional murderer awakens one morning, his panic gone and his life returned to normal. The blind rabbi feels "with all [his] heart a moral structure with real meaning" and "some kind of higher power." He is unaware that Judah is a murderer as he is blind to the rain, and he dances with his daughter at the end of the movie in simple contentment. Lester, for his part, is aware of no rain that could cause him a problem, just as he finds a device—caviar—that he believes wins Halley's love. And so he denies the tragic character of Oedipus. His smooth recitation of Emily Dickinson, however, shows less understanding than Cliff's more awkward emphasis on death's kindness. It is not surprising that he cannot admit that he is laughable, even when he watches the satire Cliff makes of him.

Cliff does watch *Singin' in the Rain*, but it is the Hollywood version, not *Crimes and Misdemeanors*. In his own films, he documents the miseries of life and parodies Lester. His parody remains separate from his serious films. Neither has a hint of self-mockery; his laughter remains as self-righteous as his documentaries of human ills. In the end, Cliff is too proud to laugh at himself, or to admit any responsibility for those ills, and too humble before life's sufferings to assume any responsibility for them. One who can laugh at himself, in contrast, is neither so proud nor so humble. Self-laughter is that middle ground between self-conceit and self-hatred appropriate to a universe that allows human action and error. It is Allen, mocking himself in both Cliff and Lester, who is singing in the rain.

Torn between Hollywood movies and documentaries of bleak reality, Cliff recognizes neither the reality to which art points nor the moral truths to which life points. If he recognized the former, his trips to the movies with his niece would not be the mere escapism it is for him; if he recognized the latter he might have realized that his documentary on Levy could survive the man's suicide. In the first instance, Cliff downplays the potential of art to reflect life; in the second, he downplays the potential of life to reflect art. He does a disservice to both. He is a maker of films, but he is no Woody Allen.

Allen's use of the eye metaphor, somewhat overdone as critics have noted, may be an attempt to mock his own Lester-like attempts at profundity.[32] "Heavy-handed" though that metaphor may be, it suggests the possibility of insight supportive of moral responsibility. Just as the rabbi's literal blindness does not imply an inability to see the truth, the blindness of God in the simple sense is required by his goodness.

11

The Detectives

(Manhattan Murder Mystery)

Allen regards *Manhattan Murder Mystery* as merely "an escapist movie . . . a vacation from film-making," and "not ambitious enough for [him]." He thinks it "a trivial picture, but . . . fun for me . . . an indulgence . . . something I've always wanted to do . . . like a little dessert . . . not a real meal."[1] But a vacation is not simply a pause from work that makes possible more work; it can also serve as a celebration that work makes possible. It is in the latter sense, I believe, that *Manhattan Murder Mystery* is Allen's vacation. He has gotten so good at what he does that it comes easily. A dessert may be the crowning glory of a good meal, and *Manhattan Murder Mystery* features a woman whose desserts are works of art. What is fun is not necessarily trivial, any more than what is good is necessarily painful. This, in fact, is the truth that emerges from *Manhattan Murder Mystery*.

Manhattan Murder Mystery is a combination of murder mystery and domestic comedy. It falls within the genre of the old *Thin Man* movies, as many critics have noted.[2] In those films, Nora Charles often leads her husband, private detective Nick Charles, into a case, usually in an attempt to help someone out. She also insists on providing unwanted amateur assistance to her professional husband, gets herself into dangerous but amusing situations, to her husband's chagrin, and in the end does help out, albeit in a supportive and wifely role. Nora resembles Dr. Watson in Arthur Conan

165

Doyle's adventures of Sherlock Holmes, and her participation makes the *Thin Man* into a detective story that is also about a marriage. *Manhattan Murder Mystery* follows in this tradition, a tradition that is an offshoot of the classic detective story in the English language, that of Sherlock Holmes. It is an offshoot because the stories of Sherlock Holmes are not domestic comedies.

Holmes may have his Irene Adler, but she is an enigmatic figure of questionable character and represents an object of admiration for Holmes rather than a faithful helpmate. To Holmes, Irene Adler "is always the woman," Dr. Watson tells us,[3] just as romantics admire an unattainable and elusive ideal. Like Goethe's young Werther, for example, Holmes watches "the woman" become married to another. And it is a nice touch on the part of Arthur Conan Doyle to have Holmes, disguised as a lower-class coachman, pulled off the street into church to serve as the official witness of Irene's marriage. It is also a nice touch that Holmes asks only for Irene's photograph in payment for his services. He keeps the image, as the real woman goes off with her husband. The figure of Holmes thus oddly combines the infinite and unfulfilled longing of modern romanticism with a cold logic in the service of justice. Thus, in Holmes we find soulful violin playing and cocaine use alongside keen powers of observation and impeccable deductive reasoning. He is divided between using science to protect human beings from crime and a melancholy that no sleuthing success can relieve. The *Thin Man* reveals no such anguish. Even if Nick Charles's martinis are a sign of his boredom between mysteries, he is simply not attracted to cocaine. His is a more conventional, more social indulgence. Holmes sometimes takes along a bloodhound, but Nick and Nora have a cute little terrier named Asta, who typically confuses matters by carrying away and burying the evidence.

It is not that the *Thin Man* is less profound than Sherlock Holmes. Rather, the *Thin Man* is informed by a vision that brings the excitement of a mystery into a marriage, and thereby demonstrates that happiness is possible because the "ordinary" life of Nick and Nora's marriage is not simply ordinary. Nick and Nora have adventure, love, and light-hearted fun. They are within our reach in a way that Irene Adler and Sherlock Holmes are not. Doyle reminds us of this through his narrator Dr. Watson, who must leave Holmes for long periods because of his marriage and his medical practice. Holmes is not his life, even if he is an important element in his life. The *Thin Man* movies, in contrast, may be "romantic" comedies, but not in the sense of the European romanticism originating in Rousseau. It is Sherlock Holmes to whom music and drugs offer the solitary reveries of the romantic soul. If there are any solitary walks in the *Thin Man* movies, they are for solving the mystery at hand rather than for facing the irresolvable mystery of life.

Manhattan Murder Mystery is Woody Allen's version of the *Thin Man* movies, in which the mystery of life becomes accessible only through the mystery at hand. Like the *Thin Man* (and unlike Sherlock Holmes), *Manhattan Murder Mystery* is about a marriage. But like Sherlock Holmes, the principal character, Carol Lipton (Diane Keaton), longs for something she knows not what. She is Sherlock Holmes placed in a *Thin Man* movie. She is attracted to Wagnerian opera as Holmes is to his violin, but she is also married to a successful if slightly neurotic publisher, Larry (Woody Allen), who likes hockey games and Bob Hope movies. Their son has gone off to college; their child has been raised. What next? Larry is a contented publisher. But what is she? Carol wonders if she and her husband are becoming "a dull aging couple," like their next-door neighbors, who are made happy by the thought of their twin cemetery plots. She is thus not entirely satisfied by her marriage.

At the beginning of the movie, Carol is thinking of starting a restaurant, for she is a great cook whose repertoire includes exotic desserts. "You are an artist," their neighbor Mr. House (Jerry Adler) tells her when she brings him "floating islands." She is happy at the thought that her restaurant will be in a "tucked away, romantic" setting. In Carol, Allen presents a version of the romantic, artistic type, who like Joey in *Interiors* does not want to become stifled by domesticity. She too is looking for some undetermined means of self-expression. Unlike Joey, she does have a talent, even if it is only fancy cooking, especially desserts. Like Allen himself, she too will get her dessert in this movie, come what may. It is not surprising that she becomes attracted to their friend Ted (Alan Alda), who is recently divorced and therefore eligible. Ted is "more adventuresome" than Larry, "a fun guy," and, as Larry says sarcastically, "great on a scavenger hunt." The murder mystery comes at an opportune time in her life, for she is looking for something to do.

Allen reveals the tension between Larry and Carol in the first scene of the movie, when the couple watch a hockey game. The entertainment is clearly Larry's choice, and Carol is bored. The first scene symbolizes an underlying problem in their lives together— they are living Larry's life. He is the successful publisher; he is content with his work and with his life. Unlike Joey in *Interiors*, Larry shows no dissatisfaction from editing the work of others rather than creating his own. He is not fascinated, as is Carol, by the prospect of a murderer living next door, and he tells her to "save some of [her] craziness for menopause." He insists to Carol, "I don't need a murder to enliven my life." And he is appalled when his wife tells him that she has broken into their neighbor's apartment. "I don't break the law," he proclaims to her, "I live within the Constitution." Later we see the couple at a Wagnerian opera. This is obviously Carol's choice of entertainment, in contrast to the hockey game. Larry finds the opera too pretentious, too romantic. He mocks its inspiration: much more of this opera, he claims, and he will get the urge to conquer Poland.

Differences between Carol and Larry also become manifest when they meet the Houses in the elevator of their apartment building. Mrs. House (Lynn Cohen) mentions that she has seen Carol at the gym, while Larry jokes that he prefers "atrophy" to exercise. His association with exercise is *watching* others, as in the hockey game. Similarly, he wants to go home to *watch* a Bob Hope movie, when the neighbors invite him and Carol in for a cup of coffee. Carol might have accused Larry of what Nancy accused her husband of in *Play It Again, Sam*—being "one of the world's great watchers." Like Nancy, Carol wants excitement. And she wants to accept the Houses' invitation for coffee. She ignores Larry's preference, just as she will later ignore his command not to pursue the mystery further, especially in the middle of the night: "I am your husband," he asserts, and "I command you to sleep. . . . I forbid you to go." Carol goes and drags him with her, just as she drags him to the Houses' for coffee. When there, Larry forgets about the coffee and tries to go home before it is served. But Carol helps Mrs. House serve, and Larry partakes, even if against his inclination. When Carol wonders if they too will become like the Houses, a "dull aging couple," Larry claims that they already are a dull aging couple, and doesn't seem to mind. Not surprisingly, he later advises Carol to spit out the wine at a wine tasting. And not surprisingly, she ignores him. When Carol breaks into Mr. House's apartment to look for clues, she calls her friend Ted on the phone: "I'm just dizzy with freedom," she excitedly proclaims. "This is the craziest thing I've ever done."

Allen hints at a happy reconciliation between Carol and Larry even near the beginning when the couple go on a third outing—with friends to see a replay of the old movie *Double Indemnity*. They are happier seeing this movie with friends than they were at either the hockey game or the opera. Although they disagree about sports and opera, they both like movies. The key to the solution of the tension between them lies in art (movies) rather then in sports (hockey), but not in romantic art (Wagner). This movie explores whether we can have some of Nick and Nora's fun if we have the romantic longing of a Sherlock Holmes, whether Carol and Larry must be like the separate "floating islands" that Carol creates at the beginning, or whether the pursuit of art and romance might be consistent with the ties of marriage. By the end of the movie, Larry comes to enjoy adventure, while Carol comes to appreciate Larry's initial reservations about the dangers of sleuthing. The excitement and the exhilaration that Carol felt while breaking into Mr. House's apartment she and Larry at the end both feel from their relationship. The Houses turn out to be anything but a dull, aging couple, as Carol discovers. And her discovery about them leads her to a similar discovery about Larry and herself.[4]

When Carol imagines something suspicious in Mrs. House's heart attack, Larry thinks that Carol finds "a mystery where there is none." He claims she has seen "too much *Double Indemnity*." Movies are having a bad effect on her life, not because they are removing her from life, but because she is understanding life in light of them. There are no murder mysteries next door. As Leopold in *Sex Comedy*, Gil Shepherd in *Purple Rose*, and even Marion in

Another Woman all in one way or another assert, there is nothing
more than meets the eye.

Like each of these characters, Larry learns that he is wrong. Leopold admits that the forest is enchanted, as Andrew and Adrian
claimed; Gil discovers that Tom really did walk off the screen; and
Marion acknowledges that Larry Lewis was correct about life. In
the course of *Manhattan Murder Mystery*, Larry also recognizes that
he is wrong, that his wife really is onto a mystery; this amounts to
a recognition that the ideal is connected to the real, or art to life.
That the romance and adventure of sleuthing can be embodied in a
marriage thus serves as an illustration of how art can inform life.

By profession Larry is a publisher of fiction and advises authors
like Marcia Fox (Anjelica Huston) about their novels. How much is
she, Larry asks Marcia, in Dorothy, the character in her current
novel? How much is based on her own life? The best fiction, they
acknowledge, is neither simply autobiography nor utter fantasy—it
is somewhere in-between. And so Marcia is not Dorothy, her character, but she is like Dorothy. She did not live with a blackjack
dealer, like Dorothy, but she did put herself through college playing poker. Her novel should be neither too transparent, as she fears
it is, nor should it be so distant from ordinary experience that it
makes *Finnegan's Wake* look like airport reading. Larry and Marcia
know that good art is neither the same nor absolutely different
from what it represents. But do they fully understand why? And
do they know it only from the side of art, but not when it comes to
life? Larry doesn't believe that there could be a mystery next door,
denying that life could imitate art. And Marcia, as we shall see,
proposes solving the mystery in a way that misfires because it tries
to perfectly reproduce art.

Larry watches *Double Indemnity* but denies that anything like its
crimes and intrigues could touch his own life. Surprisingly, Mr.
House, the murderer, shares a version of Larry's oblivion. Allen
shows us Mr. House and his mistress, or at least one of them, returning from watching a movie, *Madame Bovary*, just as we see Larry
and Carol come out of *Double Indemnity*. Like Madame Bovary, Mr.
House is involved in adultery and will soon suffer an unhappy fate.
But he is not forewarned, for he supposes he can get away with
adultery, and even murder.[5] And, curiously enough, Mr. House,

like Larry, also makes it his business to publicize art, for he is reno-vating an old movie theater, where he plays movie classics. Art and its popularization are central to both Larry's and Mr. House's professional lives, but it takes a woman in both cases to demon-strate art's reality to them.

Startling evidence finally persuades Larry that something is up, and the couple meet Ted and Marcia to discuss the situation. Marcia eagerly embraces Carol's murder case and proposes following to the letter a device she read about in a detective novel: they will record a fake audition that captures the voice of the killer's trusted accomplice, edit it, and play it on the phone to trap the killer. By chance, the "bimbo" for whom Paul House murdered his wife, Helen Moss, is a model who aspires to be an actress and would jump at the opportunity for an audition. And playwright Ted has a studio in which such an audition might be staged as well as the necessary equipment. They will then play a skillfully edited record-ing of Helen's voice to Mr. House over the phone. "Paul," they will have Helen say, "they have your wife's body, they showed it to

Amateur sleuths (Diane Keaton, Alan Alda, Anjelica Huston, and Woody Allen) try to solve a murder mystery. Credit: Tri Star (courtesy Kobal); photographer Brian Hamill.

me," and they are asking to be paid for it. "You have to pay them off or get rid of them." Whether Mr. House tries to do the former or the latter, he will reveal his guilt.

Marcia had earlier claimed that "to me it's obvious, obvious that he's committed the perfect murder." But this clever novelist, with the help of a murder novel, also believes that she can create the perfect trap. Life will work as a novel does. Not only is life connected to art, Marcia assumes, but it can model itself simply on art. Allen shows us that there is as much wrong with this assumption as there is in denying any connection at all. This time it is Carol who expresses the gravest reservation: "You're basing your plan on some dumb paperback." She claims to see "many fallacies" in the plan. Most important, they do not really have Mrs. House's body, which she and Larry watched Mr. House destroy in an incinerator. The story they tell him, she believes, will fail because it is *merely* fiction, words without the reality to back them up. And Larry, who has read this novel too, knows that the plan was not successful, for the killer kills those who try to trap him. For life to imitate art in this case would destroy the lives of the protagonists. Luckily for them, life does not in this instance imitate art perfectly.

When the detectives play the recording of Helen Moss's words over the phone to Mr. House, chance threatens the drama they stage. Their recording answers the questions they imagine that Mr. House will ask, such as "Who has my wife's body?" and "How much do they want for it?" And when Mr. House asks "Helen" to "say that again," they are able to replay the exact words. But Mr. House detects an echo. "Are you using a speaker phone?" he asks Helen. The amateur detectives of course had not foreseen this question, and have no answer in Helen's voice. That Helen does not respond might follow from her obvious agitation, and Mr. House is not alerted to the plot. Chance, however, always lurks in the background and soon determines the course of events.

Carol has been becoming progressively unhappy with sleuthing, although she seems to have gotten exactly what she wanted—the excitement of pursuing a murderer and even Larry's enthusiastic involvement. After the telephone scene, however, she no longer wants to participate in the plot and claims that she wants to be alone for a while. What she earlier asserted was "her case" she abandons when it becomes a group effort. She leaves, not primarily because she is jealous of Marcia, who has taken the lead in pursuing the murderer, but because she is also beginning to realize what she really wants. It is not the excitement of solving a murder, which actually comes too close to art, for it is like acting out something in a book (as at that point it literally is), but the excitement of her marriage with Larry. "A few years ago," she tells the cautious Larry when he holds back from sleuthing, "you would be doing the same too." She wants primarily a renewal of their love, not simply the excitement of solving a murder mystery.

When Carol goes home alone, however, Mr. House kidnaps her. Larry calls him to enact the next step of the plan, but Mr. House tells Larry that he must turn over Mrs. House's body if he wants Carol back alive. Events are not going according to script. And as Carol had earlier pointed out, they have no body. Larry is caught in the fiction that they have created. But his love for Carol prompts him to act. Although he claims not to be a bluffer, and he has lost a fortune in cards over the years, he realizes he must bluff. His love must teach him to do what he had earlier sought to learn from the poker-playing expert Marcia—"when to bet, and when to fold." Earlier, he suggested calling the police when faced with danger and Carol wanted "to check it out." Later, when he was finally absorbed by the case, he proposed driving to New Jersey to get Ted and Marcia's help. Now he does not think of calling anyone. He is on his own, but precisely because he is not on his own, precisely because of his love for Carol. And he does bluff, even though he fails at it. He shows Mr. House his murdered wife's wedding ring, which he and Carol had found, but this does not prove that he has her body. Mr. House finds only a mannequin in the trunk of Larry's car. But what doesn't fail Larry is the courage he shows when he rescues Carol. "Larry, you were surprisingly brave," she tells him afterward. And the lovers know that Ted and Marcia hold no threat for their marriage.

As he pursues Larry through his theater with a gun, Mr. House is diverted by the appearance of his earlier mistress, the middle-

Novelist Marcia (Anjelica Huston) tries to teach Larry (Woody Allen) how to play poker in *Manhattan Murder Mystery*. Credit: Tri Star (courtesy Kobal); photographer Brian Hamill.

aged and crippled Mrs. Dalton (Marge Redmont). "Hello, Paul, didn't you expect me?" she asks. Just as the detectives' plan did not go according to expectation when House snatched Carol, so now Paul House has an unexpected problem with which to deal. His past has in fact caught up with him. "You made a lot of promises to me over the years, and then you dumped me for that young model," she says as she points a gun at him.

Allen highlights the drama of this scene—as Mr. House pursues Larry and is cornered in turn by Mrs. Dalton—by means of the movie that happens to be playing larger than life on the screen in the background. Orson Welles's *Lady from Shanghai* is running, and indeed nearing its conclusion, as is *Manhattan Murder Mystery*. The various broken mirrors in the theater reflect both movie and real events, which happen to reflect each other. Not only are there similar chases, and sounds of gunshots from both sources, but the words of the people in the theater echo those of the characters on the screen. "I'm aiming at you, lover," Mrs. Dalton says to House, almost as if she had walked out of Welles's movie. "Of course killing you is like killing myself," a character on the screen says, and Mrs. Dalton repeats it, apparently unaware that the words from the movie function as her cue. She then finishes the lines from the movie just ahead of the character on the screen, "but you know I'm pretty tired of both of us." From this scene it is as impossible to say whether life imitates art or art imitates life as it is certain that they reflect each other.

Mrs. Dalton proceeds to kill the man she loves when she recognizes that she cannot have him. With Mr. House out of the picture, Larry is able to rescue Carol. "I'll never say that life doesn't imitate art again," Larry muses, as he rescues his wife from the murderer's clutches. Larry has not merely come to see the mystery next door, but also a connection between art and life.

Although Allen has artfully contrived parallel scenes between *Manhattan Murder Mystery* and *Lady from Shanghai*, in the end, life's imitation of art both falls short and goes beyond such artful exactitude. *Manhattan Murder Mystery* as a whole suggests that life imitates art most importantly when the uncontrived and unforeseen events of life bring forth opportunities for such acts of courage and love as are found in and encouraged by the images of art. Because Larry has demonstrated courage and love, Allen's art supports life. But courage and love are fully expressed only in action. Larry must do more than watch movies or help edit books. He must play a part, as he does in the end, and as Kugelmass does in *Madame Bovary*. Allen's art is thus an image of life that points to the imperfection of images, even though its images themselves inspire the deeds that are their most important justification. Life uninformed by the courage and love revealed by art is, as Larry complacently said of himself earlier, "a bore" and encourages escapes into romanticism of one form or another.

When at the end of the movie Carol and Larry go off happily together, they tease each other about their jealousy, Carol's of Marcia and Larry's of Ted, making a joke of what had come between them. What is Ted, after all, Larry asks, if you "take away his elevated shoes, his fake suntan, his capped teeth?" "You," Carol replies. Larry likes her answer, for it implies that she loves, without any of the embellishments with which art can adorn us. There is a romantic art that hides life's imperfections, as do elevated shoes, a fake suntan, or capped teeth, and as does the Houses' "romantic" suggestion of "twin cemetery plots" that hides death with the illusion of "spend[ing] eternity with the beloved." The Houses, however, are not grounded together for all eternity, if only because Mrs. House's body is incinerated. And they are hardly bound together even in this life, for Mr. House has mistresses. They are more like "floating islands," and Carol has by chance brought them the appropriate dessert.

At the end Carol and Larry are going out to dinner. They are not looking for some romantic, tucked-away place as Carol and Ted had imagined opening together, where Carol would cook and Ted "run the joint like Rick in *Casablanca*." They will be satisfied, they laugh, by any restaurant that does not serve cowards. But it is such a restaurant, the movie suggests, that would more likely serve true lovers than the romantic one Carol sought at the beginning. Carol has learned at first hand the dangers of sleuthing and will be less eager, we suspect, to go to Wagnerian operas. The skeptical Larry, for his part, has come to accept that there was a mystery next door and has even played a part in its solution. Even though he remains dubious about elevated shoes, fake suntans, and capped teeth, he has come to see the importance of art to human life. His remark that he takes back everything he said about life not imitating art, Allen acknowledges, is key to the movie and resolves in Carol's favor an argument that Larry and she have always had.[6]

What is the significance, however, of life imitating a detective story rather than, for example, a simple romance or a tragic drama? In spite of the movie's title, some critics dismiss the murder mystery as inessential to the movie: "The murder mystery itself can't be taken too seriously—it's just Allen's fanciful pretext for making another movie about relationships."[7] To see the connection between life's imitation of art and a detective story, I believe, Hitchcock's *Rear Window* is helpful.

Several critics have noticed a close connection between *Rear Window* and *Manhattan Murder Mystery*. The movies share "virtually the same plot"—the protagonist L. B. Jeffries comes to suspect a neighbor of murdering his wife and becomes obsessed with a mystery that at first seems concocted and imaginary. There are even parallel scenes in the two movies in which Jeffries's girlfriend in the one, and Carol Lipton in the other, sneak into the suspect's apartment to look for clues and the suspect unexpectedly returns.[8] But even more important is the analogy between the detective and the artist, especially the moviemaker, which Allen adapts from Hitchcock's movie.

"Like a director," Robert Stam writes, Hitchcock's protagonist in *Rear Window* "channels and guides [the] glance [of others in the movie such as his girlfriend, his nurse, and his detective friend], framing their vision and imposing his interpretation."[9] Jeffries does so, in fact, when he acts like a detective trying to solve a crime he imagines was committed next door. Detectives are like poets who construct tales. They attempt to put together the pieces of a puzzle that emerge in their investigation, just as poets piece together stories from the elements of human life that they discover. Like classic detectives who solve mysteries, Carol and her friend Ted construct a variety of versions of what might have happened to Mrs. House, as they acquire more and more information. And it is Marcia, the novelist, who in the end explains what has happened to the still-confused Ted. Appropriately, both she and Ted are writers of fiction. As Carol tells Larry at one point, "if Ted were with us, he would have a million theories by now."

A detective is a particularly useful image for a poet, however, because detectives do not simply create stories but they create stories in order to uncover truth, for detectives fit their theories to the evidence.[10] Fantasies unrelated to reality fail, as Larry learns when he gets caught without the body. The detective may be like an artist, but he is like an artist who tries to construct a story that uncovers what actually happens. Thus he is a particularly good image for an art that is not arbitrary or autonomous, but truth-seeking as it weaves its stories.

There is nevertheless one way in which artists do not necessarily imitate detectives. Detectives investigate and uncover crimes. They dissect evil, as the doctor in *Shadows and Fog* wants to do when he wants to dissect the body of a serial murderer. As Larry says after they find—and then lose—Mrs. House's body, "this is deep stuff," but unlike the mad doctor, Larry does not want to come face to face with evil, for he utters in almost the same breath, "we shouldn't be here." The "stuff" that Allen uncovers in the lives of his characters, in contrast, is not only evil but also good, beautiful as well as ugly.

What the murderer and his wife look forward to at the beginning of the movie—a renewal of their love and marriage in their celebration of their twenty-eighth wedding anniversary—Larry and Carol find by the end of the movie. Like Marion in *Another Woman*, Carol has reassessed her life and her marriage, and she has even had thoughts of an unfulfilled opportunity with Ted, as Marion does with Larry Lewis, and Andrew with Ariel. Unlike Marion, but like Andrew, Carol comes to understand that she has just what she wants. Since Allen's resolution in *Manhattan Murder Mystery* demonstrates that good can be deeper than evil, we are able to look at the "deep stuff" of life that he uncovers without feeling Larry's fear, and without having to echo Larry's words, "we shouldn't be here."

12

The Murderer and the Playwright

(Bullets over Broadway)

Throughout his career, Woody Allen has expressed reservations about Hollywood and its movie establishment, often commenting on its "bad faith" and low ambitions of money and fame. Allen, in contrast, has higher goals for his films. In *Interiors*, as we have seen, he aimed at what he thought was the highest kind of drama. Allen's first filmscript, *What's New Pussycat?* (1965), was, he complains, turned over to "the quintessential Hollywood machine." "Nobody understood what to do with the film." The director "was hemmed in on all sides" with "people putting their girlfriends in roles," and "writing special roles just to accommodate stars."[1] Allen determined that he would never write another filmscript unless he could be the movie's director.[2]

In *Bullets over Broadway*, then, we are not surprised to hear its star, an idealistic young playwright named David Shayne (John Cusack), begin the movie by proclaiming to his agent (Jack Warden), "I'm an artist. And I won't change a word of my play to pander to some commercial Broadway audience." Art is not to entertain, he insists, but to transform people's souls. Moreover, David insists on directing his play himself. He doesn't want "to see [his] work mangled," or "actors change [his] dialogue." His more business-minded agent tells him that it's a real world out there, and a lot rougher than he thinks. The first dialogue of the movie thus concerns the purity of art and hints at the compromises necessary in the real world. The scene suggests a conflict between beauty and reality, art and life. After his agent refers David to the real world, the scene shifts immediately to a gang of mobsters engaged in a waterfront killing of four. The gangsters breathe a sigh of contentment at a job well done and go out for a meal of ribs. Whether David's agent had anything quite so rough in mind we doubt, but he soon introduces the playwright to the boss of these hoods, Nick Valenti (Joe Viterelli), who offers to back his play if his girlfriend Olive (Jennifer Tilly), an aspiring actress, is given a role in it.

David is at first horrified, not merely by Olive's lack of talent but also by the moral implications of such a compromise. He knows that to agree to have his play "backed by hoodlums" is to make "a deal with the devil," but the temptation is too great. This compromise on David's part is the first of many. Given his initial declaration of the purity of his art, followed by his many compromises, we expect that the movie will be about the corruption of the artist by the necessities of real life, and the difficulties artists have in resisting such corruptions.

The story does not turn out, however, as we might expect. David, far from being a true artist, proves to have scarcely any talent at all. He is no more able to produce "real" art than he is at home in the dog-eat-dog world of the mobster. The man most representative of the "real" world, on the other hand, at least as that world immediately surfaces in the movie, is a gangster's hit man, Cheech (Chazz Palminteri), whom we see at work on the waterfront. After David enters the world of hoodlums in order to have his play produced, Cheech enters David's world of art to act as Olive's bodyguard as she rehearses her part in the theater. Cheech turns out to be the artist of the movie. He may have never seen a play in his life, but he knows that people don't sound like David's characters, and that the plot is not "the way it would happen in real life." Like Sandy in *Stardust Memories*, Cheech believes that art should reflect life. He makes a few suggestions and eventually rewrites David's "tepid and cerebral" play into a success. It is Cheech's understanding of life that makes him an artist, and his refusal to compromise that, like Sandy's, preserves the play's integrity. After all, he is a hoodlum and unaccustomed to letting anything get in his way.

If it is comforting to find that art and life are not as divorced as the opening scene implies—inasmuch as it is the artist who knows most about life—it is less comforting that the greatest artistic talent in the movie is possessed by a murderer. Of course, it is funny for an uneducated, uncultured, unsophisticated hoodlum to turn out to be an artistic genius. It is funny when the idealistic (but now plagiarizing) David joins Cheech for a beer and asks the hard-nosed murderer whether he has ever thought of going into another line of work, perhaps writing. Critics see that it is Cheech's role that makes a good comic movie into a brilliant one. Janet Maslin, for example, calls Cheech "a stunning wild card."[3] And Roger Ebert says it well: "The twist involving the bodyguard is what makes 'Bullets over Broadway' more than what it could have been, a funny but routine backstage comedy. Allen follows the simple logic of this character until it leads to a moment both shocking and incredibly funny . . . taboos were being broken even as inexorable logic was being followed."[4] The inexorable logic that Allen follows has to do with the integrity of art. If art is as important as David and his sophisticated friends claim, one should subordinate everything to it. Indeed, if artistic integrity allows absolutely no compromises, as David states at the outset, an artist should be willing to kill for art. And this is the very thing that Cheech eventually does.

A deeper opposition between life and art emerges, however, if the perfect artist murders for the sake of art. It is not so much that life compromises art, but that art compromises life. And with the destruction of life comes the immorality of the artist, at least by ordinary moral standards. As David's artist friend Flender (Rob Reiner) advises him, "the artist creates his own moral universe." Since that "moral" universe justifies betrayal of close relationships—and, by extension, murder—it contains no moral standards that qualify the demands of art. Earlier Flender poses to a group of friends a version of the old dilemma of choosing whether to rescue from a burning building the last known copy of Shakespeare's plays or an anonymous human being. One of the group insists that art is not "an anonymous object," for "it lives." They are artists, and to them the choice is clear. But does Allen, also an artist, agree?

The discussion occurs at the beginning of the movie, and the rest of the movie serves as a reflection on that discussion.

One of the women in the group disagrees with David's artist friends. For example, she thinks that loving the artist and not the man is a mistake that women make. Others in the group deny it is a mistake. For them, the most important thing about the man is his art. Flender, who most forcefully advocates this position, has even "raised intercourse to an art form." For him art is everything. When he advises David that the artist can create his own moral universe, he suggests that artists are not subject to the limits that bind other human beings. David thus supposes that he is justified in betraying his girlfriend Ellen (Mary-Louise Parker) with his lead actress Helen Sinclair (Dianne Wiest), for Helen Sinclair is "an artist," and "we speak the same language."

David is of course deluding himself. The man is not simply the artist, and for that reason alone cannot escape the norms that apply to others. He must recognize that, as he says to Ellen, "I'm David," a line that echoes his opening words that "I'm an artist." He is unfortunately lying to Ellen about his affair with the actress when he reminds her of who he is. He must learn that when he says "I'm David," he is not saying merely, "I'm an artist." Like Marion in *Another Woman* he will come to admit that he has been lying to both himself and others.

Before any of this happens, however, the play must go on. And this requires Nick Valenti's backing and therefore David's giving Nick's girlfriend Olive a part in the play. When we first meet Olive, she is dissatisfied with the anniversary gift Nick brings her, with Nick, and with her life. Like Joey in *Interiors*, like Carol in *Manhattan Murder Mystery*, she aspires to something more. She demands that Nick get her out of "this lousy chorus line," for she wants to be an actress. As for the black pearls that Nick gives her, she has never heard of such things and supposes that "they probably came from defective oysters." Olive wants to be an actress as badly as David wants to have his play produced, and like David she wants a kind of perfection—pearls that are pure white. Neither wants bullets over Broadway, yet they both need Nick and at least the threat of his bullets to get what they want. Nick knows the value of black pearls, just as he does of bullets, and he hardly deserves Olive's disdain. He is willing to celebrate only a "six-month" anniversary. He knows that life is always only halfway to where we would like it to be. It is appropriate that while he does not give defective pearls, as Olive in her ignorance supposes, he does love what is defective, Olive herself. Olive, in her aspirations, is a comic version of David. She can no more act than David can write. It is appropriate, as well as funny, that Allen teams them up so that each's artistic fulfillment depends on the other's.

Once David accepts Valenti's backing—and Valenti's terms—he must determine the other members of the cast. And they are quite a crew. There is the star, Helen Sinclair, "a scene-stealing granddame who is a teensy bit over the hill."[5] Her agent only partially encourages her self-image: "You are a great star," he tells her, "but in the last few years you are better known as an adulterer and a drunk." Her first lines in the movie, "I am Helen Sinclair," and I won't act under the direction of a novice, echoes David's assertion, "I'm an artist, and I won't change a word of my play." To say "I am Helen Sinclair" says it all, at least for Helen, just as did David's assertion for him. She subordinates everything to Helen Sinclair, just as David at least thought he could subordinate everything to art. But David is no match for Helen. She offers him "Broadway" as if it were hers to give, as well as the opportunity of writing his next play as "a vehicle for Helen Sinclair." Her flattery aims at manipulating the pliable playwright to make changes in her part in his play, which is "not a very glamorous role," she tells him, and could use something "to brighten it up." She wants major changes in the role of the frigid wife she plays, for "I'm used to playing more overtly heroic women." Sylvia Postum's role should therefore be "less tentative, more alluring, certainly not frigid." David agrees to change "a touch here or there," for Helen's "instincts as an actress are impeccable."

Allen himself has described his own reliance on the "instincts" of his actors and actresses. "In general," he says, "I like to trust the actors; when an actor is doing something good and meaningful, I just like to leave the camera on them and let them be there and not bother them." And so he can tell them not to feel bound by the script: "If something makes you feel uncomfortable, just change it! Just feel free!" Allen mentions Geraldine Page, who played the lead in *Interiors*, as such an actress whom he could trust.[6] But while Allen might similarly trust Dianne Wiest, who plays Helen Sinclair, David Shayne should not trust Helen Sinclair. Helen Sinclair is no Dianne Wiest, and David Shayne no Woody Allen. David thinks he can trust Helen's "instincts as an actress," with no hint that her "instincts" are less those of an actress than of a scheming woman bent on magnifying her role to suit herself.

David therefore destroys whatever integrity his play had by changing the parts to suit Helen, without regard for their place in the whole. David had wanted to direct his own play, so that no director would compromise his vision. Only he himself, he thought, could preserve the integrity of the whole that he created. But David loses control, first by accepting Olive in a major part as the condition for its production, and then by modifying the lead to suit its temperamental and egotistical actress. It is not without reason that her role is called the "lead."

Neither is Olive entirely satisfied with her role as a psychiatrist: "It ain't the lead," she complains, and "I know the lead when I see the lead." She believes that actors and actresses "are allowed to add things," and that this is called "ad-libbing." And like Helen Sinclair, she too has "a lot of ideas how we can goose it up." Olive's disgruntled remarks come after David gives the "lead" to Helen Sinclair, without seeing the sense in which he has given her—and will give others including Olive—the lead. And it is finally the hit man Cheech himself who takes over from behind the scenes to make the play a hit.

On the first day of rehearsal, the cast arrives, one by one. The male lead is to be played by famous actor Warner Purcell (Jim Broadbent). Although Warner is David's first choice for the lieutenant, David's agent has some doubts, for Warner's eating habits typically escalate as the stress of the production increases. A director can no more control Warner than Warner can himself, either with regard to food or, even worse, his desire for Olive. The progressive expansion of Warner's girth in the course of the rehearsals symbolizes each part's magnification of itself at the expense of the whole.

Each grows to a disproportionate size, making the whole monstrous. Drastic cuttings are required, and finally murder.

After Warner, Eden Brent (Tracey Ullman), the actress who plays the "other woman" in the love triangle, arrives. She insists on carrying her pet chihuahua to every rehearsal, to which Helen Sinclair soon takes a dislike, for she "hates mutts." She has an even greater dislike, however, for the dog's owner. How could the lieutenant leave her for *that* woman, she asks, as the play takes on a life of its own. Helen Sinclair has begun to act like the character she is playing, as she extends Sylvia Postum's animus against the other woman in the story to the actress who plays her. It is difficult for quarreling actresses to play any kind of characters, quarreling or not. David's play is like a many-headed Galatea that has come alive to cause him problems. When the various parts assert their integrity, the whole loses *its* integrity.

When Olive arrives at rehearsal with Cheech, David objects to his presence. His agent, who knows only too well about the relation of art to necessity, or at least of David's play to Nick Valenti's money, claims that Cheech will be "unobtrusive." Olive says that "he just wants to watch." Their words foreshadow the obtrusive role he comes to play in the drama, both rewriting it to give it an integrity it never had, and then obtrusively removing Olive so that a more talented understudy can take her place. At first, Cheech is merely a spectator who sits in the back of the theater watching the play, much as we are watching Allen's movie. This spectator, however, soon becomes a key player, even if few see the part he plays when David sneaks to the pool hall to get Cheech's revisions of the play. Cheech must go to the play's opening night, he tells other members of Valenti's gang, for he has become friendly with some stage hands and wants to wish them luck. Of course it is an excuse, for Cheech wants to see his handiwork, just as Sandy Bates watches his movie at the end of *Stardust Memories*.

Helen Sinclair is the last to arrive at rehearsal. Like everyone else who acts in the play, she stands out. She stands out most explicitly by arriving half an hour late: her pedicurist, she explains, had a stroke, fell forward onto the orange stick, and plunged it into Helen's toe, which then required bandaging. She notes the lives of others only as they relate to her own. Her entrance is staged in other ways as well, for she dramatically discourses on her past great roles in the theater, from Ophelia to Clytemnestra, "each perform-ance a birth, each curtain a death." Helen Sinclair's theatrical past is more on her mind than the work at hand. Like Eden Brent who arrives with "the mutt" Helen so disdains, Helen herself carries baggage that will threaten the new production.

When work finally begins and the members of the cast read their parts, poor Olive's vocabulary makes it impossible for her to read the lines of her character with any intelligence. She has never heard of "masochistic," for example, and when its meaning is explained, understands only some kind of "retard." Although Allen like Shakespeare often lets his fools utter words of wisdom, the unso-phisticated Olive is nevertheless incapable of acting the part of a sophisticated psychiatrist. She remains outside the character she plays because she does not have in herself the intelligence or experi-ence to get inside the part. She must bring something of her own to the role the playwright has created in order not to bring too much

Cheech (Chazz Palminteri) coaches his boss's girlfriend Olive (Jennifer Tilly) about her lines in the play. Credit: Miramax (courtesy Kobal); photographer Brian Hamill.

of herself to the role in a way that ruins the play. "Ad-libbing" of a sort thus turns out to be necessary to the play, for actors and actresses must make contributions of their own for the play to work. This is why not just any actor or actress can play any role. Acting is not all. Olive cannot utter a psychiatrist's reflections on masochism persuasively if she doesn't know what masochism is. An artistic whole that relies on actors and actresses to play parts within it must count on them to be both more than and not more than the parts they play. That is why casting is so important to a drama's success. David's play loses its integrity, such as it had, on both counts.

If the parts of a play grow to a size disproportionate to the whole, a director or writer should cut for the sake of the whole. As director, David does try to cut. The lines of the psychiatrist are ruining the whole play because Olive is speaking them. Since David obviously can't fire Olive, he tries to minimize the damage. But David wants to cut the psychiatrist's lines not because they are unnecessary to the whole but because Olive is speaking them, because of the actress rather than because of the character. Unfortunately, he does not have even this minimal control, for Cheech will not let him diminish Olive's part by removing any of the lines she has painstakingly memorized. By protecting Olive's part, the bodyguard inadvertently happens to protect the integrity of the play. He is already guarding the play itself.

Cheech soon begins to play this role intentionally, for art seems to be his calling at least as much as the job he does for Nick Valenti. Cheech turns out to be what Nick claimed of Olive when David asked about her previous experience: "She ain't got no experience, she's a natural." Olive, in fact, is so naturally deficient that no experience can help her, while Cheech is a natural artist without any experience of playwriting. When Cheech gives David's play an integrity that it never had, David's loss of his own integrity becomes even more obvious. When Helen Sinclair praises David for Cheech's new version of his play, he is unable to own up that the "eunuch version" she first saw is the reach of his talents. Both by yielding to the seductions of Helen Sinclair and by using Cheech's rewrite as his own, David suffers moral failure. With Helen, he betrays Ellen, not recognizing the extent to which Helen is using him

David Shayne (John Cusack) confers with hit man Cheech (Chazz Palminteri) about the revisions of his play. Credit: Miramax (courtesy Kobal); photographer Richard Cartwright.

for her own purposes. It is Cheech who reproaches David for this affair, when David tries to take the high moral ground with the gangster. And when he first hesitates to take credit for Cheech's writing, Cheech supposes that his moral scruples are delusions: I saw you enjoying playing the artist, he tells David, and assures him that he will not tell. It is Cheech who has moral scruples: "Where I come from nobody squeals." And he earlier confided to David, "I never rubbed out a guy who didn't deserve it." Just as easily as a playwright erases characters who do not fit the play, Cheech rubs out human beings who deserve to die.

But does Olive "deserve it"? As opening night approaches in *Bullets*, the murdering gangster turned artist murders again, but this time to preserve what has become "his" play. Olive, unfortunately, is mangling her lines and ruining the whole in which she has a part to play. Cheech observes to David that Olive is "killing" his words, and that "every time I hear that voice it is like a knife cutting through my fucking heart." David must warn him that "you are too close to this." The play, in David's hands, does not come close enough to life, while its truly artistic creator comes close to having no life apart from it and its production. Since David can hardly fire Olive, to remove her from the play Cheech must kill her. Since David entitled his play "God of Our Fathers" before Cheech took it over, his hint at its future was purely fortuitous. But as the play's "godfather," Cheech leaves nothing to chance. Having seen by chance what an understudy can do for Olive's part, David may hope that Olive will get sick before the play's opening on Broadway, but Cheech takes Olive for a ride to his favorite pier. Cheech says to Olive just before shooting her, "Olive, I think that you should know this: you're a horrible actress." For Cheech it is a moral choice. He does not think that "it's right" for "some tootsy" to "ruin a thing of beauty."

For Cheech it is a moral choice because beauty is a standard of morality. There is precedent for this in his past, for his father once killed a bad opera singer in Palermo. His "morality" carries to its logical conclusion the morality of the "sophisticated" artists who would save "a thing of beauty" from a burning building—for it is the art that is "alive"—rather than an "anonymous" human being. Their morality, the movie shows, is only gangster morality. David's opening lines, "I'm an artist. And I won't change a word of my play," are echoed in Cheech's "nobody, nobody is going to ruin my work, nobody."

The brutality of Cheech's deed brings David to his senses. He recognizes the immorality of what Cheech has done: "You've killed Olive, Cheech, and for that I can't forgive you. I don't care what kind of genius you are." Neither can Nick Valenti forgive Cheech. "Fix him," he tells members of his gang. They pursue Cheech to the theater, where he is watching the play from backstage, as he earlier watched from the back of the empty theater. Unlike Sandy Bates, he never joins the audience to look with them at his own work. The audience hears gunshots as the play draws to a close, and David reaches Cheech in time to hear his dying words. They concern the last line in the play.

The "great finish" that Cheech recommends for the play as he dies is that Sylvia Postum announce that she is pregnant.[7] But the play that he has written ends simultaneously with his own death.

Instead of ending with the promise of life onstage, it ends with death backstage. It accidentally demonstrates the words of the failing actress Helen Sinclair about the theater, "every performance a birth, every curtain a death." But Cheech's last words about his play suggest a different possibility—that the curtain should close not with death but with the promise of new life. For a woman to announce a pregnancy is for her to acknowledge that her life is not a perfect whole but connected to life that exists outside herself and restricts her own. For a play to end with a pregnancy is for it to look forward to life beyond itself. It is for it to close, as it were, without closing, much as the series of finishes in *Stardust Memories* suggest that the movie's finish is somewhat arbitrary. The integrity of art lies in its reflection of life, in its pointing to its own incompleteness, in its recognition that it is an abstraction from the life that exists beyond itself. With Cheech's "finish," the play, like Sylvia herself, would acknowledge that as art it too is connected to life outside itself that limits its own.

Cheech dies thinking only of the play's finish rather than of his own. He dies, as it were, without noticing it. David tries to talk to him, presumably about Cheech's own condition; with Cheech dying, David shows little interest in the play's proper ending. Cheech tells him, as Helen Sinclair did earlier when he tried to declare his love for her, "Don't speak." But then David is no artist, and his own final words in the movie are appropriately his declaration to Ellen of the two things of which he is "certain": that he loves her and that he is not an artist. Ellen lets him speak. And David finally realizes the meaning of saying, "I'm David."

Like Cheech, David leaves the play unfinished, for he leaves Broadway to go back to Pittsburgh with Ellen. What Cheech suggests for the play—the announcement of new life to come—is thus found instead in Allen's movie. *Bullets* ends not with the death of Cheech but with David's declaration that he loves Ellen and that he wants to get married and have children. Allen's movie comes closer to Cheech's dying vision than anything Cheech himself produces.

The integrity of art in which Cheech believes is a delusion that Allen mocks even in David's opening assertion that he will not change a word of his play. Allen has revealed the bullets over

Broadway, that is, the seamy backdrop that allows Broadway to flourish. The connection between Broadway and the mob was a theme of Allen's earlier film *Broadway Danny Rose*, although there the connection was not as stark or pointed, if only because while murder is threatened it does not occur. In *Bullets*, the bullets are real, and they do their job more than once. Inasmuch as Cheech is both Olive's bodyguard and her murderer, he is the person who should be most aware that bullets hover over Broadway. The greatest testament to the power of art and beauty over human life is that it is Cheech who is most deluded about art's integrity. He is the last person, we might think, who would die without noticing it.

As it turns out, the play is critically acclaimed, even without Cheech's new ending. The critics have no sense that the play lacks anything, or that art is incomplete if it does not recognize its own dependence on life. They find the play that Cheech finally regards as incomplete as "a masterpiece, a theatrical stunner." They think that "one of the greatest moments" occurs in the last act, when gunshots from behind the stage get "louder and louder" as an "echo" of "the lieutenant's violent past." They understand the accidental as if it were intentional; they take an event independent of the play as if it were a crucial part of the whole. They interpret life—and death—as if they were simply parts of a play. The critics are as little aware of Cheech's murder as Cheech is of his own death. Both take the artistic imitation to be the whole. To the critics the bullets are not real, to Cheech he does the right thing when he kills Olive, and to the intellectuals art rather than human beings live.

David's question echoes at the end: Olive may have been "ruining the play, but does that mean she deserves to die?" Can the integrity of art be purchased with the integrity of human beings? Allen's movie is the story of David's learning to raise this question. It is a question unknown to "artist" Flender, who thinks of human beings as anonymous, and to actress Helen Sinclair, who silences David before she hears what David intends to tell her about his own limitations as an artist. When David asks Cheech whether Olive deserves to die, the artist-murderer does not take the question seriously. Similarly, his moral declaration that he does not squeal abstracts from the question of that to which he is loyal, just as the integrity of art abstracts from the ongoing life in which it plays a part. Both Cheech's moral declaration and the integrity of art resemble, in Frederick's words about Flyn, "form without content." Cheech is unlike Pearl, who sympathizes with the character in a play who does not squeal, but who is loyal to Arthur and saves Joey's life. Cheech simply does not squeal. As an artist, he too is a failure, like Flender and Helen Sinclair. Like Flender he leaves his "finished" art unproduced. And like Helen Sinclair, he tells David not to speak just when David, about to call attention to his dying, will remind him that art is not the whole that he supposes it to be.

Olive believes, as we have seen, that actors and actresses are "allowed to add things" or to "ad-lib." She supposes that they may act "at will," although she hardly knows that "ad-libbing" comes from *ad libitum*. They are artists, after all, and artists are free spirits. We have seen the way in which ad-libbing is part of acting and how as director Allen seeks actors and actresses whom he can allow the freedom they need for them to play their parts. David Shayne, in contrast, does not have either the freedom or the good sense to select such actors and actresses. Just as character Tom Baxter ruined the Hollywood *Purple Rose* when he walked off the screen to gain his freedom, David's cast ruins his play when each member walks onstage without giving up any freedom. While the character wants to be real, the actors refuse to (or, in the case of Olive, is unable to) play characters. But when ad-libbing, they neglect the conditions under which they are artists, that they are acting in a play and playing characters created by another. Like a playwright who will tolerate no compromises, they forget about the dependence of their art. They consequently ignore their parts as artists.

The actors in David's play assert their integrity and thereby destroy the integrity of the whole in which they play a part. In doing so, they mirror an artist's insistence on the integrity of art, which denies the whole of life of which art is a part. But artistic integrity is a delusion if it does not in some way reflect that whole. That whole includes David's ethical concerns that come to the fore when Cheech murders Olive. And it includes the words of David that affirm personal moral integrity, words that both Helen and Cheech refuse to hear, but that Allen nevertheless lets us hear in his movie.

Artistic integrity at the cost of moral integrity is therefore a contradiction in terms, just as is an artistic integrity that does not recognize its dependence on the life that it reflects and serves. *Bullets over Broadway*, inasmuch as it does not ignore David's ethical concerns, does not make this mistake. The preservation of moral integrity is necessary for artistic integrity.

13

The Sportswriter and the Whore

(Mighty Aphrodite)

Aphrodite is the Greek goddess of love, and Allen's story of Manhattan sportswriter Lenny Weinrib (Woody Allen) begins in Greece, or at least in an amphitheater where a chorus in tragic masks introduces Lenny's story—"a tale as Greek and timeless as fate itself." From time to time in the movie the scene shifts back to the chorus, which comments on the action amid references to ancient heroes, such as "brave Achilles," and calls upon Zeus to come to the rescue. The chorus leader himself (F. Murray Abraham) even appears in New York City to advise Lenny directly, and messengers report to the chorus news from Manhattan. Lenny Weinrib is cast in the role of a Greek-style tragic hero. Allen now seems to be replaying ancient tragedy itself. There may be "timeless" tales, but can Greek tragedy be replayed in the modern world? And why does Allen's replay turn into a comedy?

In the opening scene, the chorus refers us to the fate of Oedipus as well as Achilles, and Jocasta (Olympia Dukakis) herself emerges from the chorus with references to her son. In *Crimes and Misdemeanors*, Lester described Oedipus as "the structure of funny." To *New York Stories* Allen contributed "Oedipus Wrecks," a story of a successful New York attorney who attempted to deny his Jewish origins with consequences that came back to haunt him. *Mighty Aphrodite* is a more sustained and developed treatment of the possibility of tragedy in the modern world and of its relation to comedy.

195

The chorus begins by lamenting a litany of evils that human beings, even the greatest of human beings, have suffered. "Brave Achilles" was "slain in trial by blood, the prize—the bride of Menelaus." There is Jason's wife, who fared "little better," as well as the "father of Antigone, ruler of Thebes, self-rendered sightless by lust for expiation, lost victim of bewildered desire." However much Oedipus may seem to be the author of his actions, and his blindness "self-rendered," he is a victim, and the chorus claims that "to understand the ways of the heart" is "to grasp the malice or ineptitude of the gods." The Greek view of the world, insofar as it is embodied in Allen's tragic chorus, broadcasts the sufferings of human beings, sufferings that are inevitable and for which they are not fully responsible. No wonder the chorus refers to the timelessness of the fates as it turns to Lenny Weinrib.

"Lenny Weinrib" of course does not sound Greek, and the camera soon switches to a contemporary New York Jew enjoying dinner with his wife and friends. Lenny seems to be an ordinary New Yorker, as ardent about his profession of sportswriting as Allan Felix was about his as movie critic, for in both cases they make a living by watching the events they love. Lenny is interested in such things as baseball, hockey, and boxing, and there is no sign that he has anything as elevated—or as depressing—as Greek tragedy on his mind. He does not see himself as fated. He watches sports, where success accompanies merit and hard work. He may "watch," like Allan Felix, but we see him act throughout the movie. He supposes that it is he who is in charge of his life. The only "curse" he recognizes is the Weinrib name, and that is merely because it does not sound good with anything when he is trying to name his son. In his modern self-assurance, he has lost sight of the inevitability of human suffering, something of which the Greeks were aware—at least according to the chorus. *Mighty Aphrodite* begins as a reminder, at least to the audience.

At dinner, casually, and among friends, Lenny's wife Amanda (Helena Bonham Carter) mentions to Lenny that she wants to have a child. The chorus, from whom we hear again, does not take it so casually. It knows the trials and tribulations children can present to their parents, and calls upon "Laius, proud father," to speak. Jo-

casta speaks as well: "My son did slay, unwittingly, my noble husband, and did without realizing hasten with me his loving mother
to lustful bed." But even if today's parents have less traumatic experiences, "children grow up," the chorus points out, "they move out,
sometimes to ridiculous places like Cincinnati, or Boise, Idaho, and
you never see them again. You would think once in a while they
would pick up a phone," the chorus continues, complaining somewhat like a Jewish mother. The chorus may have its origins in ancient times, but its focus is on modern America where there seem
to be very few ties that bind, where the technological advances that
make long-distance communication possible occur in egalitarian
social conditions that attenuate links between family members. Jocasta, in contrast, still shows affection for her ill-fated son, even
after all these years: "I hate to tell you," she laments, "what they
call my son in Harlem." While modern Americans may take children lightly, children are, even after all these years, as the chorus
says, "serious business." But the only "heavyweight" Lenny fore-
sees his son becoming is a boxer.

As suggested by the chorus's reference to the mobility of modern
American life, there is something very modern about Lenny's and
Amanda's lives. Western civilization may have its origins in the
Greeks, but the Acropolis has become merely a Greek deli on the
Upper West Side. Lenny Weinrib and Amanda Sloan are the prod-
ucts of an egalitarian age, an age characterized, as Tocqueville observed, by a kind of individualism in which people see themselves
as autonomous units with minimal obligations to the past, to the
future, to society, and to others. Lenny, for example, at first rejects
his wife Amanda's proposal to have a child. And he seems equally
unconnected with past generations: this is one of the few movies in
which Allen plays a Jew whose Jewishness seems to have no effect
on who he is and how he lives. Unlike Alvy Singer, for example, or
Sandy Bates, Lenny makes no references to his parents, his other
relatives, or even his childhood. He and Amanda wrangle over
names for their son, like Strepsiades and his wife in Aristophanes'
Clouds. But unlike this couple in ancient Greek comedy, Lenny suggests not names connected with family members for their new son,
but the heroes of his chosen occupation, such as Sugar Ray, or of

comedy such as Groucho or Harpo. The Marx Brothers may be Jewish, but theirs are not Biblical names like Judah, Sol, or Ben. When Amanda suggests Ben, Lenny immediately moves to other possibilities. Although we meet Amanda's parents in the movie, there are no signs of Lenny's. It is as if Lenny has succeeded in wishing away his origins. And there are no flashbacks in the movie.

Hearing of Amanda's desire for a child, Jocasta observes that "a woman's urge to motherhood is as old as the earth," but Amanda suggests adoption. It is not that she or Lenny suffers from any natural limits, but that an adoption would preserve her freedom. She "can't give up the time right now, there are too many exciting things happening in [her] business," or, as Lenny more cynically suggests, she doesn't want to have morning sickness. Like the young Marion Post, who aborted her child, Amanda has not yet achieved the success she desires. She is interested in opening her own art gallery, and, unlike Carol Lipton in *Manhattan Murder Mystery*, she does not want to wait until her child has grown to do something with her life. But she supposes she can have it all—child and career at the same time. With adoption, moreover, even the sex of one's child might be a matter of choice; "Why can't we adopt a girl?" Amanda asks. References to a possible "bad seed" mean nothing to her, and through an adoption agency she finds a child "with no strings" if they act quickly. Theirs is a no-strings approach to life, and they have, appropriately, a perfectly modern marriage, which leaves each free for a rewarding career. That Lenny says no to adopting a child does not affect Amanda's decision to do so.

Of course, raising a child does make demands. And it is Lenny, not Amanda, who spends time with Max as he grows up. We see him playing basketball with his son in a gym, for example, and taking him to other sports events. We see him offering to go home and put him to bed when Amanda must stay late at her new art gallery to discuss changes with architects. In another scene an educator is telling the couple about "a special program we have for bright students," when a phone call and dinner invitation for Amanda derail the discussion. Her thoughts are on the Amanda Sloan Gallery, not on Max, and certainly not on Lenny, who complains more than once about how her business associate and friend Jerry Bender (Peter Weller) has been eyeing her. No wonder that Lenny has doubts about his marriage and is suddenly struck by the thought of Max's unwed mother. Such a wonderful kid, he muses, must "come from great stock: a good father, a dynamite mother." It was Lenny who had feared a "bad seed," and now that he sees that the growth is good, he becomes interested in its origin. An "unwed" mother is, after all, free. And his troubled marriage with Amanda makes him all the more interested in looking elsewhere.

Lenny now begins his search for the perfect woman who could produce such a son as Max. Looking for origins may seem to be a recognition of ties, of the past, and of obligations, but Lenny, paradoxically, is looking for a kind of perfection, even a freedom from the limits of his own marriage. The chorus warns that Lenny should not meddle. "Let sleeping dogs lie," it advises, and it is "curiosity" that "kills us." When Lenny starts rifling through the files at the adoption agency, the chorus leader points out to him that he is breaking the law. Proceed "no further," he advises Lenny, just as Jocasta advised Oedipus in Sophocles' play. But Lenny's pursuit of his son's origins is as relentless as Oedipus's of his own. Curiosity evidently gets the better of him, or perhaps Mighty Aphrodite is at work again. On the other hand, the chorus leader's cautious advice is not necessarily authoritative; it shows why, Lenny tells him, he'll "always be a chorus leader." "I act; I take action; I make things happen," Lenny asserts. And after he succeeds in obtaining the forbidden information, he is on his way to Pennsylvania in search of a "Leslie Wright."

His search brings him back to Manhattan, where the sought-for woman has gone with aspirations to be an actress. When he finds Leslie Wright, or perhaps Leslie St. James, or perhaps Linda Ash (Mira Sorvino), as she now calls herself, no more than Oedipus himself does he find what he thought he was looking for. If he ever meant to tell her that he has adopted her child, he doesn't mention it now.

Far from being the "dynamite mother" of his dreams, Linda has starred in a number of porn movies, such as *The Enchanted Pussy*, and works primarily as a hooker. But there is nevertheless something delightful about this sweet-natured, kind-hearted innocent, who confides in Lenny that abandoning her child was "the sorriest thing" she ever did in her life. "A whore without a heart of gold is unthinkable [in Woody Allen's universe]," as movie critic Anthony Lake has said.[1] Of course, Linda has more than a heart of gold: she is attractive, and quick, and a "state-of-the-art fellatrix," Lenny tells her to console her for her bad luck. Her bad luck started as a child, for her epileptic father was a drug pusher and "burgled and stuff"; she ran away at fourteen and ended up with a magician who committed suicide. Her tale, you might say, goes downhill from there, which is not to say that she had no "regular jobs," she tells Lenny, such as waitressing, massage parlors, and phone sex. No wonder Lenny looks more than "a little white," when he meets her. There is no promising hereditary material here, other than Linda's uncle, a genius, who might have done well at math if he had not become a serial rapist.

Like so many of Allen's characters, Linda aspires to be an artist—she wants to study acting and to be in a Broadway musical. Lenny encourages her until he hears her read Katharine Hepburn's lines from *The Philadelphia Story*. Not as smart as Joey in *Interiors*, she is blithely oblivious of her lack of talent. A part closer to herself, Lenny advises, would not be such a struggle. Indeed, acting is "a tough life," Lenny observes, but a hairdresser can always make a buck. Fortunately, she would like to get married and have kids, she tells Lenny, but her husband would have to be as smart as she is. And Lenny sets out to find her "equal" somewhere. He has found his son's mother, and undertakes to befriend and save her for a more promising and conventional life. After all, he must help her for Max's sake, he protests to the chorus when it reproaches him for hubris, for his drive to find Max's mother and now to change her life.

It looks at first as if the chorus's warning of danger and of the hubris involved in "playing God" is an overreaction, for Lenny succeeds not only in freeing Linda from her pimp, but in finding a potential match for her. Kevin (Michael Rapaport) is a not-so-bright young boxer who plans to return to upstate New York to work on his brother's onion farm. He is looking for "a nice church girl, a nice homely girl, to raise a family," "an old fashioned girl, like [his] Mom," and supposes (with Lenny's help) that he has found it in Linda. The chorus starts expatiating on the joys of "true love . . . refreshing as Spring," and singing of "voodoo" love in music more akin to the romantic scores of Broadway than the foreign Zorba-like notes that opened the movie. We are moving from ancient Greece to modern America, and the chorus is, so to speak, coming along too, acting more like a "chorus line" than foreboders of doom. Modern optimism replaces ancient pessimism, as the movie seems to move to a close, with a bright future on the horizon.

Lenny was seeking his son's origin, expecting her to be a dynamite mother and her family "good stock." But he learns that origins are not determinative. In fact, given what we know of Max it would be difficult to see his resemblance to his birth mother. As for his biological father, Linda admits, it could have been any one of a hundred men. His origin in this sense is lost in time—unrecoverable and seemingly irrelevant. Human beings are free to be themselves; they are not reflections of their parents.

But not only is our present free from our past, we can affect the future. Lenny can make Linda a reformed woman, so that should Max ever seek her out, he would find something quite different from what Lenny found. He would find, given what Kevin wants in a woman, a homemaker on an onion farm, who cleans, cooks, takes care of the lawn, and walks the dogs, someone as American as apple pie. Wampsville, the site of the onion farm, Lenny explains to Linda, is "a place rich in American heritage."

The chorus accuses Lenny of "playing God," of hubris, of trying to control Linda's life, especially by inducing a match between her and the onion farmer. But Lenny is not simply playing God, or at least not the great Zeus upon whom the chorus calls. If there has been any Zeus in Linda's life, he has been the source of only unbelievably bad luck. Lenny clearly is a better provider. When the chorus calls on Zeus for help, it hears merely the voice of an answering machine: "This is Zeus, I'm not home right now." We do not know if Zeus ever gets his messages, but we have seen Lenny act. The chorus began this movie speaking of the "malice and ineptitude of the gods," but Lenny demonstrates care and competence.

If Lenny has played God, he has improved upon the role. Linda's dream, she tells her onion farmer, is that "someone would come along and think that I'm special, and want to change my life for me." Kevin supposes that he fits the role, but Lenny himself has done just this for Linda. But this is no special providence from above. It takes Lenny to see that Linda is special and to provide accordingly.

Lenny has provided, moreover, not by means of ancient virtue, but by his ability to make use of the opportunities that present themselves, or, as Machiavelli advises, by conquering fortune. As he tells the chorus leader who reminds him of "brave Achilles," as he faces Linda's "two-bit pimp," "Achilles had only a heel, I have a full Achilles body." Linda relies on him to free her from her "business representative," she tells him, because he is "smart and bright" and has "a way with words." Spotting the "common interest" he shares with the pimp in professional basketball, Lenny offers to deal—a trade of hard-to-get seats at a Knicks game in exchange for Linda. The pimp too is not bound by his origins, for he would "give [his] mother for courtside seats, much less this stupid little whore." And Lenny knows how to accommodate him, for his own business connections give him access to courtside seats.

Lenny provides for Linda as well by introducing her to Kevin. He also spends a lot of time preparing her to meet him, buying her different clothes, having her change her hairdo, and cautioning against her typical approach to men. While he gives Kevin a "great build-up" to Linda and tells her that he is just "finishing a very productive career as a boxer," he tells Kevin that Linda is "church-people . . . practically a virgin," and loves the prospect of living on an onion farm. He has heard what each of them desires in a mate and gives each of them an appropriate image of the other before they meet. When they meet, they are ready to fall in love. Linda said more than she knew when she thought that Lenny would outsmart her pimp because he had "a way with words." Lenny is in fact like a moviemaker, who creates characters who fit together in a story and prepares actors for their roles.

Mighty Aphrodite therefore promises a triumph not of ancient courage but of Yankee ingenuity. Woody Allen has shown how the

Kevin (Michael Rapaport) takes lessons from Lenny (Woody Allen) before his blind date. Credit: Miramax (courtesy Kobal); photographer Brian Hamill.

modern world, free from belief in the past, in the fates, and in the gods, can find sustenance in human provision, both in the sense of care and know-how, especially the know-how to create and to manipulate images. This provision is a virtue appropriate for an age of equality, where success need not be connected to class or wealth and is a provision possessed par excellence by the movie-maker, who can give us images through which we can understand our lives that are more benevolent than images of malicious or inept fates. Just as Lenny reforms Linda, Allen reforms Greek tragedy, with its view of the malice or ineptitude of the universe, the view that Linda herself expresses in a modern form when Lenny takes her to the racetrack and she says that there is no way, just no way, that she could ever pick a winner. Lenny tells her that she must "learn to be a graceful loser." Lenny is nevertheless able to pick a winner for her—at least the favorite to show. One can "win" if one lowers one's goals. One can win if one is content to be a loser, or in Linda's case, if she settles for Kevin. In this way Allen's comedy can win a contest with Greek tragedy. Has Allen finally revealed himself to be the self-satisfied liberal his critics say he is, who believes that individuals can replace God and that no sense of traditional virtue is possible or necessary?

But wait. The chorus's happy musings about the budding romance between Linda and Kevin are interrupted by "Ms. Party-Pooper," Cassandra herself (Danielle Ferland), who comes with a vision of the blind seer Tiresias (Jack Warden) and Lenny Weinrib at the Acropolis, the Upper West Side deli. A blind beggar reports to Lenny that Jerry has been kissing Amanda, and she responding to him. The "virtuous" Lenny has not been minding his own house. And while he may be making the world a better place for his son by improving the lot of Max's birth mother, his wife has fallen prey to the lurking Jerry Bender. Amanda wants to move out, for she can't cheat, and Jerry is in love with her. The devastated Lenny wanders out to "get his thoughts together," and he meets Kevin, furious at him for setting him up with a "stupid" girl, a hooker, who does porn films. Lenny's matchmaking fails due in part to chance—for the porn movie Kevin watches with his buddies is one of Linda's. But if Kevin is watching a porn movie, he is not quite the clean-cut, apple-pie American that Lenny billed. And far from being the man Lenny described, who would take care of Linda and respect her, Kevin hits Linda when she confesses her past. Although he watches porn movies, he will not go out with a porn actress. Lenny's weaving has unraveled, and he goes to tell Linda that she was right—they are both losers. Linda finally gives Lenny what one aspect of her past prepares her to give, and what he has amply paid for with his time and concern, but the experience is bittersweet for both of them. The chorus is in a position to say to Lenny, even if it does not, "I told you so."

The unraveling of Lenny and Amanda's marriage, as well as of Lenny's matchmaking, reveals the limits to human action about which the chorus had warned. The past is more important than it had seemed to Lenny. "People change," he pleads with Kevin, and begs him not to hold up Linda's past. But his words are to no avail. Some pasts are just too much, at least for Kevin. There are limits to the images that can be created. When Lenny warned Linda that

Kevin thought that she was a hairdresser, she expresses reservations: "You lied?" Images cannot work if they are simply "lies." "Buildup" must utilize materials that are real. And Lenny should have known. After all, he advised Linda when he heard her read from *The Philadelphia Story* that she should find a part closer to herself.

Lenny's defense of Linda speaks for human freedom: Linda has changed, he insists, she is a reformed woman. His words about the possibility of change, however, sadly echo Amanda's announcement to him that things have changed between the two of them. If Linda can outgrow her past as a hooker, so can Amanda outgrow hers as Lenny's wife. Lenny's attention to reforming Linda has distracted him from attending to his and Amanda's relationship. Lenny spends time raising his son, but he doesn't seem to learn the truth about the continuity of life and time, of past and future, that nurturing might reveal. After all, his one conversation with an educator about Max's schooling was interrupted by a phone call. Lenny is thus a double loser—both in his efforts to provide for Linda's happiness and in his failure to provide for his own. The comedy may be a tragedy after all, and the Greek chorus that warned of hubris may have been proven right.

The tragedy of the modern age lies in its exaggerated notion of human freedom and autonomy, in its supposition that it can bypass tragedy. Like Oedipus, today's children leave home without even an occasional phone call. But unlike Oedipus, they have no oracle impelling them to do so. Rather, the modern ethic commands that children become autonomous. Lenny thinks that he can find an ideal woman, and when he finds her less than ideal, he thinks that he can reform her. Amanda thinks that she should move out, and even that it might be better for Max if they are apart rather than quarreling all the time.

But there is a kind of logic that says a double loser is impossible. There is hope for Lenny, for if Linda cannot deny her past entirely, can Amanda? Another ending is yet in sight. Tiresias had reported that Amanda had "responded" to Jerry's overtures, but Tiresias is blind. When with Jerry, Amanda can think only of Lenny, and realizes how much she loves him. Lenny, of course, misses Amanda, for it was only when he was distressed by Amanda's leaving him that his relationship with Linda became anything more than platonic. Amanda finds Lenny, and they determine "to put things right" between them. Past ties and present efforts hold out hope for the future.

Meanwhile, Linda, who really did want a husband and children all along, determines to make another attempt with Kevin, pursues him to Wampsville, and begs him to take her back. But Kevin is simply not the man for her, nor is she the woman for an onion farm. To think so is to suppose that she can become anything, or that she can fit the image that Lenny created for her. He—and we—should have been forewarned when Linda proved allergic to the daisies Kevin gave her. How would someone allergic to daisies do around onions? But salvation comes in strange ways. "Talk about a deus ex machina," the chorus observes, as a helicopter makes a forced landing beside Linda's car as she is driving back from upstate New York. The helicopter pilot is "a wonderful man, who was not uptight and repressed and accepted [Linda]." Accepting the past, they have a future—married and raising children in Connecticut. After all, Linda always thought that she would be a great mother, and she regretted every day of her life giving up her son for adoption. It is a future more appropriate to Linda than either life on an onion farm or a life acting in Katharine Hepburn roles like *The Philadelphia Story*. Married life with children in Connecticut is an image, to be sure, but it is more than an image. It is a part such as Lenny told her she should seek when he heard her read Hepburn's lines—one closer to herself.

Mighty Aphrodite is a movie for a liberal or modern polity. It points out the tragic potential in its characteristic error, its assumption of freedom and control, and its indifference to the past. Allen's movie also demonstrates the potential of art to call forth liberalism's best self. It is one of the brilliant moves of Allen's film that Kevin discovers the truth about Linda's past from watching a porn movie in which she acts. The images of art themselves reveal that some images, such as the one that Lenny gave to Kevin of Linda, and to Linda of Kevin, are lies. Kevin and Linda are simply not "church people." Like Linda's porn movie that Kevin watches, Allen's film reveals limits to liberal individuals' power to create their lives, and corrects their images of their own freedom.

Lenny knows that Amanda is "crazy" to think that Max could be better off with his parents apart, and his actions to help Linda demonstrate not just his common human decency but also his recognition that Max's origins may be important to him. Lenny is a liberal in the best sense when he makes a deal with Linda's pimp for her freedom, not when he acknowledges that the pimp's assertion that "[his] girls do what [he] tells them" is "a work ethic specific to [his] needs." The latter is only a joke, even if it is also a bitter comment on the cruelties to which liberal principles might lead if not reined in by good sense and laughter.

In spite of the chorus's statement about the past and the limits of freedom, however, *Mighty Aphrodite* is not a return to any fatalistic view of life or tragic view from the past. Kevin is clearly wrong to identify Linda only with her past, or with any character she plays in a porn film. Being Katharine Hepburn may not be possible for Linda, but other things are. Images of the past can unduly restrict freedom, and art can mislead as well as reveal. The porn film does both for Kevin. But then he wants to marry someone, he tells Lenny, just "like his mom."

When Lenny and Linda make love, the chorus finally reports, Linda conceives a child, but not wanting to complicate his life with Amanda, she never tells him. Thus, Lenny and Linda have each other's child, but they don't know it, the chorus points out. Is there tragic potential here? A possible brother-sister incest? Hardly. Neither parent may know the full story, but each knows enough— Lenny knows that Linda is Max's mother, and Linda knows that Lenny is her child's father. We cannot conquer chance, just as we have no perfect knowledge, but we know what we need to know. If chance continues to play a role, there is the chance that luck may be good as well as bad. There may be no god in the machine, but there might be a wonderful helicopter pilot. And that is why *Mighty Aphrodite* is neither a Greek tragedy of fate nor simply a Hollywood comedy.

Allen's revision of Greek tragedy is a contest for virtue. If life is fated, if the gods determine our actions, there is no space for virtue.

Virtue requires freedom to act, in situations where acting makes a difference. That Zeus has no more than an answering machine, and that he is not the one who comes down in the helicopter, preserves the possibility of human virtue. The chorus regards Oedipus as "a victim," as we have seen. Of course, the chorus also speaks of "brave Achilles." But how brave can anyone be if his actions are controlled by fate? Lenny expresses the difficulty with the view of fate when he reminds the chorus leader who urges him to imitate Achilles of his "whole Achilles body." As no less an authority on ancient virtue than Rousseau once observed, by making Achilles invulnerable, Homer deprived him of "the merit of valor."[2] A fatalistic view of life produces Cassandras, who forestall action by anticipating its inevitable consequences, like heavy mortgages and beach erosion. And besides, such a view does not give its due to all that human beings have accomplished, especially by means of Yankee ingenuity. For Allen to offer us an updated version of a Greek tragedy is even further afield than Linda Ash acting in *The Philadelphia Story*. Allen is searching for something in his art "closer to himself," and to us all.

Just as a view of the world that allows no room for freedom leaves no room for virtue, so too does a view of the world that has no room for failure. If risks are not risks, for example, courage is not needed, and moderation appears only as a vice. Such a view threatens when Yankee ingenuity meets only with success. It appears when people believe that with a certain know-how, perhaps an understanding of how the forces of nature work, all can be controlled, or when they believe that the world is constituted solely by the images we create of it. Such a view believes that a cure can be found for Linda's allergies, or that Lenny's "way with words," as Linda said, is sufficient to meet all obstacles, that Lenny can both deal with the pimp and also create the images of Linda and Kevin that make them a perfect match. It is when Lenny acts as matchmaker that the chorus observes that he is "playing God." He is acting as if there were a god in the machine, not because he believes in God, but because he put the god there. If Allen showed Lenny's success, his movie might entertain but it would not educate. But the highest aspiration of art, as David Shayne stated at the beginning of

Bullets over Broadway, is not to entertain but "to transform men's souls." Allen uses ancient tragedy to correct modern excesses, to inform liberal freedom with a sense of limit. His search for virtue is a contest not only with ancient tragedy but with liberalism itself. In the end, Allen's art comes closer to traditional piety than to Greek fatalism, for it does not foreclose the possibility that our prayers are answered while it insists on human freedom. "Great Zeus," after all, does have an answering machine. We have no evidence that he sent the helicopter, but we do not know. And that is fortunate.

Critics over the years have accused Allen of pandering to the worst kind of liberal self-indulgence and neurotic pessimism that characterizes the contemporary intellectual. But whatever failures of virtue or self-restraint Allen may exhibit in his personal life, in his art he has consistently tried to come to grips with what it means to be a good artist and what such an artist has to contribute to a good life. In *Play It Again Sam,* for example, he explored the extent to which the heroes of the screen lead viewers to virtuous conduct. *Stardust Memories* is about a director's searching for—and finding—a proper ending for his movie. It is an ending that affirms the goodness of life without misleading about human suffering. *Mighty Aphrodite,* in converting tragedy into comedy, illustrates that Aphrodite is mightiest not when she impels humans to their doom, but when human beings reflect on their passions and make moral choices. For only then does she support ongoing human life.

Life is something neither tragic nor comic but, as the chorus concludes, "ironic" as well as "unbelievable, miraculous, sad, and wonderful." Because this is "all true," the chorus members pull off their masks and sing a second time. This time they celebrate not the romantic "voodoo" power of Kevin and Linda's love, which turned out not to be very powerful at all, but a more ambiguous but nevertheless happier vision. "If you smile, the whole world smiles with you," the chorus sings and dances, whereas "if you cry, you bring on the rain."

Our options are open, but in every case, what we do has its effect on others. Nor is Woody Allen indifferent to the options. His unmasked chorus speaks for him, advising to "keep on smiling," and "be happy again."

14

The Comic

From at least the time of Aristotle, comedy has been viewed as inferior to tragedy. Whereas tragedy involves those better than ourselves, the noble, or the dignified, Aristotle claims, comedy involves the vulgar, the ridiculous, and the shameful (*Poetics*, I. ii. 1 and 7; and v. 1–2). While tragedy, in the words of Ortega y Gasset "opens [us] to the heroic in reality," comedy reabsorbs a hero into reality and mocks his pretensions as "a mask beneath which a vulgar creature moves."[1] Comedy in this view reveals the limits to human aspiration, the extent to which the hero who wills greatness is just another human being, as bound to the earth as the rest of humanity.[2] Thus, Allan Felix sees in a romantic scene only "eagles flying over a cesspool," and Andrew Hobbes's flying bicycle sinks into a lake.

Allen claims to accept the traditional hierarchy between tragedy and comedy: "I have always felt that tragedy was the highest art form, even as a child, before I could articulate it."[3] In comedy, "there is not the same level of . . . confrontation with issues or with oneself," Allen says.[4] "When you do comedy you're not sitting at the grown-ups' table, you're sitting at the children's table."[5] And yet Allen also senses that there is something more to comedy than puncturing pretension. "In the end, we are earthbound," he observes, but far from accentuating and reveling in our materiality, comedy "def[ies] all that pulls [us] down." The comedian, he continues, always attempts "somehow, through some artifice or trick, to get you airborne. Being able to suggest that something magical is possible, that something other than what you see with your eyes and your senses is possible, opens up a whole crack in the negative."[6] Allen is groping for an alternative beyond a comedy that merely mocks aspiration. He suggested this as early as *Annie Hall*, for he wanted to make "a deeper film" and be funny in a way different from his earlier zany comedies, where everything was "subjugated to the joke." Instead he sought a comedy that would allow "other values" to emerge, that would be "interesting or nourishing for the audience."[7]

Among Alvy's memories in *Annie Hall* is his first live performance, when he finally summons the courage to do his own jokes rather than write them for others. He tells of being expelled from college for cheating on his metaphysics exam. He looked into the soul of the student sitting next to him. As a stand-up comic, Alvy appears as a nervous, neurotic, whining hypochondriac, self-absorbed, anxious about the world and victimized by it, a real "loser." Instead of looking into the soul of others, stand-up comic Alvy lets others look into his own. Although his self-revelations appear as self-absorption, he has gained enough distance from himself to share his neuroses with others and to make himself the butt of their laughter. He selects tales of himself that are funny.[8] With his audience, he laughs at himself.

As a loser, the stand-up comic gains his audience's sympathy. What happens to him could happen to them. His foibles and weaknesses are theirs. And their laughter turns to the human condition, which they themselves share. In the best case, those laughing at the stand-up comic are also laughing at themselves. He lets them look into his own soul not so that they can avoid looking into their own, but so that they can see and laugh at themselves. As Mike tells Joey to do in *Interiors*, the stand-up comic tells his audience to "get off themselves." His self-absorption self-destructs. And the loser turns himself into a winner precisely because he helps others win as well.

Alvy's doing his own jokes is a reflection of Allen's putting himself in his own movies—what critics see as an inexcusable manifestation of self-absorption. If Allen as filmmaker is absorbed in his own problems, those problems are very much humanity's problems. Allen's movies—at least from the time of *Play It Again, Sam*—

address fundamental human concerns, questions of love and friendship, alienation and community, justice and cynicism, freedom and courage. Allen risks his reputation to open up for his audiences "a crack in the negative." And that requires reflecting on art and its relation to life.

The year after he made *Annie Hall*, Allen made *Interiors*, a movie about characters too self-absorbed to laugh at themselves. This is especially true of Eve, who attempts to impose order on the world in the way that an artist might do on his or her art. As Arthur said of her, she "created a world around us that we existed in . . . where everything had its place." Eve wants the perfection of art reflected in life. She is, as Joey says to her just before Eve commits suicide, "too perfect . . . to live in this world." She wants no cracks in her sealed-up interiors. Lacking the comic's distance from himself, Eve becomes destructive of others and of herself.

Whereas Allen thrusts comedy into Eve's serious world when Arthur brings Pearl to meet his daughters, he puts a tragic figure into a comedy when he gives us Cheech in *Bullets*. Cheech is an artist who kills in order to protect the integrity of art and, in effect, signs his own death warrant by doing so. He is willing to destroy and be destroyed for the sake of "a thing of beauty." In him too we see the tragic consequences of confusing art with life: like his father before him, he believes that bad actresses deserve to die. Life and art become one: removing Olive from life is as justifiable as removing her from the play. He acts not simply as the godfather of the play, but as a god who controls life and death.

David's original play lacked the integrity and beauty of Cheech's revision, but it pointed in its title to a moral understanding that its amoral godfather lacks. The "God of Our Fathers" may be harsh, but he is also just. And our fathers who obeyed such a God knew at least enough not to act as if they possess divine power and righteousness. Cheech, in contrast, who blurs the line between life and art, also blurs the line between human beings and God. It is Sandy in *Stardust Memories* who better understands these distinctions. When Sandy plays God in one of his movies, he knows that it is only a role. He is aware that he does not have the voice for the part, and therefore had his lines dubbed.

In trying to create perfection, Cheech resembles the mad doctor we saw in one of Sandy's movies who tries to create the perfect woman. While the mad doctor succeeds in his creation, he also falls in love with the perfectly imperfect one who is her by-product. Cheech's desire to create a thing of beauty also destroys life, including his own. There is irony, however, in Cheech's "great finish," which looks forward to new life beyond the play. Far from making his play into a whole, a perfect work of art as he intends, his "finish" suggests that even the most perfect art is necessarily unfinished and that life eludes the control of any artist. In *Bullets*, tragedy corrects itself and unfolds into Allen's comedy. And while Cheech is unaware that his "finish" affirms the goodness of life rather than perfects his art, Allen uses a version of Cheech's "finish" for his own movie.

David announces to Ellen that he is not an artist and that he wants to go back to Pittsburgh with her and raise a family. It is he and Ellen who promise new life. Unlike Cheech, David has learned in the course of the movie to compromise, but in positive as well as negative ways. In returning to Pittsburgh, he leaves the almost perfect play imperfect. He gets the message of Cheech's "great finish" in time to understand and reject any destructive pursuit of art and beauty. By the same token, he would not regard his children, as Renata did hers, merely as "great potential raw material."[9] The true godfather nurtures, and therefore recognizes limits to his control. Beauty is not all.

For Cheech, "beauty is truth, and truth beauty." But that is not all that Allen "knows," or all that we need to know. Just as *Crimes and Misdemeanors* is about a murderer's lack of "emotional vision" and "moral vision,"[10] *Bullets* is about the dependence of art not primarily on a gangster's bullets, as the title suggests, but on the moral integrity that gives a work of art its aesthetic integrity. While Flender claims that the artist creates his own moral universe, Allen thinks that when "the artist considers himself not like other people," it is mere vanity. Although he "doesn't agree that the artist is superior," he nevertheless implies that there is something special about the artist, for artistic talent is "a gift from God" and that "with that . . . comes a certain responsibility."[11]

Commenting on *Stardust Memories,* Graham McCann observes that while "the producer sees the ideal movie as a screen that shields us from harsh realities," Sandy "sees it as a screen that reveals such realities." That Allen's movies "acknowledge both of these functions," he concludes, "is a source of their ambivalence."[12] McCann shares the perspective of Nancy Pogel, who thinks Allen's films offer "intersecting optimistic and pessimistic images . . . as unresolved possibilities."[13] If McCann and Pogel were right, Allen's movies would vacillate between showing that life ends in a garbage heap and that it ends in a Jazz Heaven. And to the extent that there is a reality, it is a harsh one, whether art should reveal it to us or screen us from it, or do a bit of both. McCann and Pogel thus miss what happens in New Jersey.[14]

Sandy's finish for his movie, not to mention other later Allen movies I have discussed, suggests that there is more to life than the harsh realities that too often meet the eye. To point to goodness in reality—from Allan Felix's act of friendship to Lenny Weinrib's attempt to help Linda Ash—is a higher function of art than those McCann mentions. This is the effect of Allen's mature art, and this is its greatest justification. The values that emerge from Allen's new kind of comedies, the values that might well "interest" and "nourish" his audiences, are closer to joy and hope than to anguish and despair. If, as some contend, *the* "great synthesis of the twentieth century" is "humor and despair,"[15] Allen offers an alternative. He is untimely in the best sense.

Like Eve in *Interiors,* Cheech dies near the end of *Bullets.* But while Eve's suicide is the product of despair, Cheech is punished for a murder, even if his punishment comes from a man for whom Cheech committed many other murders. Ironically, the godfather gives Cheech what he deserves. Although there is hope at the end of *Interiors,* it has an abstract quality, and Pearl has only begun to melt Eve's "ice palace." *Bullets*'s ending, in contrast, is part of a world that is warmer and more just. It is not a perfectly just and ordered world, but the worst offender is mortally punished, and David finds the possibility of human happiness without the illusion of perfection. But then *Bullets* is a later movie than *Interiors.*

Girgus refers to some critics who object to Allen's inclusion of

laughter and comedy in his "serious" movies, inasmuch as it provides relief from "the despair and anguish in the human condition." To them comedy is a cop-out. They would rather have
Interiors without Pearl. Girgus, in contrast, defends Allen's use of
humor, for he thinks that humor, far from being escapist, "under-
scores" the vision of anguish and "gives a cutting edge to it."[16] He
here implies that the inclusion of Pearl in *Interiors* is good because
it deepens our sense of life's futility. But his view hardly does justice to Pearl. Girgus and these critics to whom he objects, whether
they approve or disapprove of Allen's use of humor, use the same
criterion. They would presumably applaud the twentieth-century
synthesis of humor and despair.

One of the captions in *Hannah and Her Sisters* is that "the only
absolute knowledge attainable by man is that life is meaningless,"
and Allen affirms that this is the message of *Hannah*. Thus, he sees
the positive ending of that film, which shows the happiness of
Mickey Sachs and his new wife over her pregnancy, as a sign of his
lack of nerve, for he "copped out a little on the film."[17] And he finds
"no great affirmation" in Mickey's conclusion that *maybe* life isn't
meaningless.[18] This is one instance, however, in which we can trust
the tale, not the teller.

There are any number of objections that might be raised to this
understanding of Allen's art. When Alvy Singer tells Annie Hall
that he has "a very pessimistic view of life," he explains that life is
divided into the horrible and the miserable. The horrible include
"terminal cases," the "blind," the "crippled." He doesn't "know
how they get through life. It's amazing to [him]." The rest of us are
miserable, and "you should be thankful that you're miserable," he
advises her.

Allen claims that he agrees with Alvy that life is divided into the
horrible and the miserable.[19] But there may be more optimism in
his own movie than Allen admits. When Alvy tells Annie about his
pessimistic view of life, he makes Annie laugh. They proceed to
have fun as they identify types of people they see in Central Park.
Although Annie accuses Alvy of being unable to enjoy life, Alvy
admits at the end "how much fun it was just knowing [Annie]."
He realizes "what a terrific person she was," just as Sandy realizes

in *Stardust Memories* that "it's not as terrible as I originally thought." Alvy may think that his view of life is pessimistic, but he is also thankful that he is among the miserable rather than the horrible. And he is aware that he is lucky to be so. We must trust the tale, not the teller; we must trust Allen's movie, not Alvy, not even Allen.

Although Allen "aspire[s] to tragedy,"[20] he includes Pearl in *Interiors* and Mickey Sachs in *Hannah*, which, without him, Allen admits, "would have gone in a much more serious direction."[21] While Mickey is not sure whether there is a God, he wants to be part of the experience of life and is able to enjoy himself. And he is happy over his wife's pregnancy. He wants to have a child, like Marion's first husband. Mickey suffers the inconsistency of which Marion accuses her husband, that despite believing in "the pointlessness of existence" he wants to bring a child into the world. Fortunately, Mickey is married to Holly, not Marion. And Marion herself, as we have seen, comes to regret her words. She becomes more like Holly. *Another Woman* as well as *Bullets* tells us that the ending of *Hannah* fits. Perhaps we should say to Allen what the graduate student in *Deconstructing Harry* said to Harry Block about his books: while "on the surface they all seem a little sad, underneath they're really happy. It's just that you don't know it."

In his later movies, however, Allen's characters are less the unhappy intellectuals absorbed in life's problems (like Alvy Singer or Sandy Bates) and more happy with their place in the world. To many, movies like *Manhattan Murder Mystery*, *Bullets over Broadway*, and *Mighty Aphrodite* (and of course his musical *Everyone Says I Love You*) are less profound because the characters are less alienated. Sander H. Lee worries about David Shayne's renunciation of art in *Bullets*, for example, his return to Pittsburgh, and his desire to marry and have children. Lee wonders whether Allen is telling us by this that his own "return to comedy marks the end of his 'serious phase' that began with *Annie Hall* and *Interiors*?"[22] He hopes not, but then he is interested in Woody Allen's "angst." And there is surely less angst in Allen's more recent movies.

My analysis suggests, in contrast, that as Allen matures as a filmmaker, he takes more seriously the relation of the individual to the larger community, the limits to human freedom imposed by the past, and freedom's obligations toward others. He is as concerned as he has always been with individual happiness, but he is more likely to explore the links between individual happiness and the moral and social structures that support it, especially those of family. Allen's protagonists live their lives less and less in their own minds than in the external world. Their possibilities are greater and yet more limited. They see themselves in relation to others and to the society in which they live. Allen doesn't frequently raise political issues in the narrow sense, but as he reflects more on human life in contemporary America, he inevitably is drawn outside of himself.

The protagonist of *Mighty Aphrodite* is a sportswriter rather than an intellectual. Lenny Weinrib, like Allan Felix, is still watching and writing, but we also see him playing on a basketball court with his son. He contrasts himself with the chorus leader in much the same language as Allan Felix's wife contrasts herself with her husband:

Lenny Weinrib (Woody Allen) and wife Amanda Sloan (Helena Bonham Carter) spend time with their son (Jimmy McQuaid) before bedtime. Credit: Miramax (courtesy Kobal)

you are a great watcher, I take action. More important, Lenny watches and enjoys what his society is more likely to watch and enjoy, for it is in sports that our heroes are often found. There are hints of this in Larry Lipton's dragging his wife to a hockey game, Zelig's attempt to join the Yankees at spring training, and even in Alvy Singer's preferring to watch the Knicks on television to cocktail party talk about alienation.

In his movie following *Mighty Aphrodite*, *Everyone Says I Love You*, Allen plays Joe Berlin, a writer living in Paris but whose books sell in a stall on Fifth Avenue in the ninety-nine-cent bin. Although we don't know if his books are accessible to mass audiences, their price is certainly right for it. And when he becomes interested in a woman who loves Tintoretto, he absorbs knowledge of the famous painter from an art book and mouths to her its textbook words about him. That he is a sophisticated romantic who has a passion for Mahler's Fourth, eats snails in his garret, and visits Bora Bora in the summer is only an image he adopts to make himself attractive to her. As compared to Alvy Singer or Sandy Bates, he is just an ordinary "Joe." His best friends, his former wife and her attorney husband, have conventional prejudices and reactions. And they all sing—ordinary voices though they may have.

If the turn from art to sports, or from high-brow to low-brow art, suggests Allen lowers his sights in some respects, it suggests that he has raised them in others. He has connected both himself and the concerns of the Western tradition to life as we live it. He has a more comprehensive view of himself and the world. He sees the connection between himself and that world, and in so doing he is able to see both a timeliness and timelessness to human life. He is also able to overcome alienation from himself and his world, or, more accurately, he has come to put that alienation in perspective and put it to good use. Woody Allen is not sportswriter Lenny Weinrib, and he does not follow David Shayne to Pittsburgh, but his vision now includes Lenny Weinrib and David Shayne as well as those things that he shares with them. They share a detachment, a desire to make the world better, and ultimately a recognition of the limits of their ability to understand and control, a recognition that is not only conducive to success but essential to happiness.

Although Allen began his career with "escapist" comedies, and then courageously refused to escape, he never entirely lost sight of the goodness of life. And in his later movies, such as *Another Woman*, we can find stronger and stronger affirmations of that fact. *Manhattan Murder Mystery* is about a marriage that comes to work, and *Bullets* looks forward to one. *Mighty Aphrodite* ends with the renewal of one and the beginning of another. These last movies in different ways transform tragedies into comedies. It is not so much tragedy to which the greatest artists should aspire but comedies that without being escapist demonstrate that life is good—from the peace that Marion Post achieves by the end of *Another Woman* to its comic reflection in Leopold's admission that the woods are enchanted, after all.

This understanding of life that emerges from my interpretation of Allen's films is neither the playfulness of the deconstructionist in the face of an ever-receding reality nor a Sartrean angst as we face moral chaos and out of which we create meaning or value for our lives. Rather, the vision that emerges comes closer to that of Kierkegaard, who insisted that faith was not a result of human will but a gift analogous to grace.[23] That is why Allen's reference to artistic talent as "a gift from God" is not mere slippage into conventional beliefs that he more characteristically rejects.[24] And he accepts a responsibility to give gifts in turn. Near the end of *Manhattan*, Isaac Davis asks, "why is life worth living?" and proceeds to give a list of things that "make it worthwhile": Groucho Marx, Willie Mays, the second movement of the Jupiter Symphony, Louie Armstrong's recording of "Potatohead Blues," Swedish movies, *Sentimental Education* by Flaubert, Marlon Brando, Frank Sinatra, those incredible apples and pears by Cezanne, the crabs at Sam Wo's, Tracy's face. Isaac leaves the list unfinished. To it we can add Woody Allen's movies.

I have tried to interpret Allen's movies, which Allen himself claims result in part from instinct, although a disciplined and educated instinct. I have tried to show how various elements of his stories fit. While critics have accused Allen of arrogance and boasting, I do not know whether Allen understands how good his movies are. I have said not only that they are good, but why they are good. They are good, most importantly, because they reveal what is good in the reality they reflect. In interpreting Allen's art, I am not trying to understand Allen as he understands himself. I have tried to understand the movies he has made, and often Allen's own reflections have been helpful, but not always.

Like Sandy at the end of *Stardust Memories*, the moviegoer must look upon the story, the text, the film. He or she must find the distance to judge, to see it whole. The viewer cannot be, as David finds Cheech, "too close" to it. But to have distance from something does not mean that one cannot appreciate its goodness; distance is, in fact, necessary for such an appreciation. When Sandy looks upon his creation, we can assume that he judges it good, even if he doesn't say it. After all, he doesn't have the voice for playing God. *Stardust Memories* thus does nothing to preempt our own judgment about the worth of Sandy's movie and even presents us with the conflicting judgments of viewers. Its goodness lies in part in the fact that Sandy does not pronounce its goodness. This movie may be about the artist's control of his material, but it is about the kind of control that allows for freedom, for it calls attention to the fact that it is "only" a movie. It is like ending with a happy announcement of pregnancy, and like accepting that time will tell.

Notes

Preface

1. Pauline Kael, "The Frog Who Turned into a Prince," *New Yorker* (October 27, 1980), 183.

2. Maureen Dowd, "Grow Up, Harry," *New York Times* (January 11, 1998), 19.

3. John Podhoretz, "Missing Heaven, Making Hell," *Weekly Standard* (December 17, 1997), 38.

4. Jami Bernard, "Woody's Dirty Harry," *Daily News* (December 12, 1997), 69.

5. Janet Maslin, "Gleefully Skewering His Own Monsters," *New York Times* (December 12, 1997), E1.

6. Dowd, "Grow Up, Harry," 19.

7. The theme is not a new one to Allen. As early as *Manhattan* (1979), protagonist Isaac Davis reproaches his ex-wife for writing about their marriage.

8. Ed Siegel, "When Harry Met Woody," *The Sunday Boston Globe* (January 11, 1998), N1.

9. Podhoretz finds *Deconstructing Harry* "shocking" and "the most foul-mouthed and pornographically suggestive mainstream American movie yet made" and blames Allen for his "sadly puerile" intellectual obsessions. He nevertheless admits that the movie is "the funniest Allen film in fifteen years" and contains "moments more inspired than any in contemporary cinema," 37–38.

10. Nancy Pogel, *Woody Allen* (Boston: Twayne Publishers, 1987), 150 (see also 8, 34, 48, 54, 146). Pogel takes the phrase "dialogic imagination" from Mikhail Bakhtin, *The Dialogic Imagination*, ed. Michael Holquist (Austin: University of Texas Press, 1981).

223

11. Sam B. Girgus, *The Films of Woody Allen* (Cambridge: Cambridge University Press, 1993), 2 and 9.

12. Allan Bloom, *The Closing of the American Mind* (New York: Basic Books, 1987), 155.

13. Sander H. Lee, *Woody Allen's Angst: Philosophical Commentaries on His Serious Films* (Jefferson, N.C.: McFarland and Company, 1997), 1–9. Although my own manuscript on Allen was complete before Lee's was available to me, I have nevertheless attempted to acknowledge his sometimes supportive and sometimes conflicting interpretations whenever possible. Even where we disagree, I find Lee's observations and arguments thoughtful and helpful.

14. Lee, *Woody Allen's Angst*, 55.

15. Lee, *Woody Allen's Angst*, 5.

Chapter 1

1. Interested readers may find the texts of some of Allen's films in Woody Allen, *Four Films of Woody Allen: Annie Hall, Interiors, Manhattan, Stardust Memories* (New York: Random House, 1997) and Woody Allen, *Three Films of Woody Allen: Zelig, Broadway Danny Rose, The Purple Rose of Cairo* (New York: Random House, 1987).

2. Susan Sontag, *Against Interpretation* (New York: Farrar, Straus & Giroux, 1961), 6–7.

3. Stig Bjorkman, *Woody Allen on Woody Allen: In Conversation with Stig Bjorkman* (London: Faber and Faber, 1994), 124. Bjorkman's book, a series of interviews with Allen on each of his films, is an invaluable source for the study of Woody Allen's art.

4. Bjorkman, *Woody Allen on Woody Allen*, 121, 122, 124, and 128. Allen explains that critics "got angry because *I* was that character, Sandy, the film director, and I said that they were stupid for liking my comic films. If I did think that, which I don't, I would be smart enough not to say it in a movie," 128.

5. See, for example, David Denby, "Woody's Poison-Pen Letter," *New York* (October 13, 1990), 61.

6. See Allan Bloom, "Interpretive Essay," to *The Republic of Plato*, trans. with notes and interpretive essay by Allan Bloom (New York: Basic Books, 1968), 428–29.

7. Bjorkman, *Woody Allen on Woody Allen*, 263.

8. What does the "autobiographical" approach do, for example, when the character whom Allen plays in *Husbands and Wives* resists the advances of an attractive young woman? Should we not find more self-criticism here than self-justification?

9. Bjorkman, *Woody Allen on Woody Allen*, 126–27.

10. Bjorkman, *Woody Allen on Woody Allen*, 200 and 139.

11. Bjorkman, *Woody Allen on Woody Allen*, 213–14.

12. See, for example, Bjorkman, *Woody Allen on Woody Allen*, 161.

13. Bjorkman, *Woody Allen on Woody Allen*, 97.

14. Bjorkman, *Woody Allen on Woody Allen*, 262–63.

15. Bjorkman, *Woody Allen on Woody Allen*, 244–45.

16. Bjorkman, *Woody Allen on Woody Allen*, 8–9.

17. Bjorkman, *Woody Allen on Woody Allen*, 98.

18. See Allen's description of how, when he is writing a script, his "unconscious is cooking," Bjorkman, *Woody Allen on Woody Allen*, 263, and also 77, 92, and 249 for other examples of Allen's instinct at work.

19. Susan Sontag attributes to D. H. Lawrence, for example, the statement, "Never trust the teller, trust the tale"(*Against Interpretation*, 9). She interprets the significance of this differently, however.

20. Bjorkman, *Woody Allen on Woody Allen*, 252.

21. Bjorkman, *Woody Allen on Woody Allen*, 252.

22. Bjorkman, *Woody Allen on Woody Allen*, 6. Even apart from his earlier comedies, Allen describes the more recent *Manhattan Murder Mystery* as "nice, light entertainment," 255.

23. "My Apology," *Side Effects* (New York: Ballantine Books, 1975), 49–57.

24. Bjorkman, *Woody Allen on Woody Allen*, 209–11. Allen contrasts the themes emerging from Kierkegaard and Dostoyevsky with those of linguistic philosophy: "dramatizing linguistic philosophy . . . is not much fun," 209.

25. "The Kugelmass Episode," *Side Effects*, 59–78.

26. As Lee points out, Rick himself utters a version of the line to Sam, "You played it for her, you can play it for me. Play!" (*Woody Allen's Angst*, 27). Is the misquote a misquote of Ilsa, or a misquote of Rick?

27. Bjorkman, *Woody Allen on Woody Allen*, 6.

28. He actually uses this expression to refer to Rilke (Bjorkman, *Woody Allen on Woody Allen*, 200).

29. "My Apology," *Side Effects*, 49.

30. Bjorkman, *Woody Allen on Woody Allen*, 6.

31. Lee, *Woody Allen's Angst*, 27.

32. "Selections from the Allen Notebooks," *Without Feathers* (New York: Ballantine Books, 1972), 10.

33. Diogenes Laertius, *Lives of Eminent Philosophers* (Cambridge: Harvard University Press, 1966), trans. R. D. Hicks, Vol. I, Book III. 5.

34. Bjorkman, *Woody Allen on Woody Allen*, 5–6.

35. Allen, "Selections from the Allen Notebooks," *Without Feathers*, 10.

36. *God*, in *Without Feathers*, 129–190.

Chapter 2

1. Girgus, *The Films of Woody Allen*, 12. See also Lee, *Woody Allen's Angst*, 26. *Play It Again, Sam* was directed by Herbert Ross; the screenplay was written by Allen, itself an adaptation of his original Broadway play. I agree with Girgus, however, that "Allen's creative imagination as articulated and presented in the screenplay clearly dominates the film and places it within the Allen canon," 12. See also Lee, *Woody Allen's Angst*, 35.

2. See, for example, Annette Wernblad, *Brooklyn Is Not Expanding: Woody Allen's Comic Universe* (Rutherford, N.J.: Farleigh Dickinson University Press, 1992), ch. 1, "A Shlemiel [sic] Is Born," 15–31, and Sanford Pinsker, "Woody Allen's Lovably Anxious *Schlemeils* [sic]," *Studies in American Humor* 5 (1986): 177–89. Consider also the title of Maurice Yacowar's perceptive study of Allen's work, *Loser Take All: The Comic Art of Woody Allen*, New Expanded Edition (New York: Continuum, 1991).

3. For a good analysis of Dick's own insecurities, see Lee, *Woody Allen's Angst*, 33–34.

4. Lee, *Woody Allen's Angst*, 35.

5. Girgus, *The Films of Woody Allen*, 18–19.

6. Girgus, *The Films of Woody Allen*, 13.

7. Girgus refers to the "invention of identity and reality" and "the continuous construction of the subject" (*The Films of Woody Allen*, 13; see also 11). When Girgus states that Allan Felix "overcome[s] his obsession with Bogart in order to become his own man," he may therefore mean simply that Allan has achieved a kind of fluctuating self-creation that reflects the film's own creation of him.

8. Girgus, *The Films of Woody Allen*, 18.

9. Diane Jacobs, *. . . but we need the eggs: The Magic of Woody Allen* (New York: St. Martin's Press, 1982), 46.

10. Pogel, *Woody Allen*, 53–54 and 48.

11. As Lee observes, "the *Casablanca* of the first few minutes of *Sam* is not the 'real' *Casablanca*. . . . Major bits of action and dialogue are left out. For example, we see no Major Strasser, nor do we hear the famous line, 'Round up the usual suspects' " (*Woody Allen's Angst*, 27).

12. As Allen asks in one of his early sketches, "Did anyone I know have a 'meaningful relationship'? My parents stayed together forty years, but that was out of spite. . . . Nobody's relationship could actually be called happy" (*Side Effects*, 104).

Chapter 3

1. Bjorkman, *Woody Allen on Woody Allen*, 75. I agree with Sander H. Lee that *Annie Hall* "introduced, for the first time in a serious manner,

many of the most important philosophical themes that would concern Allen throughout the next two decades" (*Woody Allen's Angst*, 49).

2. Yacowar, *Loser Take All*, 171. See also Lee, *Woody Allen's Angst*, 51.

3. Yacowar claims that "suddenly the clown's mask drops," *Loser Take All*, 171–72.

4. Girgus, *The Films of Woody Allen*, 31.

5. Sigmund Freud, *Civilization and Its Discontents*, trans. James Stachey (New York: W. W. Norton & Company, 1961), 22–24.

6. *Four Films*, 167–68. See Bjorkman, *Woody Allen on Woody Allen*, 3–5. In *Hannah and Her Sisters*, Mickey Sachs starts enjoying life while viewing the Marx Brothers' *Duck Soup*. And in *Mighty Aphrodite*, Lenny Weinrib suggests naming their adopted son Groucho. And then of course there is the New Year's party where almost everyone wears Groucho Marx masks in *Everyone Says I Love You*.

7. Girgus clearly states that "for Allen . . . Freudian theory fails as a total solution to life's dilemmas" (*The Films of Woody Allen*, 9). The issue, however, is not whether Freud fails to offer a total solution for Allen, but whether Freud has correctly understood the character of life's dilemmas. And, for that matter, did even Freud understand himself as offering "a total solution" to life's dilemmas?

8. Allen claims that he firmly believes in the ideas in *The Denial of Death* (Bjorkman, *Woody Allen on Woody Allen*, 106).

9. Ernest Becker, *The Denial of Death* (New York: The Free Press, 1973), 99, 69, and 96.

10. Becker, *The Denial of Death*, 199.

11. Becker continues, "Neurosis is another word for describing a complicated technique for avoiding misery, but reality is the misery" (*The Denial of Death*, 57).

12. Girgus understands *Annie Hall* as "a retrospection" that returns to "the repressed and unconscious in a manner similar to psychoanalysis" (*The Films of Woody Allen*, 31).

13. Pogel, *Woody Allen*, 90 and Wernblad, *Brooklyn Is Not Expanding*, 64.

14. Wernblad, *Brooklyn Is Not Expanding*, 64.

15. Freud, *Civilization and Its Discontents*, 25.

16. Freud, *Civilization and Its Discontents*, 31.

17. Wernblad, who sees Annie as a humanizing life force, does note her neuroses, although she implies they come in a "healthier" form than Alvy's: "While Annie is neurotic, her neuroses manifest themselves not in depression and paranoia, but in a tendency to babble, make silly sounds, and occasionally laugh out of context" (*Brooklyn Is Not Expanding*, 64).

18. Yacowar does an excellent job of pointing out how the movie is structured around this halfway point, with parallel scenes coming before and after. Alvy's despair at the expanding universe at the beginning, for

example, is matched near the end by his anxiety attack in Los Angeles. Before the dinner, Alvy encourages Annie to take adult education classes; afterward he expresses jealousy of her teachers when she does so. Alvy's fear of commitment appears in his concerns over Annie's moving into his apartment in the first half of the movie; Annie's fears come out in her dream in the second half of the movie (*Loser Take All*, 176–77).

19. Allen emphasizes the gulf that separates them not simply by the split screen, but also by the differences in the settings—the office of Annie's therapist is bright, its furniture and art modern and sparse, while that of Alvy's is dark, its furniture heavy and traditional (Yacowar, *Loser Take All*, 175). The former recalls sunny California, the latter gloomy New York City. Yacowar points out as well that while Alvy lies on a couch, Annie sits up, supposing that whereas "Alvy is prone to stasis or regression, Annie is perched to advance" (*Loser Take All*, 175). While Yacowar is one of the most insightful of Allen's critics, and sensitive to the complexities of Allen's films, I disagree with his preference for Annie over Alvy. Allen's use of images of light and darkness, as in the respective doctors' offices, comes closer to that of Thomas Mann in "Tonio Kroger," where light represents a kind of unself-conscious happiness or wholeness and darkness represents the conscious longing for that wholeness. Alvy's lying on the couch rather than sitting erect might therefore indicate a greater depth of analysis rather than stasis or regression. See also Lee, *Woody Allen's Angst* (63–71), who is also more critical of Alvy than I am.

20. For a different, but interesting interpretation of this scene, see Lee, *Woody Allen's Angst*, 65–66.

21. As Allen says, "when you're writing literary things, the fun has to be in the writing of them because there's very little feedback on them. I'm never around when anyone reads them." In contrast, "with a play or a movie you can actually hear the audience laughing. It's a more vivid response," quoted in Robert F. Moss, "Creators on Creating: Woody Allen," *Saturday Review* (November, 1980), 42.

22. *Four Films of Woody Allen*, p. 53.

23. *Four Films of Woody Allen*, p. 105.

Chapter 4

1. Bjorkman, *Woody Allen on Woody Allen*, 101. See also 95 for Allen's distinction between comedy and drama.

2. See, for example, Vernon Young, "Autumn Interiors," *Commentary* (January, 1979), 60–64, especially 64. As Neil Sinyard writes, "*Interiors* seemed to many American critics a perverse denial by Allen of his unique

comic gifts in favor of humorless pretentiousness" (*The Films of Woody Allen* [Lincoln, Neb.: Bison Books, 1987], 50).

3. Bjorkman, *Woody Allen on Woody Allen*, 95. See also Eric Lax, "Woody Allen—Not Only a Comic," *New York Times* (February 24, 1985).

4. Bjorkman, *Woody Allen on Woody Allen*, 95.

5. When Bjorkman observes to Allen that the images at the beginning of *Interiors* are like still-life pictures, Allen agrees: "I wanted to set a certain rhythm at the beginning" (Bjorkman, *Woody Allen on Woody Allen*, 96).

6. This is how Allen describes an episode he heard about where a husband did this very thing—an episode that inspired this scene in *Interiors* (Bjorkman, *Woody Allen on Woody Allen*, 99).

7. As a character in a Hollywood movie actually does in Allen's later *Purple Rose of Cairo*.

8. Maurice Yacowar points out that "in her first appearance, Pearl is shown from the waist up, as if to emphasize her bosom, her maternal softness and abundance" (*Loser Take All: The Comic Art of Woody Allen*, 188).

9. Pogel, correctly I believe, understands the camera's lingering on Flyn's tears to suggest "a genuine grief at her mother's death, a display of emotion that makes her appear less beautiful in the conventional sense" (*Woody Allen*, 113; see also Yacowar, *Loser Take All*, 192 and 196).

10. Pauline Kael, *When the Lights Go Down* (New York: Holt, Rinehart, and Winston, 1980), 440.

11. Vernon Young, "Autumn Interiors," 61.

12. Kael, *When the Lights Go Down*, 438 and 440.

13. Yacowar is a refreshing exception. See his sensitive analysis of *Interiors* in *Loser Take All* (186–96).

14. Bjorkman, *Woody Allen on Woody Allen*, 100–01.

15. Pogel, *Woody Allen*, 103. Diane Jacobs, similarly, finds a resemblance between Pearl and Miles Monroe in *Sleeper*, who like "the 'alien' [Pearl] comes to energize and threaten a homogeneous society" (. . . *but we need the eggs*, 123). And McCann claims that Pearl, the only Jewish character in the *Interiors*, "enters into the Gentile family causing the same kind of cultural discomfort that Alvy Singer brought to the Halls' dinner table" (*Woody Allen* [Cambridge: Polity Press, 1990], 115. See also Yacowar, *Loser Take All*, 191).

16. Jacobs, . . . *but we need the eggs*," 123.

17. Pogel, *Woody Allen*, 115 and 107.

18. Pogel, *Woody Allen*, 106–07. See also Jacobs, . . . *but we need the eggs*, 124. Allen, in contrast, calls Pearl "a vulgarian in the best sense" (Bjorkman, *Woody Allen on Woody Allen*, 101). For Joey and these critics, there is no good sense in which one can be a vulgarian.

19. Bjorkman, *Woody Allen on Woody Allen*, 98; see also 100.

20. For an excellent analysis of the camera shots in the scene in Renata's study where she tries to create, see Yacowar, *Loser Take All*, 193–94.

21. Bjorkman, *Woody Allen on Woody Allen*, 96.

22. Critics have noted the similarities between Allen's *Interiors* and European films, especially Bergman's, but they have also claimed that there is something distinctively Woody Allen about *Interiors*. Nancy Pogel, for example, points to *Interiors'* debt to Bergman, especially to *Cries and Whispers*, but claims that *Interiors* is nevertheless "made in Allen's own idiom" (*Woody Allen*, 99). What they sense, I suspect, has much to do with the presence of Pearl in the movie and the comic elements I have pointed out. See Jacobs, . . . *but we need the eggs*, 125.

23. Some critics find little comedy in *Interiors*. Diane Jacobs writes of the "uninterrupted seriousness" of *Interiors* (. . . *but we need the eggs*, 117). David Denby believes that "the gloominess never lets up" ("Kvetches and Whispers," *New York* [August 14, 1978], 61; see also McCann, *Woody Allen*, 113). An exception to those critics who see only gloom in *Interiors* is Neil Sinyard, who says that the film's seriousness "should not imply that the film is devoid of light, humor or irony." He "senses a delicate satire on artistic people who live their lives too intensely, particularly in an arty conversation over the dinner table about a recent evening in the theater" (*The Films of Woody Allen*, 52). And there is Penelope Gilliatt, who recognizes *Interiors* as "a serious film rooted in the temperament of someone funny" ("The Current Cinema," *The New Yorker* [August 7, 1978], 76). Critics who see *Interiors* as humorless may be making too simple a distinction between the comic and the serious, encouraged no doubt by Allen himself, who emphasizes that with *Interiors* he is attempting a different kind of movie, something serious rather than comic.

Chapter 5

1. Kael, "The Frog Who Turned into a Prince," 184. See also David Denby, "Woody's Poison-Pen Letter," 61–62.

2. Bjorkman, *Woody Allen on Woody Allen*, 122. Does Allen here assume another stereotype—that education makes people soft, that an educated man cannot be tough? Or is Allen being playful?

3. Bjorkman, *Woody Allen on Woody Allen*, 86 and 122.

4. See Michael Dunne, "*Stardust Memories, The Purple Rose of Cairo*, and the Tradition of Metafiction," *Film Criticism* 12, no. 1 (Fall, 1987): 22.

5. Kael, "The Frog Who Turned into a Prince," 184. See also Diane Jacobs, "Ineffable Dreams," *Horizon* (December, 1980), 70.

6. Vincent Canby points also to similarities between *Stardust Memories* and *La Dolce Vita* ("The Humor, Hostility, and Mystery of Woody Allen," *The New York Times* [September 28, 1980], 21).

7. The first parallel, although not the second, is often noted. See, for

example, Pogel, who gives a detailed comparison of Allen's movie and Fellini's, (*Woody Allen*, 133–49). While Pogel's analysis is sensitive and helpful, she concludes that the vision of life in Allen's movie is more ambiguous and less hopeful than in Fellini's. I believe that the opposite is the case. See also Robert Stam, *Reflexivity in Film and Literature* (Ann Arbor: UMI Research Press, 1985), 155–59, and Diane Jacobs, . . . *but we need the eggs*, 149–50. For another comparison of Allen and Fellini, see Mark Siegal, "Ozymandias Melancholy: The Nature of Parody in *Stardust Memories*," *Literature/Film Quarterly* 13, no. 2 (1985): 77–84. Siegal's conclusions are closer to my own.

8. Sandy did perform magic as a child, moreover, but he knows it was a "trick." His mother reveals that he practiced in his room for hours.

9. In Allen's later movie *Alice*, the heroine does fly over Manhattan, as Guido does over Rome, but in spite of the pleasure of her magic moments, Alice finally chooses not to control her fate by magic.

10. Canby, "The Humor, Hostility, and Mystery of Woody Allen," 38.

11. Curiously enough, Sandy himself in *Stardust Memories* praises the *Bicycle Thief* in terms similar to those in which Eve's daughters praised the play they saw with Pearl. But Sandy has no Pearl to mock his "profound" and "wonderful ambiguities." Presumably Allen finds a way to let the movie as a whole play the role of Pearl.

12. Ted Perry, *Filmguide to "8½"* (Bloomington: Indiana University Press, 1975), 64–66.

13. Pogel, *Woody Allen*, 140.

14. This scene from Sandy's movie is a version of one of Allen's sketches from *Side Effects*, "The Lunatic's Tale." So too the surgeon in that tale, after many nights "ponder[ing] the aesthetics of perfection," performs such operations on two women "in search of a fulfilling love" (Woody Allen, *Side Effects*, 104).

15. See Woody Allen, "My Apology," *Side Effects*, 47–57, in which Allen mockingly casts himself in the role of Socrates awaiting execution. Two young men, Agathon and Simmias, characters out of Platonic dialogues, come to tell Allen that he will be forced to drink hemlock. In *Zelig*, Saul Bellow comments of Zelig that he "touched a nerve in people. Perhaps in a way which they would prefer not to be touched."

16. Allen, *Side Effects*, 13.

17. Jacobs, . . . *but we need the eggs*, 152.

18. Lee argues that Sandy's new ending is simply Jazz Heaven in another guise, and that Sandy's offering it means that he has sold out to the producers. He thus understands Sandy Bates as a study in inauthenticity. See *Woody Allen's Angst*, 118 and 128, and 112–29. "As Allen presents him, Bates is the most despicable character in any of his films to date" (129).

19. In one of his fantasies in *8½*, Guido when troubled by questions

from his fans and reporters crawls under a table and shoots himself. Not even in a fantasy do we ever see Sandy consider suicide. And in spite of the fact that he is, as Allen says, experiencing some kind of nervous breakdown (Bjorkman, *Woody Allen on Woody Allen*, 121), he does not have to go, as does Dorrie (and also Guido in *8½*) to a sanitarium. Sandy suggests that he and Dorrie come from different worlds when, after hearing of her mother's schizophrenia and depression, he remarks that "in my family nobody ever committed suicide . . . this was just not a middle-class alternative, you know. . . . My mother was too busy running the boiled chicken through the deflavorizing machine to think about shooting herself or anything."

20. Allen, "My Apology," *Side Effects*, 56–57.

21. Critics who see in *Stardust Memories* Allen's hatred of his fans and respond with indignation should ponder Allen's words to Natalie Gittelson: "Audiences know I won't insult them. I may strike out—and I often do—but it won't be demeaning; they aren't going to have to sit through a lot of stupid, infantile jokes" ("The Maturing of Woody Allen," *The New York Times Magazine* [April 22, 1979], Sec. 6, 102).

22. Unless, of course, it is Allen himself. See Michael Dunne, "Metaleptical Hijinks in Woody Allen's *Stardust Memories*," *Literature/Film Quarterly* 19, no. 2 (1991): 118.

23. Pogel, *Woody Allen*, 148, 149, and 146. Pogel's view is shared by Michael Dunne, who argues that the series of endings of *Stardust Memories* disappoint the plausible expectations of the audience. One conclusion after another is "deconstructed." Allen thus offers "an aesthetic experience suited to a postmodern hypermediated audience" ("Metaleptical Hijinks," 117–18).

Chapter 6

1. My emphasis on the connections between Allen's movie and Shakespeare's *Midsummer Night's Dream* in this chapter is not meant to deny the extent to which *Sex Comedy* also "replays" scenes from other movies, especially Bergman's *Smiles* as well as several films by Jean Renoir. Nancy Pogel points out interesting parallels between *Sex Comedy* and Renoir's films (*Woody Allen*, 159–61). Nevertheless, Allen's title as well as parallels in plot justify my emphasis.

2. Lee argues that Leopold is modeled on analytic philosopher Bertrand Russell (*Woody Allen's Angst*, 130–31).

3. See Maurice Yacowar's interesting discussion of Allen's technique in this movie of holding the camera stationary so that "action and speech flow beyond the frame." This, according to Yacowar, "prepares for the

miracles later," inasmuch as it suggests that "life continues beyond what any particular sense may convey" ("Beyond Parody: Woody Allen in the 80s," *Post Script* [Winter, 1987], 33).

4. Pogel, *Woody Allen*, 156.

5. Andrew does claim to "help people with their investments until there is nothing left." Commenting on this line, Yacowar observes that Andrew is "anti-materialist even in his profession of stock-broker" ("Beyond Parody," 33).

6. By showing us Andrew leaving Adrian asleep as he goes off to pursue Ariel in the woods, Allen recalls Lysander's leaving Hermia asleep as he goes off to pursue Helena in the woods.

7. It is curious that Pauline Kael sees nothing more in this movie than "a belief in frolicking, happy sex." She therefore reproaches Allen for a message hardly needed today, when "newly discovered infections are giving [promiscuity] a bad name all over again" (*Taking It All In* [New York: Holt, Rinehart, and Winston, 1984], 368). Similarly, Richard A. Blake states with no evidence that Maxwell "will undoubtedly wander off to some other woman," (*Woody Allen: Profane and Sacred* [Lanham, Md.: Scarecrow Press, 1995], 94; see also Lee, *Woody Allen's Angst*, 139).

8. Pogel, *Woody Allen*, 159–60.

9. Pogel also points out parallels between the plot of *Sex Comedy* and another of Renoir's movies, *A Day in the Country*. In this movie, its heroine, Anatole, escapes from an unhappy marriage to relive a past moment with a young adventurer by the river. But her moment is short-lived, and she returns to her husband (*Woody Allen*, 160). Renoir's movie, Pogel writes, "like Allen's, deals with the freedom associated with nature as opposed to the restrictions of sophisticated daily life" (160). Pogel, again, fails to distinguish Anatole's return to an unhappy marriage from Andrew's return to a spouse he loves.

10. Lee emphasizes Andrew's reconciliation with Adrian, but sees it in the same hedonistic terms as Leopold's lust for Dulcy. Allen, he argues, is critical of such hedonism (inasmuch as it lacks the authentic moral commitment that characters in other Allen movies demonstrate). But since the defects of their reconciliation are not obvious to most of Allen's viewers *Sex Comedy* is a failure (*Woody Allen's Angst*, 142).

11. Sinyard, *The Films of Woody Allen*, 67.

12. Pogel notes the connection between Allen's movie and Andrew's spirit ball, which she sees as "the prototype of a moving picture projector" (*Woody Allen*, 162). But she thinks that the two function in the same way. *Sex Comedy*, she observes, "offers a release from time, and a celebration of filmmaking—in the natural immortality finally granted Leopold through the lens of Andrew's spirit ball, or prototype projector" (155). That she sees no essential difference between Andrew's spirit ball and Allen's

movie camera is not surprising, given her views of his "inconclusive text[s]," and her interpretation of *Sex Comedy* as "a postmodern commentary on classical resolutions and unitary world views" (155). I argue, in contrast, that Allen is equally critical of postmodern "irresolution" and "fragmented" world views (see Pogel, 169).

Chapter 7

1. Bjorkman, *Woody Allen on Woody Allen*, 136.

2. Girgus, *The Films of Woody Allen*, 74.

3. Bjorkman, *Woody Allen on Woody Allen*, 136.

4. The term "other-directed" was popularized by David Riesman in *The Lonely Crowd*. Allan Bloom, for example, interprets Zelig as simply "other directed" in Riesman's sense (*The Closing of the American Mind*, 144–46).

5. These are the comments of Saul Bellow in the movie. See also Bjorkman, *Woody Allen on Woody Allen*, 141.

6. Saul Bellow, the novelist, and Bruno Bettelheim, who speaks in support of a "strong personal relation" between psychiatrist and patient, in contrast do.

7. So too might disciples of Lacan. See Richard Feldstein, who argues that in *Zelig*, Woody Allen "takes a Lacanian perspective" ("The Dissolution of the Self in *Zelig*," *Literature/Film Quarterly* 13, no. 2 [1985]: 156).

8. Ruth Perlmutter, "*Zelig* According to Bakhtin," *Quarterly Review of Film and Video* 12, nos. 1–2 (1990): 38.

9. Sontag, *Against Interpretation*, 5.

10. Girgus, *The Films of Woody Allen*, 76. See also McCann, *Woody Allen*, 181–83.

11. *Woody Allen*, 171, 177, and 175.

12. Girgus, *The Films of Woody Allen*, 74. It says something about Girgus's own assumptions rather than about Allen's movie that he prefaces this statement with "of course." See also Blake, *Woody Allen: Profane and Sacred*, 109.

13. Girgus, *The Films of Woody Allen*, 75. Similarly, Daniel Green claims that *Zelig* explores "the supposed distinction between subject and medium," and "indicate[s] the extent to which the former is a function of the latter" ("The Comedian's Dilemma: Woody Allen's 'Serious' Comedy," *Literature/Film Quarterly* 19, no. 2 [1991]: 74).

14. While critics such as Girgus and Pogel praise Allen for such "deconstructive" moviemaking, others criticize Allen for not going far enough in this direction. Richard Combs, for example, notes that the structure of *Zelig* suggests "an infinite hall of mirrors" but "Allen soon closes off this

perspective by displaying little interest in the structural conundrum" ("Chameleon Days: Reflections on Non-Being," *Monthly Film Bulletin* [London], [November, 1983], 294).

15. Pogel points out that *geist*, Martin Geist's surname, is the Yiddish and German word for "ghost" (*Woody Allen*, 172). It is also the German word for "spirit," as in Hegel's *Phenomenology of the Spirit*. Perhaps only by chance is Geist's given name the same as that of Heidegger, a German philosopher who in his practical politics allied himself with the Nazis. Does Heidegger, through his understanding of authenticity, offer support for Zelig's growth and self-discovery, or does even this philosopher of the authentic self offer no ground that counters Nazism?

16. Girgus, for example, thinks that "Allen uses [these intellectuals] to deliver the social message of *Zelig*" (*The Films of Woody Allen*, 73). As I interpret *Zelig*, there is a sense in which Girgus is correct: by their deeds, not their words, the intellectuals deliver Allen's message.

17. Bjorkman, *Woody Allen on Woody Allen*, 179. See also 43.

Chapter 8

1. Richard Schickel, "Now Playing at the Jewel," *Time* (March 4, 1985), 78.

2. It is this remarkable fact that leads Arnold W. Preussner to compare Allen's *Purple Rose* to an Aristophanean comedy, which according to Northrop Frye is one of the four genres of comedy. In this genre, the action of the play is spurred by "a bright idea" that "posits a ludicrous or implausible 'what-if?' situation and then develops the ramifications of that situation to their logical (or illogical) conclusions" ("Woody Allen's *The Purple Rose of Cairo* and the Genres of Comedy," *Literature/Film Quarterly* 16, no. 1 [1988], 40). The "what-if?" question of Allen's movie is "what if a character could come off the screen and take a part in the lives of real characters?"

3. Others have noted this connection between *Purple Rose* and the "Kugelmass Episode." See, for example, Vincent Canby, "Woody Allen Journeys from Page to Screen," *New York Times* (March 17, 1985), 19. Tom Baxter's words in anticipation of his New York City visit with the group he meets in Cairo might also have been uttered by Madame Bovary when she persuades Kugelmass to take her to New York City: "I'm on the verge of a madcap Manhattan weekend." Tom utters these words in his Hollywood script at the first moment he acts outside the script, for he is uttering them when he sees Cecilia in the audience and begins to speak slowly and distractedly. His words apply more appropriately to what takes place in Allen's movie than in the one written by Hollywood. Later in the movie

Tom takes Cecilia for an outing into the Hollywood movie itself, and they frolic around the most swanky Manhattan nightclubs on the silver screen. He is thus on "the verge of a madcap weekend," not with the characters in the Hollywood movie but with Cecilia. Time after time, characters speak lines that are more relevant to a larger context than the movie within which they are uttered. Their speech thus opens them to an expanding world of which they later become aware.

4. See, for example, the sequence of Sandy's questions to the superintelligent beings in *Stardust Memories*, as well as Mickey Sachs's questions in *Hannah and Her Sisters* (New York: Random House, 1987), 133. See also Allen's comments about *Crimes and Misdemeanors*, in Bjorkman, *Woody Allen on Woody Allen*, 220.

5. Girgus, in contrast, thinks that the analogy holds. For his different interpretation, see *The Films of Woody Allen*, 86.

6. Quoted in Eric Lax, "Woody Allen—Not Only a Comic" (24). See also Bjorkman, *Woody Allen on Woody Allen*, 148.

7. My sense of the movie's ending is shared by Douglas G. Stenberg, who supposes that Cecilia "radiates the 'magical glow' at the end of the film which she had perceived as the best quality in the soon to be forgotten actor" ("Common Themes in Gogol's 'Nos' and Woody Allen's *The Purple Rose of Cairo*," *Literature/Film Quarterly* 19, no. 2 [1991]: 112).

8. Quoted by Caryn James, "Auteur, Auteur," *New York Times Magazine* (January 19, 1986), Sec. C, 27. "To hear [Allen] tell it," James observes, "his films gain their rich ambiguity in spite of him" (27).

9. Allen, *God*, in *Without Feathers*, 161–62.

10. To the extent that Gil exists only in the roles he plays, the dilemma of these characters resembles that faced by Gil himself. If his acting career were ruined by Tom's exit, and the projector turned off on him too, he too would become nothing.

11. Critics are impressed with the black humor of this joke on the film's characters, which, in Girgus's words, "cuts like a knife" (*The Films of Woody Allen*," 86).

Chapter 9

1. Bjorkman, *Woody Allen on Woody Allen*, 190.

2. In that movie a daughter eavesdrops on a woman's describing her dream man to her therapist and gives the information to her divorced father.

3. Bjorkman, *Woody Allen on Woody Allen*, 190.

4. Bjorkman, *Woody Allen on Woody Allen*, 195.

5. See Lee's discussion of Marion's relation to Heidegger's thought, *Woody Allen's Angst*, 237–38.

6. See Lee, *Woody Allen's Angst*, p. 245, and Yacowar, *Loser Take All*, 269.

7. See Allen's account of how in this literal sense as well Hope leads Marion to where she discovers things about herself (Bjorkman, *Woody Allen on Woody Allen*, 196).

8. Bjorkman, *Woody Allen on Woody Allen*, 200.

9. Roger Ebert, "Another Woman," *Go Ebert*, compuserve.

10. Bjorkman, *Woody Allen on Woody Allen*, 197.

11. Ebert, "Another Woman."

12. This is Lee's interesting suggestion (*Woody Allen's Angst*, 236). Lee also draws a parallel to *Manhattan*, where the film may be the novel Isaac Davis begins to write during the voice-over in the prologue. If Lee is correct, both Isaac's novel about Manhattan and Marion's autobiographical narrative move beyond *Annie Hall*, where Alvy Singer's play about his relationship with Annie ends in fantasy. Both Isaac's novel and Marion's book merge into Allen's movie, whereas Alvy's play does not, at the same time they are less escapist. They do not require correction by Allen himself.

13. Bjorkman, *Woody Allen on Woody Allen*, 197.

Chapter 10

1. For an interesting and sensitive analysis of the ways in which Allen verges away from Dostoyevsky toward Machiavelli in *Crimes and Misdemeanors*, see Peter Minowitz, "Crimes and Controversies: Nihilism from Machiavelli to Woody Allen," *Literature/Film Quarterly* 19 (1991): 77–88.

2. David Denby, "Beyond Good and Evil," *New York* (October 23, 1989), 128. See also Pauline Kael, "Floating," *The New Yorker* (October 30, 1989), 78.

3. James Nuechterlein, "Godless and Guiltless, A Disorderly Cosmos," *New York Times* (October 15, 1989), Sec. 2, 15. Even more extreme is the view of Leon Wieseltier: "not a frame fails to degrade, to debase, and to demean something precious" (Wieseltier, "Browbeaten," *The New Republic* [November 27, 1989], 43). Minowitz's study provides a more balanced analysis of *Crimes and Misdemeanors* that points to ways in which the movie "may diffuse its nihilistic message" (Minowitz, "Crimes and Controversies," 77). See also Lee's treatment, which presents the film as an affirmation of an existential moral stance (*Woody Allen's Angst*, 255–89). Another thought-provoking study of *Crimes and Misdemeanors* is that of M. W. Roche, "Justice and the Withdrawal of God in Woody Allen's *Crimes and*

Misdemeanors," The Journal of Value Inquiry 29, no. 4 (December, 1995): 547–63.

4. Richard Combs, "Woody's Wars: *Crimes and Misdemeanors," Sight and Sound* (Summer, 1990), 207.

5. Denby calls the movie *"serioso* with laughs" ("Beyond Good and Evil," 124).

6. Hilary Mantel, *The Spectator* (August 4, 1990), 39–40.

7. Denby, "Beyond Good and Evil," 124–26.

8. Schickel, *Time*, 82. Schickel thus sees a parallel between God's blindness and the rabbi's. See also Stephen J. Spignesi, *The Woody Allen Companion* (Kansas City: Andrew and McMeel, 1991), 214. Since the rabbi is blind to the fact that Judah has committed murder, Roche observes, as "a representative of religion, he seems to symbolize God's lack of vision or inability to offer a strong and effective moral code" ("Justice and the Withdrawal of God in Woody Allen's *Crimes and Misdemeanors*," 550).

9. Girgus, *The Films of Woody Allen*, 117 and 116. See also Denby, "Beyond Good and Evil," 124.

10. Roche, "Justice and the Withdrawal of God in Woody Allen's *Crimes and Misdemeanors*," 551. Consider also Shakespeare's *A Winter's Tale* and the appearance of Time as a character between its tragic and comic halves (IV. i).

11. That the blind rabbi dances with his daughter at her wedding to "I'll Be Seeing You," according to Wieseltier, only further insults the rabbi's faith ("Browbeaten," 43).

12. Or even Cliff, for that matter. See, for example, Wieseltier's comments about *Crimes and Misdemeanors*: "Allen is Cliff, and he has never treated himself with more solemnity. His integrity is boundless" ("Browbeaten," 43). Wieseltier sees in Cliff the flaws Allen mocks in Lester. But if he laughs at them in Lester, is he not laughing at them in Cliff as well? When critics compare Allen with any of his characters, we might suppose him saying to them what Halley says to Cliff when he thinks she has become engaged to "a creep": "Give me a little credit, will you?" For someone who gives Allen credit on this very issue, see Richard Allen, "Crimes and Misdemeanors," *Cineaste* 17 (1990): 44, and Minowitz, "Crimes and Controversies," 83–85.

13. In a similar view, Lee points out, Lester's comedy mocks the suffering of others, whereas the laughter Allen evokes for his own personas is one that shares in their suffering. Thus "Allen's humor (unlike Lester's) is not meant to distance us, but to bring us closer to our own pain and lead us to think seriously about meaning in our lives" (*Woody Allen's Angst*, 273).

14. See, for example, Mary Erler, "Morality? Don't Ask," *New York Times* (October 15, 1989), 16.

15. Later, Judah's family give him an exercise machine for his birthday. A member of his family repeats Dolores's line, "you're in great shape," and Judah repeats his words to her, "for a man my age." But this time no one repeats Dolores's denial. Instead, the phone rings, and it is Dolores demanding he see her at once. Time presses.

16. Dolores does give Judah his favorite, Schubert, for his birthday, and he returns the favor by sending her not the flowers the assassin uses as his disguise but death itself.

17. As Girgus puts it, "what follows amounts to a metacommentary on the film" (*The Film of Woody Allen*, 126).

18. Roche, "Justice and God's Withdrawal in Woody Allen's *Crimes and Misdemeanors*," 548.

19. Girgus, in contrast, supposes that the exchange between Judah and Cliff shows Judah to be "more insightful," for he can conceive "the idea of a villain who benefits from his evil and accommodates himself to his own duplicity." Judah is therefore correct, according to Girgus, to see Cliff's proposal as a naively happy ending (*The Films of Woody Allen*, 126–27). It is not exactly a "happy" ending, however, if our "worst beliefs are realized."

20. Roche believes that as Judah tells the tale of murder, he "grimaces, reliving the pain of his guilt; the effect of his facial expressions is accentuated by an exceedingly long close-up" ("Justice and God's Withdrawal in Woody Allen's *Crimes and Misdemeanors*," 555).

21. Lee, *Woody Allen's Angst*, 287.

22. While Maurice Yacowar also notes the parallel between Judah and the Ancient Mariner, he argues that by converting the events of his life into a story, "Judah manages an easy 'confession' without the costs of confessing" (*Loser Take All*, 276–77). That is, Yacowar sees in this last scene only that Judah is like the murderer of his story—whose life returns to normal and who is scot-free. In this scene, according to Yacowar, Judah does not reveal the burden that he carries but rather unburdens himself (277). But is there any reason to suppose this "unburdening" is a one-time affair? As Lee speculates, moreover, it would not be impossible for someone to connect the story with Judah's own life, and the details would be easy enough to check. While Cliff may not make the connection, "there is no reason to suppose that Judah won't repeat this incident again and again, retelling strangers his murder plot every time he's had too much to drink, until eventually he's taken seriously" (*Woody Allen's Angst*, 287).

23. Lee points out a similarity between Judah and Marion in *Another Woman*: for Judah "is trapped in a loveless marriage to a person who, like Ken, doesn't realize how lonely he really is. However, unlike Marion, he is doomed to remain trapped for a lifetime" (*Woody Allen's Angst*, 288).

24. Girgus, *The Films of Woody Allen*, 127.

25. Here Levy echoes Freud in *Civilization and Its Discontents*, 25.

26. One should not confuse the two. See Richard Allen's paraphrase of Levy's statement, "it is only we who bring meaning to an essentially hostile universe" ("Crimes and Misdemeanors," 44).

27. Lee, *Woody Allen's Angst*, 287–89.

28. Lee, *Woody Allen's Angst*, 289. See the interesting exchange Lee recounts between himself and Mark Roche on this issue (363–64).

29. *God*, in *Without Feathers*, 184 and 154.

30. These alternatives are formulated in this way by Mary Erler in "Morality? Don't Ask," 16.

31. It was Ecclesiastes itself that speaks of rain falling on good and wicked alike (Eugene B. Borowitz, "Heeding Ecclesiastes, At Long Last," *The New York Times* (October 15, 1989), 16).

32. Richard Combs also notes that "all the play on eyes . . . seems like the kind of pseudo-profound motif one might find in one of Lester's shows," but it is not clear whether he thinks this is intentional on Allen's part ("Woody's Wars," 207–08).

Chapter 11

1. Bjorkman, *Woody Allen on Woody Allen*, 192 and 255.

2. See, for example, James M. Welsh, "*Manhattan Murder Mystery*," *Films in Review* (1993), 413, and Janet Maslin, "Allen and Keaton, Together Again and Dizzy as Ever," *New York Times* (August 18, 1993), C13.

3. Arthur Conan Doyle, "Scandal in Bohemia," *The Complete Adventures of Sherlock Holmes* (Garden City: N.Y: Doubleday, 1930), 161.

4. While Lee agrees that there is more to this movie than mere entertainment, he interprets its message in a much more pessimistic vein than I do: "romantic relationships are always battlegrounds for dominance. As such, they are always grounded in self-deception and a sense of despair." The movie thus resembles "Allen's most recent and depressing films" (*Woody Allen's Angst*, 336, 342, and 346).

5. While the English professor in "The Kugelmass Episode," clearly takes into account *Madame Bovary*'s ending, he supposes he can avoid it. He insists that the magician transport him into the novel before page 120, Woody Allen ("The Kugelmass Episode," *Side Effects*, 68).

6. Bjorkman, *Woody Allen on Woody Allen*, 259.

7. "Play It Again, Woody," *Newsweek* (August 30, 1993), 43.

8. See Christopher Bray, "Woody's Genuine Froth," *The Times Literary Supplement* (January 28, 1994), 17, and James M. Welsh, "*Manhattan Murder Mystery*," *Films In Review* 44 (1993), 413–14. Welsh points out the parallel scenes. See also Lee, *Woody Allen's Angst*, 343–46.

9. Stam, *Reflexivity in Film and Literature*, 46.

10. Thus, scholars consider detective stories, especially Sherlock Holmes, to have become popular in a Victorian society threatened by social and economic change and thus a sense of a changing and chaotic world. Here, at least, in the detection of crime, is one area where there is a truth, a reality, that human beings can uncover.

Chapter 12

1. Bjorkman, *Woody Allen on Woody Allen*, 90. One wonders whether Allen is speaking tongue in cheek here. After all, he himself could be said to have given girlfriends such as Diane Keaton and Mia Farrow roles in his films, and he admits that he created characters with them in mind. He recounts, for example, how he created the feminine lead in *Broadway Danny Rose* for Mia Farrow after she expressed a desire to play that type of character, see John Lahr, "The Imperfectionist," *The New Yorker* (December 9, 1996), 76. And as for Diane Keaton, Allen explains that he wrote things that gave her an opportunity "to get out and do her thing," quoted in Lahr, 76. On the other hand, is there no difference between "people putting their girlfriends in films" such as *What's New Pussycat?* and Woody Allen's doing so in films such as *Purple Rose* and *Manhattan*? Allen may have created roles for Keaton, but he did so because he "felt [he] had a lot to learn from her," quoted in Lahr, 76. And then Allen creates parts for women other than his girlfriends. Dianne Wiest recounts that she asked Allen to create a role for her, but when she saw the script of *Bullets* she thought that Helen Sinclair could not have been written with her in mind. But play her she did: no director other than Allen, she acknowledges "has demanded of me things that I was absolutely certain that I could not do," quoted in Lahr, 76. Wiest won an Oscar for the best supporting actress for this role. Allen has indeed created roles for women in his movies, imitating the corrupt ways of the world in order to produce a work of artistic integrity.

2. Bjorkman, *Woody Allen on Woody Allen*, 10.

3. Janet Maslin, "Allen's Ode to Theater and, as Always, New York," *New York Times* (September 30, 1994), C1. Similarly, David Ansen calls Cheech Allen's "surprising trump card" (*Newsweek*, October 24, 1994).

4. Roger Ebert, "Bullets over Broadway," *Go Ebert*, compuserve.

5. Janet Maslin, "Allen's Ode to Theater and, as Always, New York," C1.

6. Bjorkman, *Woody Allen on Woody Allen*, 98 and 241. See also Caryn James, who quotes Allen's account of how his filmscript is "constantly changing" during production because of the freedom he allows his actors

and actresses to ad-lib: "I'm always telling actors, 'You can use your own words as long as you play the correct thing' " ("Auteur, Auteur," 128).

7. It is a great finish that Allen himself used for *Hannah and Her Sisters*, when one of Hannah's sisters, who is married in the movie to the character played by Allen, announces that she is pregnant.

Chapter 13

1. Anthony Lake, "Scarlet Woman," *The New Yorker* (October 30, 1995), 112–14.

2. Jean-Jacques Rousseau, *Emile*, trans, Allan Bloom (New York: Basic Books, 1979), 55.

Chapter 14

1. Jose Ortega y Gasset, *Meditations on Quixote*, trans. Evelyn Rugg and Diego Marin (New York: W. W. Norton and Company, 1961), 156 and 158.

2. See also Henri Bergson, "Laughter," in *Comedy*, ed. Wylie Sypher (Garden City, NY: Doubleday, 1956), 59–190.

3. Quoted by Frank Rich, "An Interview with Woody," *Time* (April 30, 1979), 69.

4. Natalie Gittelson, "The Maturing of Woody Allen," *New York Times Magazine* (April 22, 1979), 102.

5. Lloyd Rose, "Humor and Nothingness," *Atlantic* (May 1985), 96.

6. Quoted in Lahr, "The Imperfectionist," 71.

7. Bjorkman, *Woody Allen on Woody Allen*, 22 and 75.

8. As Allen said, his tales as a stand-up comic "were all reasonably funny because I had spent a lot of time getting the most out of them," quoted by Caryn James ("Auteur, Auteur," 25).

9. This, at any rate, was the accusation of her husband.

10. Bjorkman, *Woody Allen on Woody Allen*, 213.

11. Bjorkman, *Woody Allen on Woody Allen*, 242. The clown in *Shadows and Fog* states a version of the view Allen expresses in this interview: "We are not like other people. We are artists. With great talent comes great responsibility."

12. McCann, *Woody Allen*, 209. McCann thus likes Allen's movies for the same reason that Joey likes the play that she and her family discuss in *Interiors*.

13. Pogel, *Woody Allen*, 150.

14. See also Paul Lewis, "Painful Laughter: The Collapse of Humor in

Woody Allen's *Stardust Memories,*" *Studies in American Jewish Literature* 5 (1986): 143.

15. Lloyd Rose, "Humor and Nothingness," 96. As Arthur observed wryly in *Interiors* of his family's praises of "the futility" of a play they had seen, "Passion with pessimism is all the rage nowadays."

16. Girgus, *The Films of Woody Allen*, 77.

17. Bjorkman, *Woody Allen on Woody Allen*, 156.

18. Quoted in James, "Auteur, Auteur," 30.

19. Bjorkman, *Woody Allen on Woody Allen*, 85.

20. Quoted by Gittelson, "The Maturing of Woody Allen," 102.

21. Quoted by James, "Auteur, Auteur," 26.

22. Lee, *Woody Allen's Angst*, 356.

23. See, for example, Soren Kierkegaard, *Philosophical Fragments*, in *Kierkegaard's Writings*, vol. VII, trans. Howard V. Hong and Edna H. Hong (Princeton: Princeton University Press, 1985), 54, and especially 62–63.

24. And that is why he does not face the dilemma of Judah's father Sol, who believes he must choose either God or truth. When Lee presents these as the alternatives that Allen faces, he blurs the distinction between Sartre and Kierkegaard. See, for example, *Woody Allen's Angst*, 267, 274, and 365. In other ways, I agree with Lee that Allen does not follow Kierkegaard's more solitary path, see 307.

Bibliography

Allen, Richard. "Crimes and Misdemeanors." *Cineaste* 17 (1990): 44–46.

Allen, Woody. *Four Films of Woody Allen: Annie Hall, Interiors, Manhattan, Stardust Memories*. New York: Random House, 1997.

———. *Three Films of Woody Allen: Zelig, Broadway Danny Rose, The Purple Rose of Cairo*. New York: Random House, 1987.

———. *Side Effects*. New York: Ballantine Books, 1975.

———. *Without Feathers*. New York: Ballantine Books, 1972.

Ansen, David. "Dying for a Broadway Hit." *Newsweek* (October 24, 1994), 75.

Bakhtin, Mikhail. *The Dialogic Imagination*, ed. Michael Holquist. Austin: University of Texas Press, 1981.

Becker, Ernest. *The Denial of Death*. New York: The Free Press, 1973.

Bergson, Henri. "Laughter." In *Comedy*, ed. Wylie Sypher. Garden City, N.Y.: Doubleday, 1956.

Bernard, Jami. "Woody's Dirty Harry." *Daily News* (December 12, 1997), 69.

Bjorkman, Stig. *Woody Allen on Woody Allen*. London: Faber and Faber, 1994.

Blake, Richard A. *Woody Allen: Profane and Sacred*. Lanham, Md.: Scarecrow Press, 1995.

———. "Women's Wear." *America* (December 17, 1988), 517 and 526.

Bloom, Allan. *The Closing of the American Mind*. New York: Basic Books, 1987.

———. "Interpretive Essay," to *The Republic of Plato*, trans. with notes and interpretive essay by Allan Bloom. New York: Basic Books, 1968.

Borowitz, Eugene B. "Heeding Ecclesiastes, At Long Last." *The New York Times* (October 15, 1989), 16.

Bray, Christopher. "Woody's Genuine Froth." *The Times Literary Supplement* (January 28, 1994), 17.

Brodie, Douglas. *The Films of Woody Allen: Revised and Updated*. Secaucus, N.J.: Citadel, 1991.

Canby, Vincent. "Woody Allen Journeys from Page to Screen." *New York Times* (March 17, 1985), 19–20.

———. "The Humor, Hostility, and Mystery of Woody Allen." *New York Times* (September 28, 1980), 21 and 39.

Combs, Richard. "Woody's Wars: *Crimes and Misdemeanors*." *Sight and Sound* (Summer, 1990), 207–8.

———. "Chameleon Days: Reflections on Non-Being. *Monthly Film Bulletin* (London) (November, 1983), 295–96.

———. "Zelig." *Monthly Film Bulletin* (London) (November, 1983), 294.

Denby, David. "Woody's Poison-Pen Letter," *New York* (October 13, 1990), 61–63.

———. "Beyond Good and Evil." *New York* (October 23, 1989), 124–28.

Dowd, Maureen. "Grow Up, Harry." *New York Times* (January 11, 1998), 9.

Doyle, Arthur Conan. "Scandal in Bohemia." In *The Complete Adventures of Sherlock Holmes*. Garden City: N.Y.: Doubleday, 1930.

Dunne, Michael. "*Stardust Memories, The Purple Rose of Cairo*, and the Tradition of Metafiction." *Film Criticism* 12, no. 1 (Fall, 1987): 19–27.

Ebert, Roger. "Another Woman," *Go Ebert*, compuserve.

———. "Bullets over Broadway," *Go Ebert*, compuserve.

Erler, Mary. "Morality? Don't Ask." *New York Times* (October 15, 1989), Sec. 2, 16.

Feldstein, Richard. "The Dissolution of the Self in *Zelig*." *Literature/Film Quarterly* 13, no. 3 (1985): 155–60.

Fox, Julian. *Woody Movies from Manhattan*. Woodstock, N.Y.: The Overlook Press, 1996.

Freud, Sigmund. *Civilization and Its Discontents*, trans. James Stachey. New York: W. W. Norton & Company, 1961.

Gilliatt, Penelope. "Woody Reverberant." *The New Yorker* (August 7, 1978), 76–78.

Girgus, Sam B. *The Films of Woody Allen*. Cambridge: Cambridge University Press, 1993.

Gittleson, Natalie. "The Maturing of Woody Allen." *New York Times Magazine* (April 22, 1979), 30–37 and 102–7.

Green, Daniel. "The Comedian's Dilemma: Woody Allen's 'Serious' Comedy." *Literature/Film Quarterly* 19, no. 2 (1991): 70–76.

Halberstadt, Ira. "Scenes from a Mind." *Take One* (November, 1978), 16–20.

Howe, Desson. "Deconstructing Woody." *The Washington Post* (December 27, 1998), D1.

Jacobs, Diane. . . . *but we need the eggs: The Magic of Woody Allen*. New York: St. Martin's Press, 1982.

———. "Ineffable Dreams." *Horizon* (December, 1980), 70-72.

James, Caryn. "Auteur, Auteur." *New York Times Magazine* (January 19, 1986), C, 18–30.

Kael, Pauline. "Floating." *The New Yorker* (October 30, 1989), 74–78.

———. "What's Wrong with This Picture?" *The New Yorker* (October 3, 1988), 81–83.

———. *Taking It All In*. New York: Holt, Rinehart, and Winston, 1984.

———. "The Frog Who Turned into a Prince." *New Yorker* (October 27, 1980), 178–90.

———. *When the Lights Go Down*. New York: Holt, Rinehart, and Winston, 1980.

Kierkegaard, Soren. *Philosophical Fragments*, in *Kierkegaard's Writings* VII, trans. Howard V. Hong and Edna H. Hong. Princeton: Princeton University Press, 1985.

Laertius, Diogenes. *Lives of Eminent Philosophers* I, trans. R. D. Hicks. Cambridge: Harvard University Press, 1966.

Lahr, John. "The Imperfectionist." *The New Yorker* (December 9, 1996), 68–83.

Lake, Anthony. "Scarlet Woman." *The New Yorker* (October 30, 1995), 112–14.

Lax, Eric. "Woody Allen—Not Only a Comic." *New York Times* (February 24, 1985), 1 and 24.

Lee, Sander H. *Woody Allen's Angst: Philosophical Commentaries on His Serious Films*. Jefferson, N.C.: McFarland and Company, 1997.

Lewis, Paul. "Painful Laughter: The Collapse of Humor in Woody Allen's *Stardust Memories*." *Studies in American Jewish Literature* 5 (1986): 141–50.

Librach, Ronald S. "A Portrait of the Artist as a Neurotic." *The Missouri Review* 9, no. 2 (1986): 164–84.

Mantel, Hilary. "The Wonder of Woody." *The Spectator* (August 4, 1990), 39–40.

Maslin, Janet. "Gleefully Skewering His Own Monsters." *The New York Times* (December 12, 1997), E1 and E24.

———. "Allen's Ode to Theater and, as Always, New York." *New York Times* (September 30, 1994), C1 and C31.

———. "Allen and Keaton, Together Again and Dizzy as Ever." *New York Times* (August 18, 1993), C13 and C18.

Minowitz, Peter. "Crimes and Controversies: Nihilism from Machiavelli to Woody Allen." *Literature/Film Quarterly* 19 (1991): 77–88.

Moss, Robert F. "Creators on Creating: Woody Allen." *Saturday Review* (November, 1980), 40–44.

Nuechterlein, James. "Godless and Guiltless, A Disorderly Cosmos." *New York Times* (October 15, 1989), Sec. 2, 15.

Perry, Ted. *Filmguide to "8½"*. Bloomington: Indiana University Press, 1975.

Pinsker, Sanford. "Woody Allen's Lovably Anxious *Schlemeils.*" *Studies in American Humor* 5 (1986): 177–89.

Podhoretz, John. "Missing Heaven, Making Hell." *The Weekly Standard* (December 17, 1998), 37–39.

Pogel, Nancy. *Woody Allen.* Boston: Twayne Publishers, 1987.

Preussner, Arnold W. "Woody Allen's *The Purple Rose of Cairo* and the Genres of Comedy." *Literature/Film Quarterly* 16, no. 1 (1988): 39–43.

Rich, Frank. "An Interview with Woody." *Time* (April 30, 1979), 68–69.

Roche, M. W. "Justice and the Withdrawal of God in Woody Allen's *Crimes and Misdemeanors.*" *The Journal of Value Inquiry* 29, no. 4 (December, 1995): 547–63.

Rose, Lloyd. "Humor and Nothingness." *Atlantic* (May 1985), 94–96.

Rousseau, Jean-Jacques. *Emile*, trans. Allan Bloom. New York: Basic Books, 1979.

Schickel, Richard. "Now Playing at the Jewel." *Time* (March 4, 1985), 78.

Shales, Tom. "Woody: The First Fifty Years." *Esquire* (April, 1987), 88–95.

Siegal, Mark. "Ozymandias Melancholy: The Nature of Parody in *Stardust Memories.*" *Literature/Film Quarterly* 13, no. 2 (1985): 77–84.

Sinyard, Neil. *The Films of Woody Allen.* Lincoln, Neb: Bison Books, 1987.

Sontag, Susan. *Against Interpretation.* New York: Farrar, Straus & Giroux, 1961.

Spignesi, Stephen J. *The Woody Allen Companion.* Kansas City: Andrews and McMeel, 1991.

Stam, Robert. *Reflexivity in Film and Literature.* Ann Arbor: UMI Research Press, 1985.

Stenberg, Douglas G. "Common Themes in Gogol's 'Nos' and Woody Allen's *The Purple Rose of Cairo. Literature/Film Quarterly* 19, no. 2: 109–13.

Welsh, James M. "*Manhattan Murder Mystery.*" *Films in Review* 44 (1993): 413–14.

Wernblad, Annette. *Brooklyn Is Not Expanding: Woody Allen's Comic Universe.* (Rutherford, N.J.: Farleigh Dickinson University Press, 1992).

Wieseltier, Leon. "Browbeaten." *The New Republic* (November 27, 1989), 43.

Yacowar, Maurice. *Loser Take All: The Comic Art of Woody Allen.* New Expanded Edition. New York: Continuum, 1991.

———. "Beyond Parody: Woody Allen in the 80s." *Post Script* (Winter, 1987), 29–42.

———. "Forms of Coherence in the Woody Allen Comedies." *Wide Angle* 3, no. 2 (1979): 34–41.

Young, Vernon. "Autumn Interiors." *Commentary* (January, 1979), 60–64.

Index

Alice, 231n9

alienation, 15, 37, 40, 41, 43, 45, 51, 69, 81, 141, 213, 217, 219

Allen, Richard, 238nl2, 240n26

Allen, Woody: confusion with his characters, ix-xi, 3, 4, 59, 65–66, 154, 238nl2; film as self-reflective, xiv, 13, 112, 159; on his films, film-making, and art, 6–9, 14–15, 19, 33, 49, 110, 112, 122, 125, 131, 145, 165, 179, 183–84, 211, 217, 225n18, 228n21, 229n6, 232n21, 242n11; private life, ix–xii, 224n8, 241n1

Allen, Woody, writings. *See* "The Condemned"; "Dark Penguin"; *God*; "The Kugelmass Episode"; "Lunatic's Tale"; "My Apology"; "Selections from the Allen Note-books." *See also* art; artist

anhedonia, 15, 33, 34, 36, 39, 48

Annie Hall, 4, 15, 33–48, 49, 50, 55, 63, 64, 69, 70, 112, 153, 212, 213, 216, 217, 237n12

Another Woman, xiv, 5, 13, 15, 131–47, 170, 178, 182, 217, 220, 239n23

Aristophanes, 84, 99, 100, 197, 235n2; *Clouds*, 85, 99, 100, 197

Aristotle, 12, 14, 211; *Poetics*, 12

Armstrong, Louis, 75, 220

art: as creative, 55, 109, 204–7, 226n7; as elevating life, xi, xii–xiv, 13–17, 24, 26–31, 48, 50, 63, 72, 95, 112–13, 122, 127, 128, 147, 121, 160–63, 170, 172, 175–78, 179, 190–93, 196, 208–9, 215–21; as imitation or re-flection, xi, 3–4, 13, 16, 24, 44, 46, 67–69, 83–85, 95–97, 109, 111–13, 127, 149, 174–76, 180, 191, 213; and its relationship to life, xi, 4, 13–17, 21, 24–26, 28, 45–46, 51–52, 58, 62, 66–68, 77, 82, 96, 120–22, 124–25, 132, 146, 147, 159, 162, 166, 167, 170–71, 177, 180–82, 190–93, 204–7, 211–22; responsibility asso-ciated with, 78–79, 96, 181–82, 188–89, 192, 214–15, 242n11. *See also* artist

artist, as interpreter of own work, 4, 7, 17, 59, 65, 220–21

Astaire, Fred, 120, 125, 127

Balzac, Honoré de, 85

Becker, Ernest, 35–37; *Denial of Death*, 35, 48

Bellow, Saul, 5, 100, 105, 231n15, 234n5, 234n6

Bergman, Ingmar, 8, 63, 84, 145, 230n22; *Smiles of a Summer Night*, 84, 94, 232n1

Bergson, Henri, 242n2

Bernard, Jami, 223n4

Bettelheim, Bruno, 100, 108

249

Bjorkman, Stig, 7, 59, 145, 224nn3–4, 224n7, 225nn9–17, 225nn20–22, 225n24, 225n27, 225n28, 225n30, 225n34, 226n1, 227n8, 228n1, 229nn4–6, 229n14, 229nn18–19, 230n21, 230nn2–3, 232n19, 234n1, 234n3, 235n17, 236n44, 236n6, 236n1, 236nn3–4, 237nn7–8, 240n1, 240n6, 241n2, 241n6, 242n7, 242nn10–11, 243n17, 243n19

Blake, Richard, 233n7, 234n12
Bloom, Allan, xii, 224n12, 224n6, 234n4
Blum, John Morton, 107, 108, 111
Bogart, Humphrey, 13, 19, 20, 21, 23, 24–27, 30, 31, 64, 65, 110, 127, 129. *See also Casablanca*
Borowitz, Eugene, 240n31
Bray, Christopher, 240n8
Broadway Danny Rose, 191
Bullets over Broadway, xiv, 5, 13, 16, 179–93, 209, 213–15, 217, 220, 241n1

Canby, Vincent, 69, 230n6, 231n10, 235n3
Casablanca, 9, 10, 13, 19, 20, 23–25, 27–31, 35, 69, 83, 112, 115, 149, 176. *See also* Bogart, Humphrey
Chaplin, Charlie, 8
Civilization and Its Discontents. See Freud, Sigmund
Clouds. See Aristophanes
Coleridge, Samuel Taylor: *The Rime of the Ancient Mariner*, 159
Combs, Richard, 151, 234n14, 238n4, 240n32
comedy, xiv, 3, 8, 14, 16–17, 20, 33–35, 36, 44, 46, 49, 50, 59, 63–64, 65, 72, 80, 83–85, 100, 151, 152–55, 160–62, 165, 181, 183, 195, 197, 198, 203, 205, 207, 209, 211–17, 220, 230n23, 234n2
"The Condemned," 75
courage, 33, 95, 107, 122, 124, 129, 173, 175, 202, 208, 212, 213

Crimes and Misdemeanors, 6, 9, 13, 15, 16, 149–64, 170, 177, 195, 214

"Dark Penguin," 17
death, ix, x, 16, 35–37, 39–41, 48, 51, 52, 55, 60, 61, 73, 74, 77, 78, 93, 121, 122, 127, 129, 136, 137, 139, 155–57, 159, 176, 186, 189–91, 213
Death in Venice. See Mann, Thomas
Deconstructing Harry, ix–xiii, 217, 223n9
deconstruction, xii–xiv, 109, 220, 232n23
Denby, David, 153, 224n5, 230n23, 237n2, 238n5, 238n7
Denial of Death. See Becker, Ernest
Dickinson, Emily, 16, 156, 163
Dostoyevsky, Fedor, 8, 9, 149–51, 225n24; *Crime and Punishment*, 9, 149–51
Double Indemnity, 169, 170
Dowd, Maureen, ix, x, 223n2, 223n6
Dunne, Michael, 68, 230n4, 232nn22–23

Ebert, Roger, 143, 144, 146, 147, 181, 237n9, 237n11, 241n4
8½. See Fellini, *8½*
Erler, Mary, 238n14, 240n30
escapism, xiv, 10–12, 16, 163, 165, 216, 219, 220
Everyone Says I Love You, 131, 217, 219
existential themes, xiv, 8, 9, 11, 17, 39, 112, 154, 159

Farrow, Mia, ix, 4, 241n1
Feldstein, Richard, 234n7
Fellini, Federico, 8, 68–71, 75, 81; *8½*, 68–71, 73, 77, 80, 81
film. *See* Allen, Woody, on his films; art
Flaubert, Gustave, 30, 220. *See also Madame Bovary*
freedom, 16, 53, 54, 57, 70, 89, 121, 123, 126–28, 158, 159, 161, 169, 192, 198, 199, 205–9, 213, 217, 221
Freud, Sigmund, 1, 34–36, 40, 47, 63, 70, 227n7; *Civilization and Its Dis-*

contents, 34, 35, 41, 240n25; Freudian analysis or interpretation, 2, 108, 153; *Wit and Its Relation to the Unconscious*, 34
friendship, 23, 26, 29, 45, 50, 63, 93, 96, 143, 144, 147, 215
Frye, Northrop, 235n2

Gilliatt, Penelope, 230n23
Gittelson, Natalie, 232n21, 242n4, 243n20
Girgus, Sam B., xii, 24, 25, 100, 109, 110, 153, 159, 215, 216, 224n11, 226n1, 226nn5–8, 227n4, 227n7, 227n12, 234n2, 234n10, 234n12, 234nn13–14, 235n16, 236n5, 236n11, 238n9, 239n17, 239n19, 239n24, 242n9, 243n16
God, 17, 126, 161
Godard, Jean-Luc, 7, 8
Goethe, Johann Wolfgang von, 166
Grand Illusion, 41
Greek tragedy, 16, 195, 196, 203, 204, 207, 208
Groucho Marx. *See* Marx Brothers

Hannah and Her Sisters, 216, 217, 227n6, 236n4, 242n7
Heidegger, Martin, 136, 235n15
Hegel, G. W. F., 235n15
Hepburn, Kathryn, 200, 206, 207
Hitchcock, Alfred, 8, 176, 177
Hobbes, Thomas, 85, 89, 91, 95
Hollywood, 14, 33, 41, 45, 46, 50, 72, 115–20, 122–29, 158, 159, 161–63, 179, 192, 207
Holmes, Sherlock, 166–67, 169, 241n10
Homer, 208
Hope, Bob, 8, 167, 168
Howe, Irving, 5, 100, 108
Husbands and Wives, xiii, 4, 7

intellectuals, 5, 37, 46, 100, 108, 110–13, 191, 217
Interiors, xiv, 5, 6, 7, 15, 16, 49–65, 69, 70, 81, 101, 113, 141, 145, 167, 168,
179, 182, 194, 200, 212, 213, 215, 216, 217
interpretation, xiv, 1–5, 7, 8, 60, 61, 81, 92, 96, 107–10, 111, 113, 158, 177, 220
irony, xi, 10, 25, 37, 53, 76, 103, 111, 117, 122, 124, 128, 135, 136, 142, 156, 209, 214, 215, 230n23

Jacobs, Diane, 60, 226n9, 229nn15–16, 230nn22–23, 231n7, 231n17
James, Caryn, 150, 152, 199, 236n8, 242n8, 243n18, 243n21
Jewish character, treatment of, 39, 41–42, 55, 108, 195–98, 229n15

Kael, Pauline, 1, 59, 65, 68, 223n1, 229n10, 229n12, 230n1, 230n5, 233n7, 237n2
Keaton, Diane, 4, 241n1
Kierkegaard, Sören, 9, 220, 225n24, 243n24
"Kugelmass Episode," 9, 10, 30, 31, 63, 117, 120, 149, 175, 235n3, 240n5

Lacan, Jacques, 234n7
Lady from Shanghai. See Welles, Orson
Laertius, Diogenes, 225n33
Lahr, John, 241n1, 242n6
Lake, Anthony, 200, 242n1
laughter, xi, 2, 11, 20, 37–38, 40–41, 46, 72, 77, 78, 97, 207, 213, 216; as comic relief, 34–35, 63, 82, 153, 154, 160, 163, 212, 215, 238n13
Lawrence, D. H., 225n19
Lax, Eric, 236n6
Lee, Sander H., xiii, xiv, 23, 158, 160, 217, 224nn13–15, 225n26, 225n31, 226n1, 226nn3–4, 226n11, 228n19, 228n20, 231n18, 232n2, 233n10, 237n3, 237nn5–6, 237n12, 238n13, 239nn21–23, 240nn27–28, 240n4, 243n22, 243n24
Lewis, Paul, 243n14
Love and Death, 9
"Lunatic's Tale," 231n14

Machiavelli, Niccolo, 202, 237n1
Madame Bovary, 9, 10, 30, 63, 117, 120,
  149, 170, 175. *See also* Flaubert,
  Gustave
Manhattan, 4, 35, 223n7, 237n12
Manhattan Murder Mystery, xiv, 16,
  165–78, 182, 198, 217, 220
Mann, Thomas, 40, 228nl9; *Death in
  Venice*, 40
Mantel, Hillary, 238n6
Marx, Karl, 1, 2, 57, 63, 73, 109, 112
Marx Brothers, 8, 35, 198, 227n6;
  Groucho, 35, 198, 220
Maslin, Janet, 181, 223n5, 240n2,
  241n3, 241n5
McCann, Graham, 214, 215, 229n15,
  230n23, 242n12
McLuhan, Marshall, 45
Midsummer Night's Dream. See Shake-
  speare
Midsummer Night's Sex Comedy, 2, 3, 9,
  12, 13, 15, 83–97, 100, 113, 136, 140,
  149, 155, 169
Mighty Aphrodite, xiv, 16, 195–209,
  217–20, 227n6
Minowitz, Peter, 237n1, 237n3,
  238n12
Moss, Robert F., 171, 228n21
"My Apology," 8, 11, 78, 231n15

neuroses, x, 14, 15, 20, 21, 28, 29, 30,
  36, 167, 209, 212, 227n11
New York Stories, 9, 195
Nietzsche, Friedrich, 109
nihilism, x, xiii, xiv, 2, 5, 6, 150, 161
Nuechterlein, James, 150, 237n3

Oedipus, 9, 154, 159, 160, 163, 195,
  196, 199, 205, 208
Oedipus Wrecks, 9, 154, 195
Ortega y Gasset, 211, 242n1

Perlmutter, Ruth, 108, 234n8
Perry, Ted, 231n12
Philadelphia Story, 200, 205, 206, 208
Picnic in the Grass. See Renoir, Jean
Pinsker, Sanford, 226n2

Plato, 10, 13, 14, 79; *Republic* 3, 10, 12.
  See also Socrates
Play It Again, Sam, xiv, 6, 9, 10, 13–15,
  19–31, 33–35, 50, 63, 65, 69, 81, 83,
  110, 112, 115, 127, 131, 149, 168, 212
poetry, 3, 4, 10–14, 50, 85, 100, 115,
  133, 134, 177
Pogel, Nancy, xii, 25, 60, 80, 81, 86, 95,
  96, 109, 215, 223n10, 226n10,
  227n13, 229n9, 229n15, 229nn17–
  18, 230n22, 231n7, 231n13, 232n23,
  232n1, 233n4, 233nn8–9, 233n12,
  234n14, 235n15, 243n13
Podhoretz, John, 223n3, 223n9
Preussner, Arnold, 235n2, 242n9
psychiatry, 20, 29, 35, 74, 77, 99–104,
  108, 110, 111, 131, 132, 137, 138,
  141, 143, 184, 186, 187. *See also* psychoanalysis
psychoanalysis, 34, 36–38, 106, 112.
  See also psychiatry
Purple Rose of Cairo, 6, 11, 13–16, 115–
  29, 161, 162, 169, 192, 229n7

Rear Window, 176, 177. *See also* Hitchcock, Alfred
religion, 73, 85, 120, 155, 162
Renoir, Jean, 8, 95, 232n1, 233n9, *Picnic in the Grass*, 95
Republic. See Plato
responsibility, xiii, xiv, 94, 123, 135,
  140, 143, 158, 160–64, 214, 220
Rich, Frank, 242n3
Rilke, Ranier Maria, 134, 136, 147,
  225n28; *Torso of Apollo*, 134
Roche, M. W., 154, 237n3, 238n8,
  238n10, 239n18, 239n20
Rose, Lloyd, 242n5, 243n15
Rousseau, 35, 37, 61, 62, 84, 87, 90, 91,
  167, 208
Russell, Bertrand, 232n2

Sartre, xiii, xiv, 6, 159, 220, 243n24
Schickel, Richard, 115, 152, 235n1,
  238n8
Schopenhauer, Arthur, 55

science, 53, 73, 84–86, 88, 90–91, 102, 155, 166

"Selections from the Allen Notebooks," 13

Sentimental Education. See Flaubert, Gustave

Shadows and Fog, 177, 242n11

Shakespeare, 9, 41, 48, 83–86, 92, 97, 149, 181, 186, 238n10; *A Midsummer Night's Dream*, 9, 83, 84, 96, 97

Siegel, Ed, xi, 223n8

Siegel, Mark, 231n7

singing, 39, 40, 46, 120, 125, 162, 163, 201

Singin' in the Rain, 162, 163

Sinyard, Neil, 96, 228n2, 230n23, 233n11

Sleeper, 229n15

Smiles of a Summer Night. See Bergman, Ingmar

Socrates, 3, 8, 10–14, 55, 74, 94, 231n15

Sontag, Susan, 1, 2, 5, 100, 107–9, 111, 224n2, 225n19, 234n9

Sophocles. *See Oedipus*

The Sorrow and the Pity, 38, 45

speech, 42, 59–61

Spignesi, Stephen, 238n8

Stam, Robert, 177, 231n7, 241n9

Stardust Memories, ix, xiv, 1–4, 11, 14, 15, 65–82, 110, 112, 120, 153, 161, 180, 185, 190, 209, 213, 214, 216, 221

Stenberg, Douglas, 236n7

suffering, 2, 11, 34, 67, 69, 70, 73, 77, 102, 121, 128, 133, 137, 138, 153, 158, 160, 196, 209, 238n13

The Thin Man, 165–67

Tocqueville, Alexis de, 197

Tolstoy, Leo, 8; *War and Peace*, 9

Torso of Apollo. See Rilke, Ranier Maria

tragedy, 14, 16, 39, 152, 154, 158, 160, 163, 176, 195, 196, 203, 205, 206, 207–9, 211, 213, 214, 217, 220. *See also* comedy

virtue, xiv, 1, 16, 202–4, 207–9

War and Peace. See Tolstoy, Leo

Welles, Orson, 8, 174; *Lady from Shanghai*, 174, 175

Welsh, James M., 240n2, 240n8

Wernblad, Annette, 39, 226n2, 227n14, 227n17

What's New Pussycat?, 179, 241n1

Wieseltier, Leon, 237n3, 238n11

Wit and Its Relation to the Unconscious. See Freud, Sigmund

Yacowar, Maurice, 33, 42, 226n2, 227nn2–3, 227n18, 228n19, 229n8, 229n13, 229n15, 229n20, 232n3, 233n5, 239n22

Young, Vernon, 59, 228n2, 229n11

Zelig, 1, 2, 5, 12, 15, 99–113, 124

About the Author

Mary P. Nichols received her doctorate in political science from the University of Chicago. She is professor of political science at Fordham University. She has edited *Readings in American Government* (Dubuque: Kendall/Hunt, 1990) and has published widely in ancient and modern political thought, including *Socrates and the Political Community* (Albany: SUNY Press, 1987) and *Citizens and Statesmen: A Study of Aristotle's Politics* (Lanham, Md.: Rowman & Littlefield, 1992).